OH, NO.....JACKIE-O!

A THEORY

THE UNSPEAKABLE IS SPOKEN

JANUARY JONES

P.J. PUBLISHING

Published by P.J. Publishing

www.januaryjones.com

Cover Photo: AP/WideWorld Photos

Copyright © 1998 by January Jones

Library of Congress Catalog Card Number:98-91375

ISBN: 0-9662951-0-2

Printed in the United States of America

To my Mother and Auntie,
They taught me about love. . .
Conditional and Unconditional.

To my Husbands,
One opened the door. . .
One held my hand.

To my Daughters,
Forever our Souls will share Joy. . .
Karma, Beauty and the Magic of Life.

CONTENTS

INTRODUCTION

INTRODUCTION

I WAS LIVING IN LONDON WHEN DIANA, PRINCESS OF Wales, was going through the ordeal of the very public dismantling of her marriage. I felt so sorry for the poor woman. Here she was in a loveless marriage to a much older man who married her to sire a future king. She was nothing more than a brood mare. The public humiliation that she was being subjected to with the revelations of her husband's long time affair with the other woman was so incredibly cruel and devastating. Diana's self-esteem was taking a daily beating in all the tabloids and everyone felt so sorry for her. How Charles could have subjected her to this sham of a marriage was beyond comprehension.

So often during this time as I strolled about, I couldn't help but think about Diana and her intolerable situation. Also, during this time there were many bomb scares and threats by the IRA. The Prince of Wales' own uncle, Lord Mountbatten, had previously been assassinated on his yacht by the IRA terrorists. All the royals were targets. It easily could have been Charles rather than his uncle. As this thought crossed my mind, I felt a slight twinge of remorse for even thinking the thought. However, once it was out there it sort of took on a life of its own. I could totally fantasize about what Diana's life would be like without old Charlie around.

Well, the bottom line is that Diana's life would be blooming terrific. First of all she would be the future Queen Mother, which is probably one of the better jobs in the royal establishment. She would also be a grieving widow which is a totally sympathetic role that Diana could carry off beautifully. As for money, she would be set for life with no one to really answer to down the road except her own son, the future King. She could avoid the stigma of a divorce which always diminishes a woman in the eyes of the world, unless you are Ivana Trump.

The best part of all, Diana would have a real life of her own after a suitable period of mourning, of course. She would be her own boss and never have to stand behind or in Charles' shadow ever again.

The more I thought about it, the thought of Diana as a widow was very appealing to me. This, of course, is the most terrible karma possible to even let such thoughts exist.

I returned to the States just about the time of the Jackie-O auction, which was the classic rip off of all time, in my humble opinion. All it turned out to be was a high-class garage sale. The kids sold all of the stuff Jackie didn't care about and the kids didn't want! I started to dwell upon our dearly departed Jackie's life. I began to see the many similarities between Diana's and Jackie's married lives to Charles and JFK. Diana was on the divorce course. I thought about how much easier Jackie's life, as the sainted widow of our beloved President, had been compared to what Diana was about to go through.

I quickly got right down to the bottom line after dismissing the obvious similarities. Jackie and Diana were both young wives married to older men. Both were basic brood mares for the sake of the dynasty, who were forced to endure a public life neither enjoyed nor were suited for. Neither one had any privacy whatsoever and, oh yes, both their husbands publicly cheated on them and flaunted their mistresses in their faces. Neither husband had much dignity nor class, only money and titles.

It gradually dawned on me that Jackie was a little older and a lot more ruthless than Diana and, bingo, the light bulb went on! She did what many other women have done before her and will do after her. She had JFK knocked off. Life is so much kinder to widows than divorcees. It doesn't take a rocket scientist to figure out who was right there to carry out this dastardly deed for her. It wasn't a knight in shining armor but, what the hell, a Greek on a tanker wasn't too bad after all.

All of these thoughts took place long before poor Diana met her tragic fate in a Paris tunnel much too soon. Her death certainly changed the equation for her. Just as Jackie, Diana too found her prince charming, an Egyptian with ships, hotels and happiness. She was headed for a life similar to the one Jackie acquired with her marriage to Onassis. Sadly, this was not to be.

If the British royalty thought Diana was a thorn in their side while she was alive, they haven't seen anything yet. Diana's death puts her in the same class as Santa Evita Peron. Diana's life will be the romantic tragedy of the next century. She is now a legend and like JFK her legacy in death will far exceed anything she might have ever accomplished as a mere mortal.

Good for you, Diana.....they led you as a mere child into a marriage that would always be loveless. They all knew Charles would never give up Camilla nor did anyone expect him too. You were expected to fall in line like a good little wife. After all, you were going to get to be "The Queen" someday if you just did what was expected of you. But, no, Diana you grew up and outgrew their silly game. So then, they skinned you alive and turned you out into the world on your own. They knew you had a bounty on your head and your search for peace would be doomed until you found your grave. Little could they know that your life would be that of which legends are made . . . you touched the lepers, held the children of AIDS, walked through the mines and the mind fields of sorrow, and taught the world about the giving and receiving of love. So now, sweet Princess, may you rest in the peace you so surely deserve.

But in the meantime, lest I digress more so in sorrow, I still have stumbled on to the possible solution to the crime of the century. Who killed JFK? Well it always goes back to who really had a motive besides LBJ, who would have been incapable of organizing anything more secretive than a Texas stampede. There really is no other person who had a better motive than Jackie Kennedy. She had the most to gain. Her freedom from a demeaning marriage plus a hell of a lot more money than the Kennedys could ever dream of when she teamed up with the Greek. Isn't there a saying somewhere about "the best revenge is the good life" or maybe it was "the one with the most money wins"?

Jackie was one cool dame. She not only had it all but kept it all and everyone still thinks she is a saint. Just imagine how great she must feel knowing that she has pulled off not only a perfect crime but the crime of the century—hell, the crime of all eternity! She must be especially happy knowing that everyone else just dismissed her as another dumb dame who got lucky and married some really rich men.

Now don't get me wrong, I have nothing against JFK or Charles besides the fact that they both would be ideal candidates for penal brain transplants. Actually they sort of ended up in a very deserving state. Charles is with the enchanting Camilla who the British will never accept as Diana's replacement. Then there is Jack who is probably having a ball in eternity spiritually fornicating with Marilyn Monroe. When he gets tired of that he can always listen to her sing "Happy Birthday, Dear Mr. President" over and over.

Gosh, isn't it interesting the way theories are born?

After over thirty-five years, everyone has a theory about who really killed Kennedy. The assassination industry was only recently challenged by the Clinton's catastrophies on the best seller lists. Hardly anyone, except Gerald Ford, believes that Lee Harvey Oswald committed the crime alone. There have been so many theories through the years about who could have done it, that it has become impossible to come to any conclusion as to who really did it? Some people seem comfortable believing that it was definitely done by professional killers. These paid assassins were the very best. The real question is who hired them, or in mobster slang who ordered the hit? These were the best marksmen to be had in the entire world. This assassination ranks as one of the most successful and well-planned murders in history.

There were so many people who had good reason to kill JFK that this abundance of enemies and potential assassins boggles the mind. Was it someone or some group within our government or military establishment that did it, as Oliver Stone would have us believe? Or it could have been a political enemy such as Fidel Castro who had been targeted for assassination by the Kennedys. Then again there is the Mafia possibility since they were being harassed in a major way by the Kennedy administration, under the direction of the Attorney General Bobby Kennedy. However, one can't forget the organized unions who were being persecuted by Bobby at this time too. Also J. Edgar Hoover and the FBI felt no love lost for any of the Kennedys from a life long dislike of Joe Kennedy, Sr. Hoover had plenty of information on the entire family to be able to apply pressure anytime he wanted. Hoover invented the term job security by which every president knew who really called the shots around Washington. J. Edgar Hoover literally knew where all the bodies were buried and who had dug the graves. One must not forget the good old Ivy League boys from the CIA. Many of these patriots still to this day cannot forgive how Kennedy pulled out on them in Cuba and left their men to die while he covered his ass.

Oh yes, there were hundreds of cuckolded husbands, fathers, sons and brothers who weren't all that thrilled with the President's treatment of their loved ones. JFK's basic approach was to fuck them, then shuck them. No one was off limits for this President. It simply wasn't an issue whether they were someone's wife, daughter, mother or sister since they were all basically just a piece of ass.

Women were put on this earth to be fucked and this was JFK's main mission in life despite the consequences. Is it possible that this obsession just might have pissed off someone really big? Someone who knew how to take care of a man who crossed the line with someone else's woman? Many people who knew Kennedy well were not surprised when he was shot. The surprise was that it didn't happen to him with his pants down screwing another man's wife.

Also no one can discount the lunatic fringe in our society who just want to be famous and by murdering a president, they will ensure their place in history for all time.

The bottom line is that any one of these people might very easily have had JFK knocked off. It had to be done by professionals who would be in and out of Dallas quickly and leave no trail. Better yet, set up someone else to take the fall. There were many top-of-the line paid assassins who were available, ready and eager to take on a big job such as this. It would have been a relatively easy job since Kennedy seemed to have more enemies with valid motives than friends at the time. For a professional killer this was a slam dunk job and the financial compensation would most likely be a very satisfactory amount.

Everyone has a theory and we have been exposed to most of these scenarios over the past thirty years. I also have a theory, one that you have probably never considered even for a moment. My theory is the unthinkable, unspeakable one. Just for a moment open yourself up to the possibility that the person who ordered the hit could have been very close to the President. So close to the President that this person would have the perfect alibi since she would be sitting next to the President when he was killed!

It is not a new theory. From the beginning of time men and women have always been able to get rid of spouses who didn't quite fit into their plans. There is quite a list of historical figures who were murdered with their wives right next to them, such as Abraham Lincoln and Anwar Sadat, for example. It creates great sympathy for the wife and a terrific alibi.

Of course, there would have to be an accomplice. Who in the world would be willing to help this poor, dear wife get rid of her husband? He would have to be a man of great wealth, power and no conscience, with all sorts of connections in the shady parts of the world and underworld. He would have the ability to do anything that must be done, and be certain that no trail would ever lead back to him or his cohort. It would take great wealth and great desire to accomplish this assassination successfully.

What would the motivation be for a man of such status to risk everything in order to achieve the perfect crime of the century and perhaps of all time? First, his ego would rise to the challenge and he could propose a very simple arrangement. It was just your basic murder for a marriage deal, no big deal and very easy to do, especially when the rewards for both parties would far exceed their wildest dreams. Along with the satisfaction of committing the perfect crime, these two accomplices would then be able to tell the rest of the world to stuff it. They could eventually unite and go on to live happily ever after just like in the movies.

Impossible, ridiculous, out of the question, you say! I answer, please take a moment to consider that this new theory is no more unlikely than some other theories proposed throughout the past thirty-five years. There are a few key questions to be asked and answered. Please withhold your judgement till all the evidence has been presented to you.

I would have doubts. Then I would always go back to how any woman scorned, ignored, humiliated, with a great need for money, would feel about a husband who fucked anything that moved? JFK was unfaithful to Jacqueline Kennedy. He not only fucked around, he rubbed Jackie's nose in it for public consumption. It is not fun to be the laughing stock of a whole country. Living with it in your own home and being pitied by the servants really gave her no choice. In order to survive, the husband must be eliminated. It basically was a simple decision and one that has been made by many other people throughout the ages.

Along with the argument and logic for this theory that I will present to you, there was another big turning point for me in writing this book. I just happened to come across an incredible narrative during my research. It proved to me without a doubt that this deal of murder for a marriage actually could have taken place. I came upon a narrative written by Onassis' valet, Christian Cafarakis, which happens to be stranger than fiction. He tells all in 1972 without knowing that thirty-five years later his account would lead to a theory that might just be the truth.

His simple story, innocently told back in 1972, about his former employer's romance with the First Lady revealing the secrecy and urgency of their love story, set off the warning bells in my feminine instinct love detector. The reality for me soon became the fact that Ari and Jackie were a love story. As history has shown time and time again lovers, whether they be young or old, will do anything just to be together. For some, love cannot be denied no matter what the consequences.

It is all so simple. The missing part of the puzzle that has baffled the American public as to who killed Kennedy has been there in front of us all along. No one has been able to see the forest for the trees just because it has been so obvious. Actually no one has been encouraged to see it.

Thirty-five years ago, John F. Kennedy was our beloved, martyred President, so the American public went along with the official Kennedy-sanctioned version like little sheep being lead off to the slaughterhouse. But now, thirty-five years later, everyone knows what Jack Kennedy was like and every sordid aspect of his life is in the public domain. There is no reason any longer to protect the Kennedy legacy. Now is the time for the truth.

So perhaps my theory is wrong. The unthinkable, unspeakable theory is not possible. Well how could anyone, a Kennedy included, ever go about proving anything right or wrong about any theory of the assassination?

Everything is locked up and sealed till the year 2044.

My big question is, just who had the power to seal up all of this information?

We know that Jackie sealed her own papers, but we do not know her reasons. They must be good ones though if not even her own children will be allowed to know the truth until that time. Who was she protecting if not herself?

Why must there be such secrecy if there was nothing to hide? Jackie was still alive when much of the details of Jack's troubled Presidency and personal life became public domain, and yet it was as if she were an ostrich burying her head in the sand.

One thing for sure can be said about Jacqueline Bouvier Kennedy Onassis. . .

she never complained,

and she sure never explained!

ONE

WHAT HAPPENS WHEN
THE WORLD'S GREEDIEST WOMAN
MEETS THE WORLD'S GREATEST
SOCIAL CLIMBER?

THE PERFECT PAIR

*H*E HAD NEVER BEEN TO THE WHITE HOUSE BEFORE and he had been ordered not to even think of setting foot in the United States by the man in the coffin in the East Room. Then, in one quick moment in Dallas, everything had changed for both of these men. One was dead and one was now a welcome guest in this house of mourning.

He had received his official invitation to the funeral from the Chief of Protocol, Angier Biddle Duke, on the direct orders of the grieving widow. He knew that no one would dare challenge or question his presence since he was there at her request. No matter what anyone within the family or staff may have thought. Out of deference to the widow, there would be no unpleasantness. Her decisions on all details whether it be the eternal flame, the riderless horse, or unexpected guests, were final and not to be questioned. She was in charge here and everyone knew it.

He was not there to mourn but to silently slowly move through this sea of sorrow in a respectful, inconspicuous manner. He was not accustomed to explaining anything to anyone and he would not start now. He preferred to slip quietly into the background and take on the role of discreet supporter. He was there for only one person and for only one reason. She needed and wanted him there with her.

No one knew it then, but they were the perfect pair. They not only needed each other, they deserved each other.

History will tell us what happens when the world's greediest woman meets the world's wealthiest social climber.

Of course, they will be attracted to each other and embark on a perilous course just to be together. It will not be an easy journey. They know that, but their eyes are blinded to reality. They must possess each other since each of them has exactly what the other one wants.

The woman in this scenario is none other than the beloved Jacqueline Bouvier Kennedy, one of the world's most admired women from the moment she arrived on the political scene with her husband, the dashing Senator John F. Kennedy of Massachusetts.

The entire country and most of the world fell in love with this fabulous couple. As they stepped on center stage, they captured the hearts and souls of their country in their pursuit of the White House. They were quite a spectacular couple. They were wealthy beyond belief and they were good-looking too. Jackie was especially enchanting in the eyes of the world. She shone like a bright light and everything about her seemed so right.

Jackie had good looks, good breeding, an aristocratic appeal and an incredibly handsome husband. Their children were adorable and their life together was the kind that fairy tales are made of. Jackie had style and class and wore her clothes in such a way that she became the style-setter of the era. Everyone tried to copy the Jackie look. Her picture on any book or magazine was guaranteed to insure an immediate sellout. She was the golden girl and she could do no wrong.

Everything she said, did or wore made headlines all over the world. But while everyone sat back in awe of her, some things were carefully kept from her adoring public: her difficult childhood, her compulsive smoking and nail-biting, her lack of wealth, growing up as the poor stepsister in one of the wealthiest families in the country and, most of all, the sham of a marriage with JFK the compulsive womanizer. The electro-shock therapy to treat her depression and mood swings and the drug dependency she shared with her husband were kept secret and, finally, her desperate compulsive need to become a wealthy, independent woman. She would never be at peace until she had enough of her own money to not have to grovel to others for her security.

As Jackie became the world's greediest woman, this need for financial independence dominated her life. She would never feel secure or be happy until she could control her own fate. Her only means would be unlimited wealth. Jackie knew she could not depend on anyone else. So many people had let her down early in life. She had received so many subliminal money messages that she was a prisoner of her own need to possess great wealth.

It would not be easy, but Jackie was prepared to do whatever it took to achieve her dream. Unlimited wealth was her goal. It was essential to her very being and no one would keep her from her destiny.

Charles de Gaulle, a connoisseur of personal as well as national destiny, was fascinated by Jacqueline Kennedy. "What do you think of her?" de Gaulle privately asked his Minister of Culture, Andre Malraux. "She is unique for the wife of an American President, sir," Malraux replied. "Yes, she's unique," said de Gaulle. "I can see her in ten years from now on the yacht of a Greek oil millionaire." Within two years of this uncanny prediction, Jackie was a guest of Aristotle Onassis on his yacht, the *Christina*. Within eight years, Jackie was honeymooning with Ari on the yacht.[1]

De Gaulle had been impressed by Jackie's wit and intelligence, but what struck him most forcibly was her ornamental quality. It accounted for much of her public success and no small part of her private distress. It had been acquired at great cost, both emotional and economic, and was no less costly to maintain. The passage of time had chipped away much of the sentiment from the Kennedy marriage, revealing a husband who regularly and enthusiastically cheated on his young wife. In furthering their ambitions, it was a marriage of convenience. As a celebration of intimacy, it was not impressive.[2]

Jacqueline was the classic poor little rich girl with her nose pressed up against the window of everyone else's inherited wealth. She could occasionally share in the wealth, but could never call it her own. She was always the poor relation and, in this respect, always the outsider. This reality was the primary force in her life and decided every move she ever made.

Thus Jackie became the world's greediest woman. Money, and lots of it, became her primary goal and nothing could keep her from her destiny.

Her destiny appeared in the form of Aristotle Onassis who was one of the wealthiest men of the time. Their meeting was inevitable and nothing could keep them from each other.

Onassis was a self-made man from a poor background who eventually became one of the richest men in the world. His background was mysterious and shady, but his reputation never held him back once his wealth placed him on the world stage. He had great charisma, charm and personal appeal to many of the most famous and notable people of his time. He had a style that could be vulgar but still acceptable due to his great charm and wealth.

Aristotle Onassis was one of the world's greatest people collectors. He had tired of collecting possessions. Ari's passion had become people. He particularly adored statesmen and celebrities. His shipping career enabled him to stand at the forefront of the Greek tycoons, Greeks who wined and dined the rich and famous on their fabulous yachts in a style that would impress even the most jaded of the upper classes. His life-style was unbelievable. He not only succeeded at achieving great wealth but he was an expert at enjoying and sharing it with others. It was his entry into a world he never could have entered as just another Greek with tankers. He exemplified the classic Greek tycoon in everything he said or did. Although he was a man of small stature, there was nothing small about any other aspect of his life. He was bigger than life.

No one was richer, more powerful, more publicized or more outrageous than Aristotle Onassis. Combining shrewd cunning, extraordinary energy and amoral charm, the Greek Onassis rose from the brutal back streets of Smyrna, Turkey, to run an international business empire. He controlled one of the world's largest shipping lines and owned an international airline. He bought and sold the Bank of Monaco and made a reputation as one of the most ruthless deal-makers of his age. Counted among his closest friends were Winston Churchill, Greta Garbo, Eva Peron, Elizabeth Taylor and Richard Burton. He counted among his enemies Richard Nixon, J. Edgar Hoover and the CIA. He romanced Gloria Swanson, loved and abandoned Maria Callas and then married the crown jewel of his collection, Jacqueline Kennedy.[3]

When he met Jacqueline Kennedy, Aristotle Onassis had achieved just about everything he had ever hoped for. He had more power and wealth than he knew what to do with and, as he gradually lost his taste for acquiring things, he switched to people. People became his true passion. The more elusive and exclusive, all the better for his purposes. Until meeting and romancing Jackie Kennedy, Winston Churchill was Ari's most prized acquisition, a friendship which he cultivated with incredible care and devotion. He nurtured people in his garden of life the way some people nurture rare orchids. When he decided that a person was worth his time, he would do anything to seduce that person. He literally made himself indispensable to their every wish or whim.

Take Winston Churchill, for example. In the summer of 1958 Randolph Churchill effected an introduction between his famous father and Onassis. Sir Winston and his wife, Clementine, were with Onassis in Monte Carlo. There was an instant rapport between the two men. "We talked all through lunch, discussing politics, history, human affairs and human nature," Onassis said afterwards. It was the beginning of a remarkable friendship from which Churchill derived considerable pleasure during the final years of his life.

There was on Onassis's side a certain element of celebrity hunting. He basked in the exalted company that generally surrounded the Churchills.

They were people of real class, Onassis told a friend, very different from the international socialites who were then flocking to Monte Carlo. With Churchill aboard, the *Christina* would be met in foreign ports by ambassadors, prime ministers, even royalty.[4]

Onassis was a legendary wheeler and dealer. He had more success in the business world and more money than he knew what to do with. His multimillionaire life-style was his greatest pleasure. Ari lived his life on a grand scale and nothing was too excessive for his taste. He truly enjoyed the good life which made him very appealing to Jackie Kennedy.

What a treasure Jackie must have been in his eyes, when she first arrived on the *Christina* in the fall of 1963. He had been aware of her from the very first time they had met on his yacht in 1957. Onassis believed he could see below the surface of most men, and Kennedy did not seem to him to be a man headed for the White House. He liked the look of Jacqueline much more. He noticed everything about her. Jackie was wearing a simple white dress, the hem raised to just cover the knees, cut in the trapeze line that Saint Laurent had recently brought in. She was hatless and the evening breeze caught her short, dark hair. She had a withdrawn quality that was neither shyness nor boredom. Aristotle was surprised to hear her speaking perfect French to his guests. Her accomplishments, along with her good looks and youth, were obviously an asset to Kennedy in his public and his private life. Ari proved that he looked upon her with no careless eye. He later told his close friend, Gratos, "There's something damned willful about her; there's something provocative about that lady. She's got a carnal soul." Ari and Gratos continued constantly to give each other good advice on the dangers of womanizing and, as frequently, to confess their lapses. She's too young for you," Costa said, sensing the complexity and depth of Ari's interest.[5] The seed of interest and eventually obsession was planted deep in Ari's soul. He would not be at peace until she was his no matter how long or what he had to do to have her.

As their stars crossed in the skies, these two people came towards each other with unspoken agendas that would influence their actions and affect their future together. Along with her compulsive need and desire for money, Jackie had a greater need to even the score, so to speak, for herself on behalf of her beloved father, John Vernon "Black Jack" Bouvier, III. She had taken Black Jack's fall from grace personally. In her heart, she would never be able to forgive or forget the humiliation her father had suffered at the hands of his ex-wife and the so-called establishment. She had a great need to avenge both the Bouviers and the Auchinclosses for the tragic financial disaster of her father's life. You must remember that he was her first and greatest love. Subliminally, she felt compelled to protect his memory. As for the Kennedys, aside from old man Joe who was the ruthless, kindred spirit that Jackie adored, they could all take a flying leap with no love lost on any of them. The thought of a future on the eternal campaign trail took Jackie to new depths of depression. The Kennedy family took away her dignity, and forced her to stand on center stage putting on a good show while being humiliated publicly in her so- called private life. The first priority on Jackie's agenda would be pay back time. She didn't quite know how or when, but she would be ready when the opportunity appeared on her horizon.

Speaking of agendas, Aristotle came into this relationship with his own cargo of past relationships he wished to avenge. Aside from the basic poor boy who makes good and is shunned by the upper classes complex, Ari had a lifelong rivalry with his arch enemy, Stavros Niarchos. Ari and Stavros were both self-made men from humble origins when they burst upon the Greek shipping world. They became brothers-in-law when they married the daughters of Stavros Livanos, the patriarch of Greek shipping. The competition of these two men in their work, lives and loves reached levels of an epic, tragic Greek saga. In the late sixties, Stavros Niarchos had eclipsed Ari's affair with Maria Callas with his marriage to Charlotte Ford, the young daughter of the American Henry Ford. When Charlotte became pregnant, he quickly divorced his wife to marry this gem of an acquisition. This certainly would be a hard act to top, but Ari was on the lookout, and he would be ready when the time came to show the world, and especially Stavros that he too could capture a trophy wife who would far exceed even Niarchos's prize.

As the years passed for a man who had everything, Jackie represented the ultimate in possessions. She was the most famous woman in the world, and as the wife of the President of the United States she had entry to the most prestigious circles in the world. Jacqueline was a jewel to be cherished and someone to covet. She was young, beautiful and would be a treasure to display on any man's arm. Ari possessed a ruthless manner of pursuit combined with his sense of charm that had won over many a reluctant conquest in the past. He was confident that Jackie's path would cross his again. . . . it was their destiny.

When Jackie was invited to cruise on the *Christina* after the loss of her infant son, Patrick, Jack Kennedy was not thrilled. Eventually he gave in and Jackie was allowed to go taking along chaperons to improve the image of what might seem like a frivolous cruise. The *Christina* awaited Jackie's arrival stocked with the finest vintage wines, a crew of sixty, hairdressers, three chefs, a masseuse and a small orchestra for dancing. At the beginning of the cruise, Ari told a group of reporters witnessing the departure, "Mrs. Kennedy is in charge here."

Photographs of Jackie and Ari together disturbed Jack. Photographs of Jackie sunbathing on the deck were bad politics and photographs of Jackie water-skiing in a bikini were even worse. "Does this sort of behavior seem fitting for a woman in mourning", asked an editorial in the *Boston Globe*?[6] None of these things bothered Jackie because she was having the time of her life. Finally she was with someone who could protect and provide for her. There were so many things in her life she could barely face.

Onassis could sense her unhappiness, and he slowly would become her Lancelot in shining armor as the cruise progressed on the high seas. It is not unlikely that on their nights together alone under the stars on the deck of the Christina that certain topics would be discussed in great detail. After all, Ari was there to listen and to help. They probably talked about Jackie's unhappy marriage, Jack's womanizing, the fishbowl existence of the White House, her dire financial situation, her lack of privacy, her children's political exploitation and her inability to divorce Jack.

It appeared there was no solution, no hope, no answer. But then, wait a moment, what if Ari could help her and take care of all her problems at one time? He adores her and promises that he can solve her problems, take care of her and protect her and her children unconditionally. What woman wouldn't listen to this proposition?

The plan was simple. The President could have his precious political immortality, become a legend, and Jackie could have her freedom. Along with her freedom, Jackie would have total privacy with Ari and be done with politics forever. She would have all the money she would ever need, a husband who would take great joy in seeing her spend it anyway she chose. She would have a husband who would not only love her beyond her wildest dreams but would indulge her all the days of her life. He would never divorce her or abandon her.

It is hard to imagine any woman not being seduced by this incredible offer, especially one who has strong survival instincts. Onassis knew how to tap into Jackie's deepest fears. He was the answer to her prayers and with his unsavory background who better than Onassis. He would procure the best that money could buy and there would never be a trail leading back to either Ari or Jackie.

They would be the best professionals in the world and every thing would be carefully worked out. Jackie would not be involved in any way. Ari would take care of every detail. All she had to do was to agree?

This is a new theory. No one can prove that it didn't take place. It is a possibility of what would happen if the world's greediest, neediest woman meets the world's wealthiest man.

It is so simple . . .

a murder for a marriage!

TWO

*WHAT KIND OF CHILDHOOD,
UPBRINGING AND MOTIVATIONS
WOULD PRODUCE THE GREEDIEST
WOMAN IN THE WORLD?*

THE POOR, LITTLE RICH GIRL

*H*OW DID JACQUELINE BOUVIER KENNEDY BECOME the world's neediest, greediest woman?

It all began in Jackie's childhood and just like everyone else, this icon's personality and character were the direct result of the most early influences in her life. Although, at first glance, it would appear to most people that Jackie had an incredibly charmed, privileged life, upon closer examination Jackie had a traumatic childhood. Her parents, before and after their divorce, placed both of their children right in the middle ground of their epic war. Janet and Jack Bouvier fought from the trenches. With their daughters as the ultimate prize, they stopped at nothing to win the hearts and souls of these little girls. To say it was an ugly, vicious divorce would be an understatement.

Jacqueline was their first child in this unlikely, unstable marriage. Jack Bouvier was thirty-seven and his reputation as a ladies' man and rake was well established when he married the twenty-one-year old high strung friend of his twin sisters. Janet Lee was the petite yet athletic daughter of a nouveau-rich Irish family. An ambitious young woman, she seemed determined to marry a man who was in society, and Jack Bouvier fit that bill. The Bouviers of New York and Easthampton had been in society for several generations. Now just what criteria qualified a man to be in society?

You had to come from a gentile family of European origins that had en-
joyed wealth for at least three or four generations, a family that sent sons to
Ivy League colleges, and had at least one ancestor who had fought in the
American Revolution. The Bouviers possessed all these qualifications.[1]

During the first six or seven years of her childhood Jacqueline led
the life of a young princess, a happy privileged interlude full of accomplishments, among exquisitely beautiful and luxurious surroundings, with doting
parents and grandparents. She also developed the tastes and preferences in
people and activities that would last the rest of her life.[2] Both Jackie and her
little sister, Lee, were raised to be snobs of the first order. Their exclusive
life-styles gave them that extra advantage over those who had only recently
entered the world of wealth and privilege. Jackie was truly to the manor
born and she never forgot it. She had grown up on estates in Newport and
Southhampton perfectly comfortable with this social position. Her father,
Jack "BlackJack" Bouvier III, was a member of the New York Stock
Exchange. He was a man of inordinate charm, a legendary womanizer
who made more conquests in the bedroom than on Wall Street. He was the
classic *bon vivant* of the roaring twenties brought down by the great depression.[3] He started the depression with an estimated wealth of $750,000
and after the market collapse he ended up with only $100,000.

Jackie's mother, Janet Lee, came from an Irish family. The Lees
emigrated from Ireland to New York during the potato famine at about the
same time as the Kennedys. However unlike the Kennedys, both Janet and
her daughters chose to downplay their Irishness for the more socially prestigious French Bouvier ancestry. However Janet's remarkable father, James
T. Lee, had enjoyed a rags-to-riches career very similar to Joseph P.
Kennedy's. Jack Bouvier was well aware of the Lee family's financial
success. Constitutionally adverse to marriage, Jack would have considered
marriage only if it promised him the financial rewards that this marriage
would do.[4]

Basically Jackie's parents both got what they wanted. Janet went
into the marriage achieving her greatest ambition to enter society. Jack

achieved his main goal by marrying into a family that could aid him in his financial pursuits. They truly deserved each other and were able to pass on to their offspring their basic value system. Marriage to them was not about love but about acquisitions.

As her parent's marriage disintegrated, Jackie began exhibiting the signs of what her adult friends later described as a distinct "split personality". You never knew when it was going to happen, and she would turn on and off like a light bulb. "When the light was on, it was blindingly bright," one of her teachers said of her.[5]

Jacqueline was nearly eleven when her parents divorced. She was old enough to be aware of the collapse of her world, but too young to absorb its full significance. Instinctively, she blocked herself off, creating a refuge into which she could escape. Blocking became her main line of defense, her means of dealing with the trauma and stigma of the breakup. She taught herself how to participate in events without being seen. She became a voyeur, an onlooker. She developed an inner core, a private self that no one could ever know or touch.[6]

Jackie's reaction to the divorce was very typical of any child going through the loss of her core relationship with her parents. Life would never be the same for her. Things would only get much worse for this destroyed family unit. The parents never could get past the split up and their hostilities only served to create havoc within their childrens' lives. All the inner and outer turmoil affected every area of Jackie's existence. Jackie's cousin, Edie Beale, described her as "At age fifteen, my cousin was prissy, bookish and bossy. Jackie was too much, *dc trop* in French, a perfectly horrible child. That's why her classmates nicknamed her Jacqueline Borgia. She always knew how to get what she wanted. She was a master manipulator." Her greatest concern always seemed to be money, primarily because she didn't have any.[7]

Jackie was very much like her mother. Janet was a tough disciplined perfectionist, controlling to the point of being dictatorial. Jackie's mother was a realist who always kept her eye on the bottom line. As a young child, she had seen her father go from poor to rich. As a result, she would always live in fear of losing it,[8] a fear that Janet surely passed on to her elder daughter. It was a subliminal fear that controlled them at the deepest level. No matter how much Janet and Jackie would acquire within their respective lifetimes, they both lived in fear of losing it all. With this worry hanging over their heads, neither mother nor daughter were able to live carefree, joyful lives.

Janet also taught both her daughters the biggest lesson of their lives through her own example. The only answer to money problems was to marry a rich man. Yes, Jacqueline felt very poor as a teenager but her Mother had showed her a way out. Janet was eking out just a sparse existence on Jack Bouvier's alimony of $1000 a month. In the second year of her life as a divorcee, along came Hugh D. Auchincloss, Jr., who, in one stroke, lifted her up to be mistress of two enormous estates. He provided her with all the money she wanted, and fathered two charming children with her.[9]

As much as Janet's marriage was the answer to all her prayers, it created new problems for Jackie. Living with the incredibly wealthy Auchinclosses, and having to depend on her father for her paltry allowance of $50 a month made Jackie feel very poor indeed.[10] As Gore Vidal, another step-sibling from one of Hugh's previous marriages recalled, "You must remember that Jackie and I were in the very same boat. We were brought up in style, allowed to live in their very comfortable way. But the money was always theirs. We were penniless and were made painfully aware of the fact. So I went to work and Jackie had to look for a rich husband."[11] As a small child, little Jackie pressed her face up against the window of the Auchincloss life and learned the biggest lesson of her young life. You can never have enough money.

Janet taught her girls that they had to marry into money. Jackie and Lee were needy Bouviers whose only inheritance was the mere $3000 they received in 1948 upon the death of their paternal grandfather. Jackie didn't even own a piece of serious jewelry to call her own. The notion of money, if not the actual word itself, was never absent from Janet's conversations with Jackie. Money was the measure of every man, woman and child who entered Janet's world.[12]

This was the great lesson to be learned and it was taught in every way possible. It was taught in every action, every thought and in almost every spoken word. Janet was an excellent teacher both outwardly and, more importantly, subliminally. Janet's obsession with money and her concern for her childrens' financial situation was passed directly on to Jacqueline. It was the first message she learned and it was the one that would stay with her to the end of her life. In order to raise the world's greediest woman, this was the first and only lesson. One that Jackie would pass on to her own children. Even after her death, they followed her last wishes and amassed close to $21 million with their little garage sale at Sothebys. At this incredible event, the kids dumped all the stuff that neither of them wanted onto Jackie's adoring public. Her fans would pay anything just to have something of hers.

Looking at Jackie's background and the experience of the daily humiliation of being a poor relative, it was only natural for her to crave a life that would be cushioned by a great deal of money. However, for Jackie, money was a means to a larger end.[13] Money would give Jackie the self-esteem and security she desperately needed. From an early age, she had seen rich and she had seen poor and she knew what she had to have. It was not a matter of preference, it was essential to her very survival. The sad tragedy of her vision was that her rich and her poor were so incredibly removed from reality She was born with the proverbial silver spoon and she would fight all her life not to ever have to relinquish it. That spoon would feed the great hunger in her. It would fill up her soul and nourish her spirit.

For Jackie, Janet's example taught her the obvious lesson. Marry a rich man, the richer the better. Janet would make this very clear some years later, when Jacqueline fell in love with a young stockbroker, John G. W. Husted, Jr., the son of a prominent New York banker. Husted was a

Yale graduate whose parents knew both the Bouviers and Auchinclosses. The engagement lasted about four months. Then Janet asked the inevitable question as to how much money Husted was making on Wall Street. When she learned the answer was a mere $17,000 a year, she called off the marriage. Husted, for all his fine qualities, was not rich enough. That was all there was to it. Janet was out for far bigger game for Jacqueline and she let her daughter know it. [14]

Jackie did not question her mother's decision and quickly got on with the program. Jackie's response to her mother's advice was to do no more than occasionally flirt with a man she liked. As soon as she would discover he had no money, no big money, she dropped him like the proverbial hot potato. [15] Jackie was a quick learner and this was one lesson it was important for her to master. She was already showing signs of the world-class shopper she was to become in her future marriages. Even her beloved father, a big spender himself, was worried about her lavish spending habits. It all boils down to being too selfish, he wrote. She had to start denying herself things she wanted now. As she got older, she would find self-denial increasingly difficult. She can't expect to have her every wish fulfilled, he advised, while pointing out that character is developed through renunciation. He also pointed out that although she resembled him in many ways, she was getting to be more and more like her mother. As an example of this inherited lack of generosity, he mentioned Jackie's reactions when they had discussed some of the bequests he planned to put into his will. Jacqueline had objected to one, saying, "I don't see why she should get anything?" Thus, he adamantly advised her not to emulate her mother. He reminded her of Janet's lack of generosity, and repeated what he had told her many times before. Janet had been nothing but a gold- digger all her life. [16]

It is sad to see her father trying so desperately to prevent what is already a fact of Jackie's life. Her course was already set on what would appear to be a disastrous life when it came to ethics and morality. One can only imagine what her father's reaction would have been to Jackie's legendary spending sprees in her marriages to Kennedy and Onassis. How futile her father's lectures were to her, lectures about what he considered her selfishness, telling her that when she wanted something, she just kept insisting and insisting until she got it.[17] Boy, did she show him! What could her father have been thinking to tell her she couldn't have all the things she wanted when she wanted them? Her early life was all about wanting, getting and, then, wanting more.

As Jackie approached adulthood, her character was already becoming known to others. Elene Slocum, a close friend of Janet Auchincloss and a member of one of Newport's most formidable clans, observed that Janet and Jackie at times appeared to be different. However, Janet had a greater influence than has generally been acknowledged. Janet's drive for excellence rubbed off on Jacqueline. They were different since Jackie had far greater aspirations than her mother. "She never wanted to be an ordinary woman or lead an ordinary life, in ordinary circumstances among ordinary people. She would never have been content merely to raise a family and attend fund-raising affairs. From the very beginning, she was enormously ambitious. In her way, one of the most ambitious young people I've ever known."[18]

Another aspect of Jackie's approaching adulthood was the manifestation of her childhood preference for boys instead of girls. She never cared that much for girlfriends but always liked boys better. More than anything, Jackie took pleasure in dealing with and being close to men, men who were doing important things, not necessarily as an advisor so much as a confidant. Power and charisma seemed to override all other qualities in her estimations of people. John White remembered Jackie as, "One tough cookie, really tough. That undigested, renegade toughness that lay at the very core of Jackie's personality, and I suppose it intimidated lots of people."[19] It was this very toughness that Jackie inherited from Janet that allowed her to pursue relationships with men in which she felt she could hold her own. It also allowed her as she got older to conquer and seduce men. It gave her a tremendous edge in controlling people and situations in life to her pleasure.

After Jackie was finished with her schooling, with the help of Hugh Auchincloss, she found a job with a Washington newspaper as an around-town-reporter. Jack Kassowitz, assistant managing editor of the *Times-Herald*, became Jackie's supervising editor. He took a dim view of Jackie's professional commitment. "She was a poor little rich girl with a wealthy family but no money of her own. She behaved like a social climber. She enjoyed dancing, fancy restaurants and meeting people who were famous and had money. She seemed innocent and a bit naive on the surface, but she knew exactly where she was going and what she was doing—and it had very little to do with the newspaper business."[20]

Now it was time for Jackie to make her move into the real world and her survival instincts were honed for the kill. Looking back, her step-cousin, Louis Auchincloss said, "What no one seemed to have known about Jackie at the time was that she wasn't this soft little passive girlish person. She was tough, very tough. The major motivation in Jackie's life was money. She loved money."[21] She wasn't her mother's daughter for nothing, and just as Janet was a woman with twenty-twenty eyesight for trust funds, inheritances and property, so too, did she give her daughter an advanced degree in social calculation.[22] It comes as no surprise when her cousin, John H. Davis, tells us that, "The first twenty years of her life helped form the salient qualities of her personality, her love of beauty, her strength of will, her cynical and mercenary attitude towards men, her need for more and more money, her physical prowess and stamina, her secre-tiveness and her deep sense of history, which paradoxically, she did not apply to herself."[23]

As Jackie approached the time of life when she must choose a husband, she had a lot to consider. As the product of a broken home, Jackie's vision of marriage was marred by the cold war and passionless relationship between her parents. Their six month separation, their abys-mal reconciliation, and finally their very bitter divorce shattered any emo-tional security she ever had known. While developing a strong fixation for her father, she watched closely as her mother married a man of great wealth and position. Hugh D.Auchincloss was a good provider, by very high standards. Growing up in a subculture where women must marry well to survive and prosper, Jackie understandably gravitated to John F. Kennedy, a man who fitted into her scheme of the world as she knew it.[24]

As a child, adolescent, and adult, Jackie had always preferred being with her father rather than her mother and who could blame her? Her mother just wasn't a fun person to be around compared to all the excitement, charm and personality her father generated everywhere he went. Jacqueline would always be attracted to the "bad boys", rakes and assorted scoundrels. As she once told a friend, the one reason she was drawn to Jack Kennedy was that he was "dangerous, just like her father, BlackJack."[25]

Looking at Jackie's childhood from a distance, it is easy to understand how she would eventually become the world's greediest woman. Her parents couldn't have possibly been more different, and yet so alike in their own need and greed for money. It gave them a feeling of self-worth and security. Now there is no way on earth that any child could please each of these people without betraying the other parent. All any child looks for from the earliest years is approval. This was not a possibility for Jackie. All she could try to do was to emulate her parents in such a way as to please them. So she became her father's dream girl. She gravitated towards men that were like her father and could give her that familiar exciting feeling she had so loved about being with BlackJack. As for her mother, the only way to ever get her approval was to become wealthier than Janet. Fiscally speaking, Jackie's first marriage to JFK was a step in the right direction. On the other hand, when she married Onassis, it was as if every shopping spree and every incredible extravagance was a performance for Janet's benefit—just look at me now, Mother! Jackie had learned her lessons well from Jack and Janet. She knew that the only things that mattered were her charm, power and, above all, her money.

Now the time was approaching to choose, select, capture, seduce or whatever might be required to marry the man of her dreams. The Joseph P. Kennedy family would suit her immediate purposes perfectly. She needed a husband whose qualifications would be acceptable to both Janet and BlackJack, a man who could take her where she longed to go. Remember, this was a young woman who wanted nothing whatsoever to do with the ordinary. Jack Kennedy would be described in many terms during his short life, but ordinary would never be one of them.

What kind of family could possibly produce a mate for Jackie who would be equal to her ambitions? Jackie had to have money, the Kennedys had to have prestige.

It would appear that . . .

this would be a match made in heaven,

or hell depending on your viewpoint.

THREE

What is the description of the ideal mate for the greediest neediest woman in the world?

THE KINGDOM OF KENNEDY

THE PERFECT FAMILY TO FULFILL ALL THE DESIRES OF the young Jacqueline Bouvier already existed, not only in Jackie and her mother's dreams, but in reality. There would be no family better suited to her aspirations than the family of Joseph P. Kennedy of Boston. This family, it appeared, was on a search of its own. The heir apparent to the Kennedy crown, John F. Kennedy, the junior senator from Massachusetts, was in need of a wife. The Kennedys were not just looking for an ordinary wife, but rather a very special wife, one that would be able to be the consort to the future President of the United States. This position required a special woman of many talents. Add to this list that she would also be the wife of the first Catholic President. He would be one of the youngest, wealthiest men to ever occupy the highest position in the land. Obviously, the Kennedy's were looking for someone quite special in her own right. This union would be the culmination of the dreams of all the immigrant families who came to the new world. They had endured hardship and discrimination by the upper classes. Now it would be their time to triumph.

This young couple would represent the fulfillment of the entire country's dreams. The dream to rise up from the masses and to make one of their own the President of the United States of America.

As dreams go, this was a big one. The Kennedy family was the right family in the right time and place to fulfill this dream. "Where else but in gothic fiction, where else among real people, could one encounter such triumphs and tragedies, such beauty and charm and ambition and pride and human wreckage, such dedication to the best and lapses into the mire of life, such vulgar, noble, driven generous, self-centered, loving, suspicious, devious, honorable, vulnerable, indominatable people—who have fascinated so much of the world," observed Clare Booth Luce.[1]

Much like the Lee family, the Kennedys came from a similar Irish background. Their arrival in this country was a little later. Their rise to wealth came about through the efforts of the young, ambitious Joseph P. Kennedy and his equally ambitious wife, Rose Fitzgerald. It all began with an obsession. Joseph Kennedy wanted Rose Fitzgerald and he was willing to do anything to get her. He waited six years to get her father's approval. He would put up with Rose's religiosity and her old man's notoriety for as long as it took. Akin to so many other things he strived for, he refused to consider failure when it came to Rose. But once he had her, he would lose interest and move on to new conquests, setting a pattern that prevails among Kennedy men to this day.

Together Rose and Joe would raise nine children born during a span of almost fifteen years. So great was the age difference between the older children, Rosemary, Joe Jr., Kathleen and Jack, and the younger ones, Eunice, Patricia, Robert and Jean, along with baby Edward, that they form almost two separate generations. The older generation was the golden one. Except for Rosemary, they were all gifted with good looks, charm and serious intelligence. They were all achievers who benefited from their parents' time and attention, although as the younger children grew up, they received less attention. By this time their parents were distracted by travel, business and Joe's stint as Ambassador to the Court of St. James. Joe and Rose shared a philosophy about child rearing, raise the older ones right and they will take care of the younger ones. In Joe's master plan, it was entirely possible that once he had installed his oldest son, Joe Jr., in the White House, the others —quiet, studious Jack, devoutly religious Bobby and baby brother Teddy—would follow. In Joe's rigorous training school at Palm Beach and Hyannis Port, the boys learned that they could only trust family. Winning was everything. Kennedys were a special breed endowed by God and Joe Kennedy to someday rule America.

The boys also learned something else that the rules of responsibility, fidelity and honesty did not apply to Kennedy men. Their confidence that they were above the ordinary rules bred into Joe's sons a pattern that would ultimately destroy them. The recklessness of the Kennedy men had many facets such as a disregard for their own safety, a thirst for dangerous liaisons with unlikely women, and an unwillingness to delay their personal gratification, even when it could have life-threatening consequences.[2]

Is it no wonder that Jackie would be attracted to the whole Kennedy package. These were men just like her own father who made their own rules and defied conventions. She was especially enchanted by old Joe for he represented an attitude towards life that she wholeheartedly embraced. It was a full-speed ahead and damn the torpedoes approach to life. Jackie always said that she liked dangerous men. Now she would have the opportunity to live within a really dangerous family, a family she could relate to. Their hunger for power was as great as her hunger for wealth. She was able to hide her own ambitions under the cover of her gentility and upbringing. The Kennedys did not even bother to hide their ambitions. They hoped their lust for power would attract others to the cause of electing the first Irish Catholic president. It was an incredible dream and they were willing to share it with anyone who would help them make it come true. Rose and Joe Kennedy shared an ambition to live life to the fullest. Together they dismissed the commonplace for themselves and their prodigy.

By 1924, at thirty-five, Joe was a millionaire several times over. He drove a Rolls-Royce, hired a corps of servants and two years later sent his family to New York in a private railroad car. The stock market and real estate speculations provided a lucrative income. Joe was also involved in illegal liquor trade during prohibition. In 1922, at his tenth Harvard reunion, Joe Kennedy provided the scotch. "Joe was our chief bootlegger," said a classmate. "Of course, he didn't touch a drop himself, but he arranged with his agents to have the stuff sent in right on the beach at

Plymouth. It came ashore the way the pilgrims did."[3]   Decades later, just before his own death, mob leader Joe Costello confided to Peter Maas, the *New York Times* writer, that he and Kennedy had been partners in the liquor-smuggling business throughout the 1920s and early 1930s.[4]

To outward appearances, the Kennedys were more visible and outrageous compared to the Auchincloss environment which must have pleased Jackie and her father very much. Jack Bouvier was no fan of old Joe Kennedy and, in fact, blamed him for many of his own financial problems. Both father and daughter must have thoroughly delighted in knowing that Janet would soon have to deal with old Joe herself. Joe Kennedy was everything Janet wasn't, and he would bring back memories to Janet of where she had come from herself. After all, they were both Irish and trying to climb the same ladder. Is it no wonder that Jackie always preferred to stress her French background and her father's lineage?

This aura that both Jackie and her father had diligently worked on is exactly what made her so appealing to the Kennedy family. She had style, class and she was a fresh, beautiful face. She would provide an incredible landscape upon which to set Jack Kennedy's married life. It would be a far cry from his previous image as a ladies' man. Joe Kennedy knew what he wanted for his young heir and Jackie would fit beautifully into his plans. As one of the richest men in the country, Kennedy decided that money had meaning only when it involved power. The more power that he got, the more he wanted. A United States Supreme Court Justice said of Joe Kennedy, "Isn't he the most evil man you ever met, the most evil of the entire lot."[5]   Self-interest was Joe's motivating force. His judgments were black and white and quick, and he believed more in himself than in his God. Nor did he parade his Irish roots his sons would so later prize. More than anything else, he wanted to be assimilated and respected by the Wasp world. What better little Wasp-appearing wife for his son than Jackie? Of course, she filled all the criteria for their Catholic conscience and yet she was quite a catch. Jackie would blend into the saga that this family was about to begin. Unwittingly, they had enticed the fly into their web that would eventually cause the destruction of their entire dream.

Together, Joe and Rose Kennedy had founded a dynasty that would change the course of American history. It would create an almost century-long epic marked by more tragedy and violence than a Greek play.

Joe's father, Patrick Joseph, known as P. J. was an east Boston saloon keeper and ward boss. P.J. was a master at behind the scenes deal making and he taught his son, Joe, everything he knew. Young Joe was sent to Boston Latin school rather than to Catholic schools so that he would have a strictly secular and first class education. His parents chose Boston Latin because it was one of the finest schools in the country, and it was also a bastion of the Protestant establishment, the Boston Brahmins.

When it was time for college, Harvard was the obvious choice. Although Joe was never chosen for the prestigious clubs such as Porcelain, A.D. and Fly, he was chosen for Hasty Pudding which was a significant accomplishment for a Boston Irish Catholic at that time.[6] Perhaps this club association was a harbinger of the role theatrics would play in the future for Joe and his descendants?

Rose Elizabeth Fitzgerald was born in Boston on July 22, 1890. She was the first of six children, three of them girls. Her father was the outgoing, vivacious Honey Fitz who became mayor of Boston. Rose's mother, the former Josephine Hannon, shunned the limelight. So from an early age, Rose became her father's companion which she adored. Rose's lavish coming out party was attended by more than 450 guests including the governor of Massachusetts, but she was still ignored by the elite Wasp clubs. The greatest disappointment of her young life was that although she had been accepted at Wellesley College, she was not allowed to attend. Her father was concerned with his Irish power base and insisted that she attend a convent school. Sadly, she would return to that disappointment again and again in her later life. Even so, Rose sent all of her own daughters to the same Sacred Heart schools she herself had attended.[7] Rose returned to that topic in her later years. To be sure that everyone would appreciate the fact that she had indeed been bright enough to have been accepted into such a prestigious school. It may have been her way of trying to deflect the assessment of future historians in labeling her the compliant, dutiful wife, the one to feel sorry for or to be pitied.

Eventually Kennedy moved his family from Boston to New York because he was still frustrated by the unwillingness of the Brahmins to take the Kennedys seriously. He feared that his children would be barred from elite social events. When Joe applied for membership in the Cohasset Country Club, the summer resort of choice for many Boston families, he was blackballed. Years later, the incident still rankled him. "Those narrow minded bigoted sons of bitches barred me because I was Irish Catholic and the son of a barkeeper. You can go to Harvard and it doesn't mean a thing. The only thing these people understand is money." And Kennedy was determined to make even more of it. In early 1926, Joe entered the booming movie business. Kennedy was soon playing a major role in several key film industry mergers. In thirty-two months in the movies, Kennedy made some five million dollars and earned a reputation for shrewdness, boldness and cunning. About this time, Joe began to be known as an ardent skirt chaser. He was often away from his family for extended periods of time and, like many of the movie moguls, was unable to resist the endless stream of beauties willing to pay a price for a chance at stardom.[8]

Even though Joe was away and quite the womanizer, Rose knew her place was in the home and at his side when he needed her. Early in their marriage, she left Joe for a short time to return to the refuge of her father's home to reflect on the state of their marriage. However, at that time women from her background did not really have much choice. Most families felt that once you made your bed you had better lie in it. So Rose returned to her unrepentant husband and resigned herself to married life with her religion as her main source of comfort and consolation.

Even when he was away, the vital force in the Kennedy family was Joe who Rose called the "architect of our lives." From Hollywood, or wherever he was on his travels, he barraged the children with letters, taking an active interest in their personal lives. In the more than two hundred letters that have survived the author, Doris Kearns Goodwin reported not once did Joe raise any serious moral principles for his children to ponder. He kept in touch with Rose by telephone almost daily and on Sundays spoke with each child. When he was home, Joe became deeply involved with the children. Rose later described him as extremely affectionate, frank, outgoing and honest. He also tolerated little nonsense and no disobedience at all. Physical punishment was unnecessary. The children knew that their father was the absolute ruler of the house and the family. Rose wrote that her children "grew up with feelings of awe and reverence and respect and friendship and camaraderie and love and duty toward their father." Although a bit overstated, the description rings true since awe and respect were the primary responses. As Doris Kearns Goodwin put it, "Joe Kennedy, having achieved an almost primitive dominion over his children's youthful souls, would rule his boys and girls for the rest of their lives."[9]

Theirs was an elitist family since both Joe and Rose had grown up the favored children of their respective families who were indulged, encouraged, adored, nurtured and endowed with incredible amounts of self-esteem which they eagerly passed on to their own children. Their one early setback was the birth of their eldest daughter, Rosemary, whose development was slower than the other children. In typical can-do fashion Rose and Joe just willed her to catch up and, in fact, forced her to function at a level close to the others. In these early years of the children's lives, Rose provided the sense of what it meant to be a family and Joe supplied the emotional intensity. When they were young the children came to him for the physical love that they rarely got from their mother. Joe saw them for what they were as individuals, and had a clear vision of their capabilities. He was always there to decide who would run for what, and when— sometimes even whom they would marry.[10]

From the earliest years, the pride of the family was the eldest son and Joe's namesake, Joe, Jr. The family plan was for young Joe to become the first Irish Catholic President of the United States. After Joe was killed in World War II, Joe, Sr., selected the reluctant Jack to replace Joe in this political career. Joe Kennedy, Sr., also predicted that all three sons would be president, and if Joe, Jr., had lived it would have been four Kennedy presidents. He would even gloat that this would be better than the Adams family who only had two presidents.[11]   Joe, Sr. was relentless in his ambitions for his sons. On a golf course in Palm Beach in 1936, a friend asked Joe Kennedy, "What are you doing these days, Joe?" without taking his steely eyes from the ball, he replied, "My work is my boys." It wasn't just his work it was his life, his immortality. The driving dream of his life had been to become the President of the United States. With that dream dead for him, Joe zeroed in on his four sons. They would reach the political prize he could not reach. He shaped them in his image, instilled in them his principles and ideas. When Jack became a first term congressman, he later apologized for his conservatism, saying, "I'd just come out of my father's house at the time, and these were the things I knew."[12]

The Kennedys were raised in a cocoon of sorts, one that not only protected and valued them as young children, but, alas, insulated them from the outside world. As Rose so truthfully would put it, "Years ago, we decided that our children were going to be our best friends and that we never could see too much of them." They were a self-contained unit. If any of us wants to sail or go walking or just talk, there is always a Kennedy eager to join in. It was this tight-knit closeness that would be the political strength of the Kennedy men. Ultimately, it would also be their undoing.[13] Within the family, it was always understood that their codes, their values were the right ones.[14]

As the children grew older and began to spread their collective wings under the watchful eyes of their parents, they displayed many of their parents' attributes. Joe's sons especially displayed varying degrees of his charm, vitality and magnetism, yet they also showed some of his dark side with ruthless actions. The sons also absorbed their father's standards about women. For the sons, Joe Kennedy was a fount of constant encouragement. The father made his sons believe that no matter what they did, no matter how wrong they sometimes were, he made them all think they were wonderful. They were part of an untouchable dynasty. Such arrogance was one of invulnerability, an arrogance that began with immense wealth and was capped with driving ambition, and sometimes a sparkling brilliance that propelled them beyond themselves into the limelight of the world and into the myth of history.[15]

All aspects of their lives were in a controlled environment, a hothouse theory that was nurtured. It prepared them to take their proper places as leaders of the next generation. The children were all imbued with a strong sense of attachment to the Roman Catholic church, essential to their Irish heritage, attending weekly mass was a way of life and there were often private devotions. The girls were the most deeply affected. By stern command and example, Rose supervised their adherence to church teaching. Premarital sex, for example, so common among their upper class friends, was unthinkable for the Kennedy women. The boys, too, were compelled to attend church and go through all the motions of a proper Roman Catholic. However, Joe let them know at an early age, by his own example, that much if not most of this piety need be only superficial. Real men were profane, aggressive and ruthless. They took what they wanted and broke the rules when necessary. Each of the boys, following in their father's footsteps, would strongly identify with the church. They would attend weekly mass, while doing what was to their advantage with little or no regard to its moral content. Lechery, for example, would be a way of life for the Kennedy males. In politics they would do whatever it took to win.[16] No wonder this family would be such a perfect match for the young Jacqueline Bouvier. She, too, understood from an early age that to survive one must do what must be done. There was nothing mysterious for either Jack or Jackie about how life was to be led.

Like all his brothers and sisters, Jack would never forget what he owed to his father. He owed not only his immense wealth, but the early lessons from the patriarch's example and declared values. Indeed, these were the lessons that echoed from both the Kennedy and Fitzgerald traditions. Life was primarily about getting what you want, about winning, no matter what the cost, no matter who it hurts. Pious talk about integrity, humility and love of one's neighbor was fine in church or campaigning, but it had little or nothing to do with reality. From their earliest days, the Kennedys were trained to compete, to be second to no one and to allow no obstacles to stand in their way. Thus, the founding Father commanded.[17]

So, too, little Jackie was put on a horse from her earliest years and competed in the arena of the upper class world she inhabited. She was a thoroughbred and both her parents and extended family were there to cheer her on and commend her performance. Winning was the only thing. This was something everyone could agree upon.

From their father the Kennedy sons learned how to manipulate people and events, how to court the press and create an image. He taught them that money was the mother's milk of politics and that politics was really just another form of show business. Most of all, he poured into them from childhood that they must win, win, win—no matter what the cost. To help them win, he freely made available his vast fortune, great influence and conniving mind. So completely did Kennedy, Sr., merge his life with his sons' that their successes became his own. In doing so Kennedy, Sr., would not be deterred by obstacles of morality or law.[18] By endowing all his children with great wealth and their own trust funds, it would appear that Joe was giving them financial independence, a freedom to do as they pleased with their lives and their money. Yet by this act, Kennedy bound his children to him more closely than if he had made them totally subservient to him for their financial survival. By not having to ever earn their own money, they would never be free of their indebtedness to him. By not attaching any strings or conditions, no one could ever question his motives or generosity. He had secured all his children's and their childrens' love and loyalty for all time.

This devotion the children had for their incredibly benevolent father would go a long way in helping them accept Joe's cruel treatment of Rose. This surely had an impact on all the children in one way or another. Jack grew up with a hostile attitude toward marriage and the family. Women were at best sex objects. "Dad told all the boys to get laid as often as possible."[19]

The hypocrisy of the parents' relationship had to be a difficult bridge for even the most loyal and understanding of children to cross, especially as Joe became more blatant about his adultery during the New Deal and war years. Rose became increasingly distant from everyone groping, no doubt, for some sort of self-preservation. She was alone much of the time and traveled to Europe by herself some seventeen times during the first six years of the great depression.[20] Now keep in mind, these were not quick hops over to Europe on the Concorde. They were prolonged ocean voyages and long stays abroad to take in all the latest fashion shows, plays and museums. Jack commented about his mother saying, "Mother was not around much, she was either at a Paris fashion show or on her knees in some church."[21]

Any future wife for Jack Kennedy would have to have an understanding of the Kennedy men's sense of marital fidelity that was similar to Jack Bouvier's standards that Jackie quite understood herself. A wife would also have to accept the aloofness and disconnected emotional side of this future President. Jack was among several of the Kennedys who suffered emotional damage in their youth. Close friends would tell interviewers that while Jack appeared on the surface to be friendly and concerned about others, he suffered from severe inhibitions. "He was not the kind of person to have self-revealing conversations. Jack had a total lack of ability to relate emotionally to anyone. Everything was so surface with him in his relationships with people. All the Kennedys were blocked, totally blocked emotionally." A lifelong pal spoke often of Jack's aloofness and his inability to love or express feelings, "Mr. Kennedy had never physically touched them much when they were young, Jack was the same way....didn't touch and didn't want to be touched." The same friend related, "He was immature emotionally, he had no depth of emotion. The male side of the family was like that. They came by it naturally...from the father."[22]

Also, Rose was a distant mother. The mere fact of raising nine children, even with all the help in the world, would still make it extremely difficult to connect deeply with each child try as she might. So we now look upon these poor, little rich children who appear to have everything, yet not quite!

It is not an unusual story and, in fact, very similar to young Jacqueline's. The Kennedy family myth about JFK is that he was this kind of glorious person produced by these wonderful parents whose whole purpose was to bring up clean living, honest children dedicated to public service. That is baloney. The Kennedy household was an emotional waste-land.[23]

As Jack and Jackie's stars crossed in the skies, they had two very big things going for them. Kennedy had no interest at all in marrying a woman like his mother, and Jackie was nothing at all like Rose Kennedy. She was a complete original and a very intriguing one at that. On the other hand, Jackie wanted to marry a man just like her father. She wished to recapture that wonderful safe feeling she had with her father. Jack Kennedy came as close to being a clone of Jack Bouvier as Jackie would ever find.

Just as Jack would need a wife to validate his political quest, so too would Jackie need to marry the ideal man. That man would have to be someone who was wealthy, and could provide her with the lifestyle she so desperately needed for herself and her future children. She had spent her childhood and formative years looking through the window of the Auchincloss family's life of great wealth and security. She knew what she wanted and she knew how to get it. It was just a matter of finding the right man. She wanted a life of glamour, style and excitement, all of which the Kennedy family could do in abundance. JFK was a man on the way up. It was no secret that old Joe Kennedy deeply wanted the White House for his second son and those to follow. Joe thought big and, in this respect, he was truly admired by Jackie. The Kennedy men were much like her own father. They gave her that dangerous feeling she so loved. More importantly, the Kennedy men made her feel good when she was with them. When she first met the family, she made it her first priority to enchant old Joe right away, even if it meant talking back to him to show her spirit. She wasn't dumb. She knew he would admire that in a woman. She knew who called all the shots now and in the future. Rose was someone to be tolerated and put up with. As for the other children, they were relatively unimportant as Jack's star was in its ascendancy. JFK was the family torch-bearer and his future was the entire family's future. Everyone would be on board and do everything to help Joe achieve this dream. This was going to be quite a ride.

This was the ideal family for Jackie to marry into since their ambitions were as great as her own. They wanted to attain power to avenge all the Boston Brahmins who had snubbed Joe and his family so badly in the past. The Kennedys already had wealth and now they wanted to enter the prestigious circles from which they had so long been excluded. By achieving the White House, the ultimate power and status symbol, they would have arrived.

Jackie's motives were strictly materialistic. All she truly desired was great wealth and to eventually become a woman of independent means. As for the society she had come from, it would be nice to have the opportunity to snub them. She would do this on the day her husband became president in the future, but her real agenda was and always would be money. Money was her security, her self-esteem, her criteria by which she judged everything. She knew that she could not count on the people who claimed to love her. She knew in her heart that money would always have to be there for her to survive. It was as essential as the very air she breathed. It was the intrinsic essence of her very soul and spirit. To exist without it was unthinkable, and so she was on the lookout for the right man from the wealthiest family that she could possibly find.

When her path crossed with the young handsome, glamorous senator from Massachusetts, the stage was set for the romance of the decade, a love story for all time. The time was right and their destinies would soon join to become a legend within her lifetime. Their future looked so bright that no one could possibly foresee the tragedy that lay ahead. It would be incomprehensible to imagine what one woman's greed would do to their future. She was stepping into their midst without so much of a hint of the disaster to come. These were opportunistic people.

But not even at their very worst,

would they deserve what . . .

she would do to them.

FOUR

WHAT KIND OF COURTSHIP AND RELATIONSHIP DEVELOPS PRIOR TO THE MARRIAGE?

THE MARVELOUS MARRIAGE MERGER

*T*HE ROMANCE AND MARRIAGE OF JACK KENNEDY and Jacqueline Bouvier started out as a basic fairy tale love story, a young, wealthy, handsome senator wooing the even younger, beautiful, aristocratic lady of his dreams. The American public was presented with this union of the Kennedy and Bouvier dynasties in September of 1953 in Newport at the Hammersmith Farms. However, the events leading up to this golden moment provide a clearer look at the future Mrs. John F. Kennedy. We must examine her priorities and her personal agenda upon entering this marriage, a marriage that would so tragically end, yet survive so strongly in the myth of Camelot just ten years later.

How did it all begin? Jack and Jackie were destined to be together and many people tried to introduce them on numerous occasions. Charles and Martha Bartlett, however, were the ones who finally succeeded in bringing Jack and Jackie together.

Bartlett's interest in Jackie dated to 1948, when he first arrived in Washington, an ambitious and talented correspondent for the *Chattanoga Times*. In 1949, he invited Jackie to his brother David's wedding at East Hampton, L. I. where, so the story goes, he nearly succeeded in introducing her to his friend John F. Kennedy, Representative from the 11th Congressional District of Massachusetts. Bartlett, a native of Chicago and a graduate of Yale, had met Jack Kennedy soon after the war, when his family wintered at Hobe Sound in Florida. Also the Kennedys lived in Palm Beach, practically next door. "I knew Jack's taste in women and I thought he'd appreciate Jackie because she wasn't like anyone else," said Bartlett. "At the same wedding reception, I introduced her to former heavyweight boxing champion Gene Tunney. They stood in one corner and Jack in another talking politics as usual. Neither could be distracted nor detached, and by the time I managed to intervene in Jackie's *tet-a-tete*, Jack had already departed."

The next opportunity for an introduction came in may 1951, when Charles Bartlett had married Martha Buck, they were living in Georgetown, awaiting the birth of their first child. Although Charles Bartlett has always taken credit for introducing Jack and Jackie, the true matchmaker seems to have been his wife. Martha was the one who finally got them together. She arranged the now historic dinner party, invited Jack and Jackie and several other couples so it wouldn't look contrived. Martha pushed Jack and Jackie together on the couch, served them cocktails and let them drink their heads off.

Charles Bartlett recalled that after dinner, "Everyone repaired to our small backyard to play what was then commonly known as "the game", a form of charades. The Kennedys were as proficient at "the game" as they were at touch football and just as competitive. But Jackie, being super bright and having studied pantomime, was in a league by herself."[1]

Jack, thirty-four at the time, was intrigued by the twenty-one-year-old college senior. Jack had never met anyone quite like Jackie, all the more remarkable considering his exposure to the opposite sex. She was incredibly beautiful, to be sure, and highly intelligent. She seemed to have more substance than other girls he had known. Jack had known plenty of "substantial" women who combined beauty and brains but Jackie was special.

What drew them together? They were two lonely people who instantly recognized that in each other. It is ironic that these two people who were to eventually personify charm and grace for millions of people were really lone wolves.[2]

"Jack seemed duly impressed and when it came time to leave, he walked Jackie to her car which was parked in front of the house. As he was saying something about wanting to take her some place for a nightcap, there was a sudden commotion. The Bartlett's fox terrier had raced ahead of them and made an unexpected leap through an open window of the car, landing with a howl in someone's lap. The stranger turned out to be one of Jackie's ex-boyfriends, who lived near by. He was on his way home, spotted her car, and decided to play a practical joke. Jackie was as surprised as anybody to find him there and, when she recovered herself, made the introductions. Her friend excused himself and Jack became flustered." But he seemed interested because he telephoned the Bartletts the next day and started asking questions about Jackie.

Jack and Jackie didn't meet again until the following winter when Jackie was already engaged to John Husted, a young banker. Jackie was working at the *Times-Herald,* and Kennedy was busy preparing for his senatorial contest in Massachusetts against Henry Cabot Lodge. Again it was Martha Bartlett who instigated the meeting this time by convincing Jackie to invite Kennedy as her escort to another dinner party at the Bartletts' home. "We didn't think much of Jackie's fiance," said Charles Bartlett. "He was a nice fellow, but he didn't seem to be worthy of Jackie." The dinner went well. The first time they went out together, not long after this meeting, Kennedy took Jackie dancing in the Shoreham Hotel's Blue Room. They had a chaperon, Dave Powers, Kennedy's political aide from Boston. After that, the encounters between Jack and Jackie followed a curious private pattern—"spasmodic" was her word for it. On occasion, Jackie would visit him at his Boston apartment-cum-office.

By April, they were dating more regularly but limited their public appearances, preferring small dinner parties at the homes of friends. "Then there were the evenings," according to Jack's former roommate at Choate, Lem Billings, "when they would simply neck in the back seat of Jack's car

and afterwards he would drive her home to Merrywood. Not long after
they started dating seriously, Jack found himself in an even more awkward
situation. Once while nuzzling with Jackie in the car, they were interrupted
by a state trooper. They were parked on a secluded side street in Arlington,
the trooper drove up and shined his flashlight into the back seat of Jack's
convertible where Jack had managed to take off Jackie's brassiere. Apparently the trooper recognized Jack because he apologized and retreated. But
Jack had visions of possible headlines: *U.S. Senator Mauls Topless Inguiring
Photographer. Camera Girl Busted With Top Down,* 'She may be engaged
but at least she's not married,' he said, 'Now that could be unpleasant'."[3]

Isn't it interesting that although Jackie was currently engaged to
John Husted, it did not stop her from pursuing Jack Kennedy. The official
version is that Janet called off the engagement to Husted because he didn't
have enough real money. Perhaps it was, in truth, Jackie's decision all
along. She had found herself a bigger fish. Once she thought there was a
good chance of catching him, she was smart enough to cut her losses and
get rid of Husted. It was time to reel in the big one!

At that time in 1952, Jackie who was living with her mother and
stepfather, began pursuing Jack Kennedy in the most ingenious ways she
could devise, always being available for his last-minute calls for movies or
dinner. She once spent hours translating and summarizing a dozen French
books about Indonesia for him, laboring late at night to finish the task. "He
has got to ask me to marry him after all I've done for him," she told a
friend. She even used her newspaper column to catch his attention with
such questions as: "What do you think of marriage?" "What's your idea of
the perfect mate?" "Do you consider a wife a luxury or a necessity?" "Can
you give any reason why a contented bachelor should get married?"[4]

Jackie felt that deep within Jack was a "pool of privacy," similar to
hers. She compared herself and Jack to "icebergs," the greater part of their
lives submerged, and insisted that this was the bond between us.[5] Jackie
identified with this bond of privacy. It is not surprising that in the future
she would often feel betrayed by Jack. He would allow the political reality

to so intrude upon their private life and time together. This feeling of betrayal would haunt her, and eventually destroy her trust and loyalty to her husband.

For the present, though, Jackie had read a newspaper interview in which Jack Kennedy had elaborated on the kind of wife he wanted. "Intelligent, but not too brainy." This description disturbed her far less than the fact that she differed so drastically from the type of woman he usually dated-seductive, outgoing, curvaceous.

Jackie concentrated on molding herself into a warm, enthusiastic, lighthearted companion, a girl with a love of art, music and literature. Her most attractive feature was her ability to become a "bewitching lighthouse beacon of charm," and when the beam was on, the light was bright. "When she liked a man, she focused on him to the exclusion of everything else in the room taking him in with her wide-set eyes, listening to him 'with a shining, breathless intensity'," recalled Jackie's cousin, John Davis.

For Jack Kennedy, the light was always on. Jackie informed Mary Van Rensselaer Thayer, a journalist friend of her mother, that from the very beginning she realized that "Jack would have a profound perhaps disturbing influence" on her life. In a flash of perception, she also understood that here was a man who, despite what he told interviewers, did not really want to marry. The realization demoralized her. She envisioned heartbreak, but decided that the heartbreak might be worth the pain and effort.

Jackie's plan of action was as meticulously plotted as any of Jack Kennedy's subsequent political campaigns, very little left to chance. She learned that he sometimes brought his lunch to work in a paper bag and ate alone in his office. She made it a point of dropping in on him at lunchtime with a hot box-lunch for two.[6]

By 1952, Jackie was falling in love with John Kennedy. He had already confided to her that he intended to become President of United States. But first he had to beat Henry Cabot Lodge and be elected senator which he did. Recognizing that with Jack Kennedy she'd have it all, Jackie confided to a newspaper friend, "What I want more than anything else in the world is to be married to him." To that end she devoted all her time and attention. She tolerated what she had previously described as "a spasmodic courtship", and ignored the other women who would always be a part of his life and her life with him.[7]

Jackie had almost no money of her own. Thus when the junior Senator from Massachusetts began to pay his respects after defeating Lodge, she became highly attentive. Jack had personal charm, of course, position and a nationally recognized name, and he was worth about $10 million. "Essentially," Nancy Dickerson wrote, "she was motivated by a desire for money."[8]

In order to survive and prosper, Jackie understandably gravitated to John F. Kennedy who fit into her scheme of the world as she knew it. As one of her friends from Newport said, "During those days our future was to marry well. That's all we'd ever been trained to do and that's what we did, just like our mothers did before us."[9]

As for Jack, he liked Jackie. Jack was fascinated by her facility with foreign languages. He admired her knowledge of ancient history which surpassed his own. He respected her love of the fine arts for which he had little interest. Jack appreciated her elevated vocabulary since he regularly used vulgarities. Jack thought of Jackie as a woman of "class" someone who would elevate the Kennedy's social as well as political standing.[10]

As their courtship slowly progressed, even Jack's trusted Washington staff was kept in the dark. His personal secretary, Evelyn Lincoln, routinely telephoned girls to arrange dates for her boss. With one exception, Jack placed his calls to Jackie personally.[11]

Since his senate victory, Jack had given much thought to the idea of marriage. He liked to be petted and looked after by a woman just as much as the next man. He felt envious when his old Harvard classmates sent him invitations to their weddings. He asked so many friends for advice about marriage that they joked he should put the matter before the senate for a vote. Yet like all his brothers and sisters, with the exception of Bobby, he had trouble making a personal commitment. Something held him back. Most people just assumed that Jack was having too much fun as a bachelor to give up his independence. "The women chased him," said Evelyn Lincoln, his secretary. "I had seen nothing like it in my whole life. Half of my telephone calls were women." Jack complained to his old navy pal, Paul "Red" Fay that he was "both too young and too old for all this." "Marriage," he said, "means the end of a promising political career, as it has been based up to now almost completely on the old sex appeal."[12] He was only half kidding. The combination of power and sex was a potent fantasy for many voters, male and female alike. Jack wasn't sure that he wanted to marry a beautiful young creature like Jackie who might steal the limelight.

He did not object to marrying Jackie because it would put a crimp in his sex life; since having a wife wouldn't stop him from chasing women. But he knew that marriage would bring certain wrenching changes. For one thing, he would have to trust Jackie with his deepest secrets. Considering how he had grown up distrusting his own mother, it was hardly surprising that Jack hesitated to trust any woman.

He could not hide from a wife the facts about his health—facts that, if made public, were enough to sink his chances for the Presidency. No one would vote for a man with a congenital spinal deformation, a cripple who had to use crutches. He would not last a minute in public if people found out about his Addison's. In 1953, Addison's disease was still considered to be a fatal affliction. It was like having incurable cancer.[13]

There was also the spectre of venereal disease that carried along with it Jack's fear of impotency and infertility. JFK had contracted venereal disease in 1940, when he was 23 years old. By the fall of 1951, he was suffering from recurrent symptoms—burning urine, prostate pain, secretion of pus and anxiety about the effect on his fertility. His "nongonococcal urethritis," as it was euphemistically called on his medical charts, had become a serious problem according to Dr. William P. Herbst, a venereal specialist, who took over Jack's treatment from the Lahey Clinic in Boston.[14]

"By the time Jack met Jackie, he was thirty-five and had just been re-elected to the senate," recalls Betty Spalding, a long-time Kennedy friend, "and his wariness of marriage was being superseded by the political need for a wife." That's why he married her. He was going to be President, and he certainly couldn't take Angie Dickinson to the White House with him. Jackie filled the bill. From his father, Jack Kennedy had learned how to draw a shrewd line between women for mistresses and women for marriage. Jackie was the wife type. She was well educated and had impeccable social credentials. And of course, she was Catholic. Jack could never have married outside the church and still become President.

Such reminiscences from close friends suggest that Jack Kennedy's political ambitions motivated his marriage proposal to Jackie. He was attracted to her but it was not the romantic involvement of a young man desperately in love. "To Jack's way of thinking, women were there to serve men," said Betty Spalding, "and any wife of his would be there to do for him the same way Rose did for Joe, with the right food, good clothes, meals on time, and the house running smoothly so he could attend to business and not worry about the domestic side of life when he came home." This was completely compatible with Jackie's way of thinking as she viewed her primary role of wife and mother.[15]

However reluctant Jack was to give up his bachelor status, by late May 1953, the identity of the bride was not in question. "I think that he understood that the two of them were alike," Lem Billings said of Jack. "They had both taken circumstances that weren't the best in the world when they were younger and learned to make themselves up as they went along." Billings added, "They were so much alike. Even the names - Jack and Jackie, two halves of a single wheel. They were both actors and they appreciated each other's performance."[16]

Isn't it interesting that with the passage of time so many different memories surface that can be so different. One person sees them as actors doing an incredible performance. Perhaps no one can see at this time that Jackie is merely warming up for the performance of a lifetime. While he would seem to be the main star, Jack is doing just a short stint on center stage. Jackie, just a supporting actress in the wings, would eventually steal the show for one of the longest runs in history.

However the actress hadn't learned all her lines yet, but leading up to the proposal, she knew the way to play the scene. "Jackie was very sweet but rather shy," recalls the wife of a senator friend of Kennedy's. "She was so in love with Jack, although he barely paid any attention to her and was always making fun of her because she was so flat chested. It was obvious to us then that she wanted to marry more than he did, although he was thinking about it." [17]

As their romance progressed, Jackie struggled to keep up with the blistering Kennedy pace at Hyannis Port. She finally decided to revert to her old style, her more tranquil and reflective manner, especially after she injured her foot in one of the family touch football games. Jack's sisters needled Jackie mercilessly and bombarded her with sarcasm. Jackie in turn told her own sister, Lee, that the sisters, "Run in place and other times fall all over each other like a pack of gorillas". [18]

Jack's sisters wanted him to marry a proper political wife like Ethel Skakel, but Jackie was no Ethel. What no one in the family seemed to realize was that Jack did not want an Ethel. He had struggled all his life to cut himself loose from the raucous Kennedy herd. He was attracted by Jackie's elegant old money manners, *savoir faire*, and exotic otherness. [19]

Jackie quickly surveyed the Kennedy family scene and came to the brilliant and correct conclusion that the only one who mattered in the entire family was Joe Kennedy. Once she had him in the palm of her hand, she would then be the one who would be calling all the shots. Winning Joe over was essential to her plan to conquer the heart of the son. It didn't take a rocket scientist to figure out that all the children were merely pawns on Joe's chessboard of life. Joe was the King and his blessing upon her would ensure her marriage to the future King and her reign as Queen.

To win Joe Kennedy to her side, Jackie played upon his social insecurity. She dropped hints about her illustrious background, flaunted her French Catholic ancestry, her highly developed sense of style, while hiding the tough ambitious Irish Catholic side of her character. She sensed immediately what appealed to Joe. Despite the taunts of his daughters, he admired her refinement and polish. Every one of the Kennedy men married women more socially prominent than they. Joe had married Rose because her father was the mayor of Boston. Jackie had all the vital social ingredients Joe thought would help Jack attain the presidency. She had been debutante of the year, attended Vassar, the Sorbonne and lived at Merrywood and Hammersmith Farms. She gave the impression of having great wealth, dispelling the notion that she might possibly be a gold-digger. Her wealth was largely an illusion because in reality Jackie was almost penniless. Nobody, except Joe, realized that until after the marriage.

"Joe Kennedy not only condoned the marriage, he ordained it," claimed Lem Billings. "A politician has to have a wife, and a Catholic politician has to have a Catholic wife. She should have class. Jackie probably has more class than any girl we've seen around here,"said old Joe.[20]

Jackie was ready for the proposal to take place but Jack just couldn't seem to get the words out of his mouth. "Jack's got to ask me to marry him," Jackie told her mother. "I'm going to call him." "A girl doesn't call a gentleman, dear," Janet Auchincloss said. "You are not to go after him. You must not look too anxious or too eager. You must keep yourself scarce."[21] So following the old adage about absence making the heart grow fonder, Jackie was quick to jump at the opportunity to go to London for the coronation of Queen Elizabeth II. Jackie was gripped by royal fever and consumed every word in the British press. For Jackie, the Queen-to-be was an object of a woman who left nothing to chance. While she was there reporting on the coronation for the *Times-Herald,* she received a cablegram from Jack wanting to know if she would marry him.[22]

After London Jackie went to Paris thinking about the marriage proposal, she resumed her liaison with her old lover, Jack Marquand.[23] Gore Vidal quotes Marquand as saying, "They resumed their affair from when Jackie was studying in Paris at the Sorbonne in 1949," and that "this time he proposed to her but she turned him down." Jackie told Marquand that she was going to marry Jack Kennedy.

Marquand was appalled. "You can't marry that...that Mick.," he blurted. She was cooly to the point. "He has money, and you don't."[24]

Returning home, Jackie was ecstatic about the proposal. "Jackie immediately quit her job and started concentrating on getting married. However, Jack's reaction was somewhat different. A Newport friend of Jackie, who was also close to JFK, remembers spending the evening at a party with Kennedy before the engagement announcement appeared in the papers. "He went out to dinner with my wife and myself, got very drunk and later took a woman home and spent the night with her. But before that we were together for about three hours and he never once mentioned the engagement announcement coming out the next day, which you've got to admit doesn't sound like a man in love and looking forward to getting married."[25]

As for Joe Kennedy, he was thrilled to welcome Jackie into the family fold. He, himself, selected a most suitable "welcome to the family" gift. Joe Kennedy entered the hushed salesroom of a famous Fifth Avenue jewelry store alone to pick out Jackie's engagement ring. His son had no interest in such sentimental things. His purchase consisted of a square-cut emerald of 2.84 carats and a matching diamond of 2.88 carats. He also bought a ruby and diamond bracelet and diamond leaf pin. "Send them to Hyannis Port," he said. "These will be the first serious pieces of jewelry Jackie's ever had."[26] Joe knew exactly what would please and impress his soon-to-be daughter-in law. If it could be said that diamonds were a girl's best friend, it could be said that Joe Kennedy would turn out to be Jackie's best friend. She knew who to choose when it counted.

In Jackie, Joe saw the perfect wife for his son. She was a woman who had class, one of his favorite words, and she had enough of it to automatically elevate the family socially. Even more important, she was Catholic, the number one requirement to put his son in the White House.[27]

Joe paved the way for Jackie by giving her his imprimatur. The rest of the family did not have to embrace her, but merely accept her as he did despite her differences.[28]   Joe did not merely sanction Jack's marriage to Jackie, he demanded that it take place —and soon.[29]

      At this time, Joe had an intense conversation with Jackie that he shared with the singer Morton Downey. Joe told Downey he was impressed with the way Jackie stood up to him. She had displayed the kind of true grit he admired, and she wasn't afraid to give him the needle. "You have no nuances," Jackie teased, "everything with you is either black or white, while life is so much more complicated than that." Joe liked that. "What did you and Jackie talk about?" Downey asked. "Money," Joe said. "She talked straight to me. She makes a pathetic fifty-six bucks a week from the camera-girl job she's got on the *Times-Herald*. Her old man gives her a fifty-dollar a month allowance and he can barely afford that. Her step-father's in bad shape too. I told her that I'd fix it so Jack had his own money—he wasn't dependent on me. If she married Jack, she wouldn't have anything to worry about. And if Jack didn't look after her properly, I would."[30]   Joe had come to the conclusion that Jackie Bouvier would make Jack a swell wife. She had the three B's—Beauty, Brains, and Breeding— and what was more she had a lot of pluck. Joe and Jackie spoke the same language.[31]

      Now it was time for Jack to finally settle down and get on with the serious business of being a Kennedy on his way to the White House. For the time being at least, Jack was to try to play it straight and do his duty. Now for Jack this also meant ending his relationship with the beautiful young starlet, Audrey Hepburn. Jack's fascination with Hepburn was perfectly understandable. "She out Jackied, Jackie," said one acquaintance. "Like everyone else who met her, Jack thought Audrey was simply exquisite. She had this very sexy, very naughty side that the public never saw. She and Jack managed to keep their affair out of the press, and the fact that it was clandestine only made it that much more intense." As a foreigner, a non-Catholic, and a show business personality Audrey was not a good marital prospect.[32]

It was one thing for a Catholic politician who aspired to the White House to fool around while he was single. At the age of thirty-six, it was time for Jack Kennedy to grow up and put aside his adolescent exhibitionism. As his wedding day approached, Jack seemed willing to turn over a new leaf.[33]   Or so it seemed.

By way of one last bachelor fling, Jack flew to Europe with his old college friend Torby Mac Donald. Janet Auchincloss was outraged. "What kind of man does this sort of thing?" she demanded. " A man who is about to be married wants to be with the woman he loves. Aware that she had no power to stop Jack, Jackie told herself that perhaps he would get it out of his system once and for all. Indeed, Jack behaved as if this were a romantic farewell tour of the continent. He was halfway through his list of former flames when by chance he bumped into Gene Tierney at Maxim's in Paris.[34] Jack had instructed his secretary, Evelyn Lincoln, to charter a yacht in the south of France. For public consumption, she let it be known that the Senator was conferring with French government officials on the situation in Vietnam. Nobody was fooled by that. The captain of the charter boat later related to Betty Beale the wild behavior and orgies that went on.[35] The bridgegroom-to-be had one great time as they cruised the Riviera in their chartered yacht picking up women in Juan les pins, Nice and Antibes. It was typical Kennedy.[36]

This was just the beginning of the public humiliation that characterized the Kennedy marriage from even before their vows were taken. You may ask how could she marry him with this sort of beginning? Gore Vidal is right to the point. "Jackie married Jack for money purely. There weren't that many other openings for her. Actually if she had not married Jack, she would have married someone else with money. Although it wasn't likely, she would have gotten someone as exciting as Jack in the bargain. When given a choice of glory or money, most people choose glory. But not Jackie. She also wound up with plenty of the latter, of course, but she didn't need that like she needed to be rich."[37]

For Jack Kennedy it was never about money; for him it was always about sex. His friend, Charles Spalding, would say about Jack, "I used to say that trying to tell Jack about money was like trying to teach a nun about sex."[38] He never carried money on his person, nor did he ever think about it since it was always there whenever he needed or wanted it. In the future we would see that to compensate for his ignorance about how one handles personal finances, Jack would become overly penurious. This definitely conflicted with his future wife's approach to money.

In June, Mr. and Mrs. Hugh D. Auchincloss gave an official engagement party for Senator John F. Kennedy and Jacqueline Bouvier at Hammersmith Farms and an official announcement was made in the papers. The wedding preparations picked up steam, but the original plans hit a wall when the Auchinclosses realized how big an event the Kennedy family wanted to have. Jackie did not want a particularly big wedding and her mother, Janet, definitely didn't want any photographers there. Things were at a standstill when Joe Kennedy arrived on the scene. Joe possessed a special radar that detected weaknesses in other people, and it did not take him long to size up the real situation at Hammersmith. As Joe suspected, Hugh no longer had sufficient income to maintain his old lifestyle. The Auchincloss brokerage firm had fallen upon hard times. Now the Kennedys were proposing a wedding for 1000 guests, a circus that would cost as much as a half million dollars. The stepfather of the bride didn't have that kind of money, so he, Joe Kennedy, would pay for it.[39] Now with Joe picking up the tab, there would be no holding back. This wedding would be the political event of the year. It would be a virtual "Who's Who" of the political arena. Everyone who could possibly help Jack reach the presidency would be invited.

September 12, 1953, which should have been a day of triumph for Jacqueline, turned out to be one of the saddest days in her young life. What Jackie and Jack Bouvier should have realized was that Janet Auchincloss was dead set on excluding him from everything to do with the wedding. Her reason had nothing to do with their marital squabbles of eighteen years ago. The reason was pure jealousy. Janet was insanely jealous of her daughters' love for their father, their preference for him over her. What Janet did was to assume control of all the arrangements for the prenuptial celebrations not already appropriated by Joe Kennedy. She then pointedly excluded her ex-husband.[40] Forty years later, the wife of one of Jack Kennedy's ushers confided that the whole fiasco had been prearranged. "We all knew that Jackie's dad had a terrible drinking problem, that her mother didn't want him there, and that she'd have someone get him so drunk that he couldn't show up to embarrass her. Then, by the strangest coincidence, Hugh Auchincloss was completely outfitted in formal attire and was standing by to walk his stepdaughter down the aisle."[41]

It was a very sad day for Jackie and her father, but a very triumphant day for her mother. Although Jacqueline's wedding to John F. Kennedy received an immense amount of press attention, many people didn't have the remotest idea of what the bride had gone through that morning. The radiance she exuded came from deep reserves of emotional strength, those strengths she had displayed since childhood.[42]

Now as Jackie entered into her new life as the wife of a future President of the United States, she could not help but think of the many warnings she had received from friends about entering into this union. Also, she could think of the warning her new mother-in-law had given her prior to the marriage. Jackie was not entering her marriage as some mousey Catholic convent maiden. She knew all about Jack's exploits. She had seen the diminished figure of Rose Kennedy. She could see what Rose had sacrificed for the idea of family. Rose had come to her to prepare her for the same kind of marriage she had endured for four decades. "I warned them both Jackie and Ethel, in the beginning," Rose said. "There would be rumors. There would be letters, anonymous letters. There would be all sorts of stories. That was part of the political spectrum."[43] What could Jackie say to the poor woman who lived in a fantasy world never admitting to others the despicable condition of her marriage and the sham of a life she had been forced to live? It's a shame that Jackie's mother couldn't have clued Rose into reality, just as she would do for Jackie in the future.

Example is a powerful teacher and Janet's life taught young Jackie more than Rose could ever hope to learn herself.

What was thought of as the wedding of the century and the dream marriage of the decade wasn't met by universal approval. One of those who expressed negative opinions was Evelyn Lincoln, JFK's secretary, whose own sense of it was that, "On their wedding day, Jack and Jackie were not in love." Lincoln said, "He was a politician who wanted to be president and for that he needed a wife. I am absolutely certain they were not in love. I think he persuaded her. There was no love there. That I'm sure."[44]

Thrills aside, there is little disagreement that there was one overriding factor in Jackie's pursuit of Jack....money. "They were not a logical match," said Kennedy friend, Priscilla Mc Millan, who was working in Jack's senate office in the spring of 1953. Jackie was far more cosmopolitan than he was. I envisioned her marrying some international playboy type, Jack was not her type at all." Mc Millan continued, "Socially, Jackie was marrying beneath her. Financially she was marrying what she was raised to marry."

"She was brought up with a father who lost his money and a mother who had to marry for security, and it was drummed into her that she had to go out and find a rich man of her own. Years later, they would say her spending habits were out of scale but eventually no amount of money would really ever be enough." Nancy Dickerson agrees. "Her prime motivation in marrying Jack was money. There just weren't any others around with as much money as Jack." Betty Spalding said, "She wouldn't have given Jack a second look if he hadn't had the money."[45]

Looking back from a perspective of over thirty years, the truth of the matter is that the courtship of Jack Kennedy and Jacqueline Bouvier was devoid of the usual trappings of romance. There were no flowers, no gifts, no valentines, no love letters—and no touching ever in public.[46]

It was just one thing. It was a business deal—pure and simple.

It was simply a cash and carry sort of arrangement.

It was your basic money and marriage,

instead of love and marriage.

FIVE

WHAT WAS THE REALITY OF THE KENNEDY MARRIAGE?

THE WAR ZONE

*B*EFORE THE NEWLYWEDS HAD LEFT FOR THEIR
honeymoon or even left the church, the bride was forced to face the reality
of the union. Jack Kennedy had removed his wedding ring as soon as the
ceremony was over. He did not believe in advertising that he was, technically at least, no longer in circulation.[1]

On her honeymoon to Acapulco, Jackie didn't have to worry since
she would have Jack all to herself, but later she said the honeymoon was all
too short. It went so fast. Jackie was already preparing herself for the
worst. She teased Jack about doing to her what her father had done to her
mother, jokingly taunting him not to let his 'better part' get the best of him.[2]

Before the marriage, Jackie wrote a poem to Jack that sadly reveals
that she already knew what lay ahead.

She wrote:

> He would find love
> He would never find peace
> For he must go seeking
> The golden fleece.

This would not be an easy relationship. Jack had been so private for
so long that it was not easy to give of himself. He had friends on many
levels and for a while shared part of himself with each of them. But he had

no friend or family member in whom he could completely confide, only parts and pieces and at special times. Always, deep within him, was this reserve, this mystery.[3]

It also did not help that Jack was a most self-centered man. He truly was the star of the Kennedy family. It was expected that everyone would defer to him since he was the anointed one. All their collective hopes, dreams and ambitions lay within this one man. It would be difficult to harness him, settling down would be preposterous to expect, considering his most spirited bachelorhood.

Jackie got a good preview of coming attractions when they left Mexico and flew to Los Angeles. They spent a few days in the home of Marion Davies, better known as the the mistress of William Randolph Hearst. Later they drove up the coast north to San Francisco where they visited PT-109 resident cutup, friend of Jack, Red Fay. Married less than fourteen days, a period during which they were never alone for more than a few hours, and already Jack was eager for time away from his wife.

Their last day in California was spent apart. Instead of taking his bride for lunch atop the Mark Hopkins on Nob Hill or for a stroll along Fisherman's Wharf, Jack accompanied Fay to a 49ers game. Jackie was left behind with Fay's wife, Anita. While Anita drove Jackie across the Golden Gate bridge to Marin County, Jackie fumed in the passenger's seat. "I'm sure this didn't seem a particularly unusual arrangement to Jack," Fay said, acknowledging Jackie's resentment. "The pressures of public life, not to mention those of an old shipmate and his wife, too often intruded on the type of honeymoon any young bride anticipates."[4] It was a nice try on Fay's part but the unpleasant fact for a new wife was that the 49er game could not be considered a demand of public life in any way, shape or form. The fact that Jack would much prefer a good football game with an old buddy rather than spend time romancing his new wife, reveals a great deal about this fledgling relationship.

In the weeks preceding her marriage, Jackie had been both per-plexed and apprehensive about her impending union. She knew that besides being a womanizer, Jack very much enjoyed being with his old buddies. What was she going to do when she wanted him all to herself?

It appears she answered these very questions by deceiving herself. Self-deception, in her case a form of wishful thinking, was the way she coped with the more unpleasant realities of life. For years she had denied to herself and others that there was any trouble between Mummy and Daddy when everyone knew there was deep trouble. For years she would turn a blind eye to Jack Kennedy's innumerable infidelities, telling herself that they never happened, or, if they did, they were utterly inconsequential. As she once told Joan Kennedy, "Kennedy men are like that. They'll go after anything in skirts. It doesn't mean a thing."[5]

One can't help but feel sorry for the young bride when they attended social affairs. Jack Kennedy would later confide to Priscilla Mc Millan at a dinner party, "I only got married because I was thirty-seven years old. If I wasn't married, people would think I was queer."[6] This kind of flip comment could possibly be taken as a witty joke. Even if you put a humorous spin on it, when it is said right in front of one's new wife, it has a very uncomfortable, even cruel sound. Of course, Jack was always known for his clever wit, but it may have hit a little too close to home for the new Mrs. Kennedy.

Another problem was Kennedy's schedule. "It was most difficult our first year of marriage," said Jackie. "Being married to a senator, you have to adjust to the fact that the only routine is no routine. He is never home at night before 7:45 or 8:oo pm, often later. He's away almost every weekend, making a speech somewhere. No, I don't go along. I stay home."[7] I suppose the difference here is that the other Kennedy women would not have stayed home. They would have preferred being there to cheer their man along every step of the way. Unfortunately for this marriage, Jackie did not get the big picture. She must have been incredibly naive to think that she could even possibly begin to change Jack and his mode of operation. Jackie was no Janet Auchincloss whose will of steel could mold people and events to her liking. Of course, in all fairness to Jackie, Janet had never come up against such a formidable family as the Kennedys.

The marriage of Jacqueline Bouvier and John F. Kennedy affected many people in many different ways. For Jack, it meant the renunciation of his much beloved bachelorhood. He would give up, for a while at least, the libertine ways he had reveled in all his adult existence. For Jackie, it meant more than giving herself up to one man. It meant surrendering herself to the rambunctious, clannish family that would eventually demand considerable sacrifices of her freedom and individuality. She, of course, would be handsomely paid for those sacrifices. Finally, her money troubles would be over. She could have anything she wanted—all she had to do was send the bill to Joe Kennedy. His paymaster took care of the bills for the entire family.[8]

For the newlyweds being Catholic and Kennedys, the first order of priority was to start a family right away. Just as Bobby and Ethel Kennedy had done immediately after their marriage. It was a great idea in theory but in reality it turned out to be a most difficult undertaking for Jack and Jackie.

For her part no matter how hard she tried, Jackie could not get pregnant exactly as Joe Kennedy had predicted when he told singer, Morton Downey before the marriage, "I don't think Porcelain can carry babies." The Kennedys silently blamed her for the barren marriage, even though it was not at all clear that it was Jackie's fault.

In fact, Jack had long been concerned that his chronic venereal disease—nongonococcal urethritis or chlamydia would make him infertile. During the first year of his marriage, he visited Dr. William P. Herbst, an eminent Boston urologist, and had his sperm count tested to see if he was capable of fathering children. He shared his concerns with Jackie. She knew he was taking enormous amounts of antibiotics to eradicate the bacteria that caused the sexually transmitted disease, and she lived in fear that he might infect her. "When you have a man who carries nongonococcal urethritis," said Dr. Atilla Toth, a specialist in the relationship between infections and infertility, "the woman with whom he has sex can sometimes achieve one pregnancy. However, after the first intercourse, the woman becomes infected and the bacteria usually stays behind and multiplies, and her subsequent pregnancies can be affected. Her second baby might come to term immature, and subsequent pregnancies can be miscarried." "Further more," said Dr. Toth, "some of these bacteria may infect her ovaries and after she gives birth, those sluggish ovaries will not produce the normal complement of hormones, and she can go through hormonal withdrawal and severe depression that can last for months."[9]

In late May of their first year together, Jackie suffered a miscarriage. Langdon Marvin wondered at the time whether the loss of the baby was somehow related to Jackie's torment and anguish over Jack's philandering. "I can only guess that Jack's philandering caused a great deal of tension," he said. "I have no idea if there's any medical evidence for it, but I sometimes wondered if it wasn't the reason for all those miscarriages and other related problems that Jackie had…her doctor told her that if she remained so high-strung she might have trouble bearing children. That made Jack nervous and probably induced him to have more affairs. He wanted a large family, no fewer than five children, but realized very early in the marriage that this just isn't going to happen."[10]

After her first miscarriage, Jackie sank into a deep depression. At the beginning of July 1955, she sailed alone for England where she stayed with her sister and, her sister's husband, Michael Canfield at their mews house in the Belgravia section of London. Lee was equally unhappy with her husband and the two sisters went off to Paris. Peter Ward, brother of the Earl of Dudley, recalls staying with the sisters in the south of France that summer. "Jackie left Jack Kennedy at that time," claims Ward. "They were split. Jack was having trouble with his back and Jackie had a rather bad conscience about that, but that was all. She said, 'I'm never going back' in my presence several times. She wasn't the least upset and seemed to be having a very good time."[11] The sisters' lives were parallel since they both were miserable in their marriages. Jackie was humiliated by Jack's never-ending infidelities and Lee was miserable for different reasons but the main misery that both sisters shared was that they were childless. When not commiserating with each other, they busied themselves with fashion shows, shopping and parties—always parties. Interestingly enough, a state-side friend who ran into Jackie and Lee at one of the gatherings said that their carefree behavior "denoted the absences of husbands."[12]

At that time Jackie was looking for something - a new start in life? A make-over? A way to change her image? Every chic woman wanted to look like Audrey Hepburn in "Roman Holiday." Suddenly, curves were out, a slim-hipped, slightly boyish silhouette was in. Givenchy and Balenciaga were creating a new look for the modern well-bred woman. With her flat chest, long waist and wonderful shoulders and arms, Jackie fit the new look to a "T". She immediately adopted it as her personal style. Next, Jackie and Lee traveled to the south of France where the Canfields had rented a villa for the month of August at Cap d'Antibes. Jack showed up late in August. For the past five years his father had rented the same villa, "Vista Bella," during the height of the season. Jack moved into the villa and began working on Jackie with all his powers of charm and persuasion. Soon, Jack and Jackie appeared to have reached a reconciliation. Yet the romance seemed to be waning. "Jack and Jackie didn't seem close at all," said J.C. Irondelle, the hotel's reception manager, "She was always sitting around with her sister, while Jack was moving in a large group of people. There were many beautiful women in the area, but very few actually stayed at the hotel. It was very expensive, so they would come to spend the day around the pool."

Jack and Jackie went to Monte Carlo, then took off for a ten day tour of Poland and an audience with the Pope in Rome. They ended their European sojourn with a party aboard the yacht of Aristotle Onassis. The Greek tycoon was then entertaining Sir Winston Churchill, one of Jack's heroes. Hoping to make an impression, Jack got dressed up in a white dinner jacket, but Churchill ignored him. "I think he thought you were the waiter, Jack," Jackie said in one of her more devastating putdowns.[13]

According to a friend of the couple, Jack and Jackie separated three years after their marriage. Joe, concerned about his son's political future, met with Black Jack Bouvier. Together the two forged a reconciliation between their children. "The agreement was that Jackie would go back to Jack, but he wouldn't fling his affairs in her face," said the friend.[14] For the first three years Jackie would try to hang on, clutching at a marriage that was in her own words, "Wrong, all wrong." Rumors had been circulating in Washington for some time that the Kennedys were having marital problems, and it was no surprise to see them out at night without one another, each going separate ways. There were even published reports in *Time* magazine that Jackie had threatened divorce and Joe Kennedy had made a million-dollar deal with her to stay with his son. Joe Kennedy did talk to Jackie at length, reassuring her that despite evidence to the contrary her husband loved her very much. He impressed on her the importance of staying together, saying that the thing Jack needed most to settle him down was a child.[15]

What made the resolution of this crisis stand out was Jackie's deferral to Joe as chief negotiator in things matrimonial. Where another injured wife might extract some favor from her husband as compensation for her distress, Jackie extracted concessions from her father-in-law. When Joe sought to smooth things over with money, it would have seemed nothing short of stupid to have turned the offer down.[16] Some of the concessions were that instead of having dinner every night with Jack's parents it was agreed that, "Once a week is fine but not every night." Joe also agreed that Jack and Jackie should move back to Georgetown. At Joe's insistence, Jack gave his wife a free hand in decorating the house and Jackie took full advantage of the offer.

Despite these and several other concessions such as Jack no longer taking phone calls during the dinner hour, Jackie continued to suffer pangs of resentment.[17] As part of the deal, Jackie also asked Joe for a new car, a Thunderbird to be precise. "I mean what could be more American?" she said. Joe would have none of it. "Kennedys," he told her, "drive Buicks." As for the million dollars, "Joe told us that he did offer Jackie a million dollars not to divorce Jack, absolutely," said Clare Booth Luce, who along with her husband, Henry, was the publisher of *Time* and a close friend of Joe Kennedy. "*Time* would never have printed the story otherwise." Jackie was forthcoming on the matter with Gore Vidal. "Yes," Vidal said, "Joe did offer Jackie the money to stay with Jack and she took it. Happily."[18]

As Joe said, "It's up to the wife to keep a marriage together speaking from personal experience, I can tell you that children are the secret to any good marriage. I'm going to set up a trust fund for your children. You will have control of it when you have children. And what if I can't have children?" asked Jackie, "If you don't have children within the next ten years," said Joe, "the trust fund will revert to you. The money will be yours to do with as you wish."[19]

All of her friends knew how difficult and lonely Jackie was. "It's not the right time of life for us," she said. "We should be traveling, having fun....I was alone almost every weekend." It was all wrong. "In their strangulated way, they loved each other," said Betty Spalding. " But neither was able to relate to the other, and there was never any affection between them at any time. He was always quite indifferent toward her." Jack had a total lack of ability to relate emotionally to anyone. I think that was one of the things that was so difficult for Jack when he finally married Jackie. Both of them were blocked emotionally. Their relationship was extremely stormy.[20]

The biggest highlight of this floundering early marriage was the birth of Caroline Bouvier Kennedy, delivered by caesarian section on November 27, 1957.[21] Caroline was their long awaited dream child and Jack and Jackie were absolutely thrilled with their little girl. Their prayers were answered. Now they could settle in to the ideal marriage. However, there still remained two big problems, Jack's continual preoccupation with other women and his passion for politics. Both of these fascinations would gradually push his family life into the background.

"Jackie once described Jack Kennedy to me as somebody with a minuscule body and a huge head," said Truman Capote. "She said this in a moment of anger. I don't think she realized what she had walked into when she married him. He was in constant competition with his old man to see who could nail the most women. Jackie wasn't prepared for such blatant womanizing. She hadn't expected to find herself stranded at parties while her husband went off with somebody new. Nor did she expect to become the object of derision among those females in her own circle who knew, as did almost everyone, what was happening." Jackie herself put a softer edge on it when she confided to a friend: "I don't think there are any men who are faithful to their wives. Men are such a combination of good and evil." Capote put it far more bluntly, "All those Kennedy men are the same—they are like dogs, they have to stop and pee at every fire hydrant." Gore Vidal also felt that Jackie knew and tacitly approved of, or at least closed her eyes to Jack's meanderings. Vidal termed the Kennedy marriage "an eighteenth-century affair, a practical union on both sides."[22]

After the Chicago convention, where Jack was almost nominated for vice-president on Adlai Stevenson's ticket only to lose out to Estes Kefauver on the third ballot, the Kennedy marriage took a really steep decline. As soon as the convention ended, Jack was determined to leave for France right away to lick his wounds with his parents on the French Riviera. His plans also included a Mediterranean cruise with several of his close friends. Jackie, who was very pregnant at the time and had gone to the convention to support Jack's efforts, pleaded with him to stay home with her and go to Newport. "Jackie was so bitter about Jack's leaving her that she said she didn't care about the baby," recalls a friend who was with her in Newport at her mother's house.

A week after she arrived at Hammersmith Farm, Jackie began to hemorrhage. She was hospitalized and underwent an emergency caesarian section. The fetus, a little girl, was stillborn. The next day the *Washington Post* carried a front page story headlined; "Senator Kennedy on Mediterranean trip unaware his wife has lost baby." The newspapers said that the "nervous tension and exhaustion as a result of the Democratic convention caused the miscarriage." Jackie blamed Jack. It was three days before Kennedy, cruising off Capri in a chartered yacht, found out what had happened. When he was finally reached by ship to shore radio, he took the news calmly and decided to continue his vacation.

Only the insistence of George Smathers, a fellow senator, persuaded him to return. "If you want to run for president, you'd better get your ass back to your wife's bedside or else every wife in the country will be against you," said Smathers.[23]

The day after he arrived at Newport, with Jackie still confined to a hospital bed, Kennedy attended a dinner party given by Louis and Elaine Lorillard at the Clambake Club. Despite Kennedy's outward calm, his marriage had reached a turning point. A hospital spokesman attributed the stillbirth to nervous tension and exhaustion after the Democratic convention. However Rose Kennedy placed the blame on Jackie's nicotine addiction and Janet Auchincloss held Jack Kennedy responsible.[24]

"As often happens in times of turmoil, Jack and Jackie's differences in outlook, interests and manner became more obtrusive," said Lem Billings. "They were both bitter, disillusioned, withdrawn, silent, as if afraid that conversation would deepen the wound."[25] Jack's reaction was to leave as soon as possible to campaign for the Stevenson-Kefauver ticket all over the country.

In typical Kennedy fashion, Jack knew what his priorities were and acted accordingly. The presidency and politics came first. If there was any time left over, his wife came second. The brutal truth of the matter was that Jackie actually came third. In second place was the most important category, his sex life. This basic need for sex took on a role of great proportion in Jack's everyday life. His need and desire for sex with an incredible cast of characters was beyond belief and he took great pride in his sexual prowess. He was, in fact, a legend in his own time. The most absurd part of all was that Jackie thought she might change and shape Jack into another Bobby which was ridiculous. It was especially ludicrous when we look at the women Jackie was competing against.

Another problem in the Kennedy marriage that was kept from the American public was the use of drugs by JFK and his wife. Jack's health problems were always minimized in order to portray him as a robust, vigorous man. Most people were aware of his ongoing struggle with his back problems caused by his war-sustained injuries. The injuries were presented as more of a nuisance and everyone admired Jack's abiltiy to carry on despite the discomfort he faced everyday.

What the public did not know was that sometime in the early 1960s, John Kennedy discovered speed. Since his childhood, he had managed to function in spite of his terrible health. Cortisone had been a godsend, but he was about to get hooked on something even more powerful. He was introduced to the legendary Max Jacobson, a Manhattan doctor, who had fled Germany in 1936. He set up practice in New York and became the physician to the stars. Jacobson's fame as "Dr. Feelgood" was based on his, "miracle tissue regenerator," shots that were actually a secret combination of vitamins, painkillers, human placenta and amphetimines. His patients included Truman Capote, Emilio Pucci and Tennesse Williams. Both John and Jacqueline Kennedy began taking Dr. Jacobsen's "treatments" during JFK's presidential campaign in 1960, and he would become indispensable to Jack's future.[26] Not much was known about drug dependency in the 1960s. We now can look back and see that the combination of drugs, and an unstable marriage would definitely add to the problems Jack and Jackie were experiencing.

Early in his administration, Jack was more worried about his wife's health than any contribution she might make to his New Frontier. He had an idea of how to perk Jackie up and stop her endless moping. During the campaign, he had noticed that one of his closest friends had a new lilt to his walk, a heightened spin to his wit and enviable energy. The friend attributed it all to a marvelous Manhattan physician, Dr. Max Jacobson. The physician usually limited his treatments to one mysterious injection that Dr. Jacobsen said included a variety of elements including the blood of a young lamb. Whatever it contained, to most of his patients it seemed the pure elixir of youth.

For Jack's visits the secret service cleared the doctor's office and

Jack would slip in for his injection. Dr. Feelgood had found one of the secrets of the age. The age was the sixties and the secret was steroid and amphetamines, a short-lived secret in a syringe, for which people lived and from which they died. At Jack's request, Jacobson flew down to Palm Beach to meet with Jackie. He wanted the doctor to decide whether Jackie could go on a stressful visit to Canada and then to Europe for an extended state visit. "He was very much concerned about her condition following her last delivery," Jacobson wrote in his unpublished biography. "She suffered periodic depression and headaches." The doctor was led to his new patient who appeared unhappy, suffering from a severe headache. "After a brief conversation," I said, "the least I can do for you is to stop your migraine, which I did." Jacobson recalled, "That broke the ice and her mood changed completely."[27]

Gradually Dr. Feelgood played a big part in the lives of Jack and Jackie. Over a long course of time, the drugs would influence their relationship and their marriage. Whenever they traveled, Dr. Max would go along. He had become so indispensable that the Kennedys chartered an Air France jet to fly him to Paris. He was so much a part of their inner circle that he was included in the family pictures in the book "John F. Kennedy: A Family Album" by Mark Shaw.[28] Whenever Kennedy needed him, the doctor was there—Washington, Hyannis Port, New York City. Jacobsen's assistant, Harvey Mann, later revealed that he had mixed most of the ingredients in the doctor's famous shots that contained at least 85% amphetamine. Reporter Marianne Means later observed, "How much of JFK's personality was affected by the drugs he was taking, we don't know, but some felt it put him on an unnatural high. No president with his finger on the button has any business taking stuff like that," warned a staff doctor. Bobby had checked on the ingredients and advised his brother to stop taking the injections until he had them tested by the FDA. JFK's reply to this was, "I don't care if it's horse piss. It works."[29]

Just as Dr. Jacobson contributed to the dramatic swings within the Kennedy marriage, his own career spiralled downward six years later.

The government raided his office after a patient died of amphetamine poisoning and his license to practice was revoked after he was found guilty of fraud and forty-eight counts of unprofessional conduct.[30]

No wonder their marriage was compromised. When you factor in the other women, the political arena, their basic differences and then throw in a drug dependency, it is amazing that they ever stayed together.

Perhaps it was the combination of his ambition,

and her need for financial security. . .

that kept them together.

It was certainly not love.

SIX

How thick was Jack's little black book?

THE TABLE OF CONQUESTS

WHEN JACKIE MARRIED JFK, SHE THOUGHT SHE had a pretty good idea of what she was getting into, but as much as she thought she was prepared for taming his wandering eye she had much to learn. Kennedy men had their own code of conduct and they were all taught by their father, Joe Kennedy, that it was their birthright to enjoy themselves with women. No woman was ever off limits. If a wife had a problem with this arrangement, then it was her problem, not theirs.[1] Another friend said, "The other woman business was foremost in Jackie's mind." Sometimes she could be very adult about Jack's little flings and then at other times, she would retreat and thrash herself and mope for days.[2]

Jackie's pride and self-esteem really took a beating from the public humiliation, but she suffered in silence and tried to hold her head up in public. What woman wouldn't feel like an absolute loser with her husband screwing anything that moved. During the summer of 1958, it really all hit home. While his bride was in Hyannis Port, Jack made a late night visit to his pretty twenty-one year old secretary, Pam Turnure, who was renting an apartment in the Georgetown home of Mr. and Mrs. Leonard Kater. "We were up late one night and heard someone outside throwing pebbles at Pam's window about one a.m.," recalled Mrs. Kater. We looked out and saw Senator Kennedy standing in our garden yelling, "If you don't come down, I'll climb up your balcony," so she let him in. My husband and I were so intrigued by the whole thing that we set up a tape recorder on the kitchen cabinet and another in the basement to pick up the sounds from the bedroom. The next time Kennedy came over to visit Pam, we turned on the tapes and listened to their conversation in our living room. When they went into the bedroom, we heard the unmistakable sounds of lovemaking and intercourse.[3]

The FBI files suggest that from the mid-1955 to the end of 1959, JFK maintained a suite on the eighth floor of Washington's Mayflower Hotel. One anonymous FBI informant referred to the suite as "Kennedy's personal playpen" and notes that he attended a Mayflower party at which Senator John Kennedy and Senator Estes Kefauver, another distinguished philanderer, and "their respective dates made love in plain view of the other partygoers. When they were done, the two senators simply exchanged mates and began anew."[4] Jack hosted many big parties in suite 812 at the Mayflower Hotel, as well as intimate get-togethers and room service dinners for two. Audrey Hepburn was a guest in suite 812 as were actress Lee Remick and stripper Tempest Storm.[5]

J. Edgar Hoover continued to monitor Jack's personal life. His reports indicated that the two years before the 1960 presidential election were among the most active of JFK's sexual career.[6] This period was only a small prelude to JFK's activities. Once he reached the White House, he would have the secret service to ensure not only his safety, but also provide him with the best beard service in the world. This devoted group of men became Jack's co-horts in every amorous adventure awaiting the new President. It began at the Los Angeles convention where the secret service provided protection for all the potential nominees. It soon became apparent to all that the Kennedy contingent was all where it was happening and that JFK was an active about town type of man. He literally kept his agents hopping and jumping over fences trying to keep track of him on his various wanderings all day and far into the night.

With their triumphant arrival at the White House, Jackie's worst nightmare began when Jack promptly turned their new home into his own private, secure bordello. Jackie had such high hopes. She truly thought that things would somehow magically change. Jack had even lead her to believe this when shortly before he took office, he was talking to his old friend, Charles Bartlett. "I'll tell you something," Jack said. "I'm going to keep the White House white." Sadly, this was not to be. JFK continued to insist that married or not, president or not, he could live the life he wanted. During this time, Jackie's attitude toward her husband was one of contradictions. There was hardly an emotion that she had not experienced, from love to hate, devotion to indifference, happiness to sorrow.

Secret service agent Marty Venker observed that working the perimeter detail for Kennedy was generally considered the best assignment in secret service history. "Those fortunate enough to work it soon understood the meaning of Ted Sorensen's timeless quip: This administration is going to do for sex what the last one did for golf." Young agents newly assigned to Kennedy simply couldn't believe what they were seeing though they quickly learned to keep their comments to themselves. Kennedy enjoyed having them around. They not only pimped for him but also partied with him. This was the James Bond era, and Kennedy was intrigued by the whole mystique of the secret service. He identified with them and they never betrayed him. Any agent who talked would have been off the detail by sundown. Had an agent talked, every other agent would have clammed up or denied the stories. Although JFK's agents did not talk to the press, several of them filed confidential reports on the President's sexual activities with their home office. Copies of these reports were provided under the Freedom of Information Act in 1976.[7]

Soon Jackie began to realize that she was being forced to live within a home that had become her husband's safe sexual fortress. Here was a man who had promised both Jackie and his father that he would not flaunt his affairs in public. Now he just flaunted them in their home. He was not only subjecting Jackie to his behavior on a daily basis, but he was rubbing her nose in it. Everyone on the staff was either laughing at Jackie behind her back or worse yet, pitying her.

It would be safe to assume that not all of the secret service agents approved of JFK's sexual exploits in the White House. Some would likely be highly critical of the President's flaunting of his marriage vows and would be offended by JFK's actions. It is not inconceivable that some agents were sympathetic to Jackie. The First Lady would have her own supporters within the White House and they would be very discreet. Mrs. Kennedy's sources would keep her informed.

Jack assured journalists that they would never catch him with a woman yet, at the same time, he was maintaining simultaneous affairs with Marilyn Monroe and Judith Campbell, a beautiful, slender, blue-eyed, twenty-six-year-old passed along to Jack by Frank Sinatra.[8] In her book on their relationship, Judith Campbell Exner writes of meeting with Jack on the opening night of the convention, at which time he attempted to talk her into participating in a *menage a trois*.[9] This affair lasted well into the new presidency until FBI Director, J. Edgar Hoover, keeping a close surveillance on the President's activities, finally met with the President to warn him that his White House mistress had close ties to organized crime since she was also the mistress of Sam Giancana, a Mafia kingpin from Chicago. Hoover did not have to specify the frightening implications. The President quickly stopped seeing Miss Campbell.[10]

It is interesting to note that Jack Kennedy knew all along that Judith and Giancana were involved with each other. It never bothered him, until he found out that Hoover had documented his affair.

During this time, Jackie chose to stay at Hyannis Port awaiting the birth of their son. She didn't want to risk having another miscarriage. Jackie's absence was a green light for Jack to party and play his way through the most momentous convention of his life. After being with Judith Campbell whenever he could, Kennedy spent the remainder of the convention primarily with Marilyn Monroe. "Of all his other women, Marilyn was perhaps the best for him," said Peter Lawford. "They were good together. They both had charisma and they both had a sense of humor. Marilyn said that Jack's performance was very democratic and very penetrating."[11] News of Jack and Marilyn had filtered back to Jacqueline. She brooded about her husband's latest affair and purportedly told her friend Walter Sohier, she wasn't certain if Jack's recent nomination "signaled a beginning or an end?"[12]

Many insiders on both coasts knew about JFK's affair with Marilyn. Especially since the 1961 Christmas party at the Lawford's Santa Monica home, while Jackie and the children remained back East. The tryst would have been spoiled had they known that it was being taped. Fred Otash, the renowned private detective, had been retained by teamster boss, Jimmy Hoffa, to tape the romantic exchanges between Marilyn and Jack.

On another occasion Marilyn, disguised in a brunette wig, wearing large sunglasses and an old dress, stayed with Kennedy at the Carlyle Hotel in New York. She traveled with him aboard Air Force One and was a guest at the Lawford beach house in Santa Monica. Lawford even arranged many of their meetings and, on at least one occasion, took photographs of Marilyn performing fellatio on Kennedy.[13] Peter Lawford, the actor and brother-in-law to the future President, was a most eager supplier of women to help in quenching JFK's insatiable appetite. Peter provided him with every imaginable amenity from dates with actresses and showgirls to a California safehouse where Kennedy could carry out his West coast assignations. Lawford would often act as the beard for JFK, distracting the press and providing a convenient front for Jackie's benefit.[14]

Another Lawford inspired fling involved a high priced New York call girl named Leslie Devereux. "Peter never explained the situation, just gave me an address and told me to meet him there. It turned out to be the Hotel Carlyle. We went upstairs together to a penthouse duplex and there stood the President of the United States. I saw him four or five times. It was all pretty standard sex at first, but later it got more kinky. I'd been with a number of powerful politicians and one thing they always liked was mild S & M. So we did a little of that and he seemed to enjoy it." Miss

Devereux continues, "I visited him twice at the White House. The first time for only 15 minutes in a small room off the Oval Office, his secretaries didn't so much as blink when they saw me. They showed me in and out as naturally as they would the Secretary of State." She adds, "On my second visit, I met him upstairs in the living quarters. A secret service agent ushered me into a dark and somber room filled with heavy wood furniture and said, 'Make yourself comfortable, he'll be with you shortly.' He then motioned me to an enormous intricately carved rosewood bed. 'That's Abraham Lincoln's bed,' he said. 'You mean, I'm to lie down on Abraham Lincoln's bed?' 'Lady,' he said, 'It's the best we've got.' Soon the door opened and a white gloved butler brought champagne on a silver tray. Then the President appeared and we spent several hours together. I told him that it seemed sacrilegious to violate Abraham Lincoln's bed. He laughed and told me about the White House legend that when you make a wish on the Lincoln bed it always comes true. 'Make a wish.' I said, he closed his eyes and I mounted him. 'See,' he said, 'It never fails'."[15]

One of JFK's most memorable affairs occurred with stripper, Tempest Storm when she performed at Washington's Casino Royale. She described their relationship as stormy but sexually satisfying, commenting that Kennedy seemed to be almost insatiable in bed.[16] There were many other testimonials on Jack's behalf from many infatuated women and envious men. "There may not have been many witnesses to Jack Kennedy's love life, but there was enough circumstantial evidence to convict him a thousand times over," said Marianne Strong, the society editor for the *New York World-Telegram.*[17]

Also Emilio de Antonio, a filmmaker of some note and a mainstay on the New York arts scene, knew a number of the women Kennedy associated with during this period. "I can vouch for the fact that Jack went with a lot of high-placed women," remarked de Antonio, "and power being the ultimate aphrodisiac of our age, JFK was able to explore and realize his wildest fantasies."[18]

One fantasy that the President realized was a relationship with the lovely movie and television star, Angie Dickinson. Although Angie has never publicly confirmed an affair with Kennedy, she has made remarks of a suggestive and coy nature. However photographer, Slim Aarons, a frequent visitor to Palm Springs, recalled that, "Angie and JFK disappeared for two or three days in Palm Springs. They stayed in a cottage and never emerged. Everyone knew about it. In a profile of Angie published in the pages of *TV Guide*, she spoke frankly of her relationship with John Kennedy: "From the moment I met him, I was hooked like everybody else. He was the sexiest politician I ever met."[19]

Infidelity was the vice of choice among politicians, and Jack's problem was not his affairs but the daring indiscretion of it all, almost as if he were taunting fate. The reality was that he was taunting his young wife. He took great pleasure in his double life as a respected family man on one side and then as a world-class womanizer on the other hand. It was a Jekyll and Hyde existence. Living on the edge gave him an incredible amount of pleasure. It was a golden time for JFK since politician's sex lives were off limits to the press. He felt perfectly safe and secure doing anything he damn well pleased.

Most people would assume that Jackie had learned to live with Jack's philandering but in fact she had not. It would be foolish, of course, to state that Jackie accepted her husband's incorrigible womanizing as a mere breach of etiquette. She hated it and she let him know that she was perfectly aware of what he was doing, and even when and where. Jackie quickly realized that she had made her own bed and now she must lie in it. However, it was incredibly difficult for her especially with her very own mother as an example of controlling life's discomforts. Jackie had married into a family where the father, Joe, told his sons that, "If there's something on your plate, take it" referring mainly to the availability of women. Joe, Sr., showed by personal example that such behavior was perfectly acceptable.

Although their pre-White House years had been a disaster in terms of devotion and fidelity, Jackie hoped that as Jack's political ascendancy began, discretion and perhaps fidelity might be given more prominence in their marriage. After all, who in his right mind would continue to screw around with the entire country watching on? Well, as history has shown us, Jack Kennedy was not in his right mind. "There's no question about the fact that Jack had the most active libido of any man I've ever known," said George Smathers, his closest friend in the senate. "He really was unbelievable, absolutely incredible in that regard, and he got more so the longer he was married. I remember one night he was making it with a famous movie star and, by God, if Jackie almost didn't catch him right in the act. Jack was something, almost like a roto-rooter."[20]

The closer John Kennedy came to the presidency the more frenetic became his random search for women. The FBI file made reference to "A pair of stewardesses that the subject is seeing in California." Another item points to the Kennedy-Sinatra connection, where *Confidential* magazine was said to have affidavits from two mulatto prostitutes in New York. Another notation in the files alleges that during 1957-1958, Kennedy made several trips to Havana to visit Flo Pritchett Smith, wife of Earl E. T. Smith, Ambassador to Cuba. Other meetings between Flo and Jack took place in Miami and Palm Beach during her visits to the States.[21]

During the presidential campaign most of JFK's female companions were drawn from that transient pool known in his camp as "the Kennedy girls," the models, hostesses and college cheerleaders recruited in every city, country and state by the candidate's advance men. The girls added sparkle and zest to the race.[22] This obviously was a pattern of action continued by all Kennedy men on the campaign trail until Teddy's despicable behavior at Chappaquidick.

This picture of Kennedy never surfaced during the campaign and Kennedy never worried about his sexual indiscretions hurting him politically. He knew that no newspaper would publish a nude picture of him because of the immediate retaliation from former Ambassador Kennedy, his father. In fact, he joked with reporters about his adventures, saying, "I'm never through with a girl until I've had her three ways." As much as they might enjoy his frank comments, he knew they would never print them.[23]

One of the unprinted press jokes at the time was "Let's sack with Jack." What Kennedy knew was that the press would never print any of this in his lifetime and, as he remarked, "After I'm dead, who cares?" One wonders if he ever thought that his wife or children might care.

JFK's "daily dose of sex" as Garry Willis refers to it in *The Kennedy Imprisonment* (1981) became the most conspicuous part of his legacy. Women were Kennedy's fatal character flaw. He could not resist them.

Whenever the First Lady was away from Washington, the President frequently amused himself with nude swimming parties in the White House pool. These were followed by cozy lunches in the family quarters and a session of sexual adventures in the President's bed. Ordinarily, White House secretaries were summoned by phone to join the President for a swim before lunch. Other women would be contacted by Evelyn Lincoln, picked up in White House cars, and quietly brought into the Executive Mansion by his old buddy, Dave Powers.[24] What was particularly difficult for Jackie was that everyone on the staff from the secret service to all their aides and every servant were all a part of this conspiracy to protect Jack's privacy. This left Jackie feeling like the village idiot with all of this screwing going on right in her own home among her own family and supposed friends.

What an incredibly humiliating experience for any wife let alone the wife of a President who did not know the meaning of the word discretion! JFK was so reckless at home, maintaining simultaneous affairs with two White House secretaries whom the secret service dubbed Fiddle and Faddle. The duo, one blonde and one brunette, were said to engage in threesomes with Jack. "Aren't you afraid Jackie will come back earlier than you expect and catch you with these broads?" When he was asked in the Oval Office, Jack merely smiled. "Jackie can't get within two hundred yards of this place without my knowing about it."[25]

Welcome home, Jackie! Is it any wonder that she used any excuse to flee the White House with all its JFK loyalists. Often, she retreated to

seclusion at their rented Virginia retreat, "Flenora". Although Jackie outwardly feigned ignorance about what was so obvious to many around her,
inwardly, she protected herself by staying away as much as possible. Removed from the situation, she did not have to cope with it. Sheer mobility
allowed her to put as much distance as possible between herself and her
husband. As First Lady she spent four days of every week at the Virginia
hunt country house. [26] This self-imposed exile served her purpose.

The "other woman" syndrome touched Jackie in different ways on
different occasions. At intervals she would retreat and mope for long
stretches, aloof from everyone and glacially cold to the President. It was at
these junctures that she went on shopping binges, disbursing thousands of
dollars on jewelry, designer clothes, paintings or whatever captured her
fancy.[27]

The secret service was always electronically alerted to the specific
whereabouts of "Lancer", the President's code name, and "Lace", the
First Lady's. A secret service man always informed the President exactly
when his wife would arrive. The White House kennel keeper, Trapes
Bryant, recalled the President lounging naked around the pool and skinny
dipping with several other naked male and female swimmers when the
alarm went off, indicating Mrs. Kennedy had returned unexpectedly from
Virginia. "It was easy to get rid of the bodies," said Bryant. "But the
drinks were another matter." Bryant indicated the President had a penchant
for blondes, and the upstairs maids would complain, "Why can't he make it
easier for us? Why can't he get himself a steady brunette?" A vivid Bryant
memory was seeing a naked blonde coming out of the elevator, her breasts
swinging as she raced down the hall.[28]

On one occasion, Jackie was escorting an Italian journalist, named
Benno Gaziani, around the White House when she pointed to two young
secretaries and said, "Those are my husband's lovers." She knew about the
affairs with Jayne Mansfield and Marilyn Monroe as well as the parade of
nameless nymphos eager to notch JFK on their belts.[29] It's said that she
once discovered a woman's undergarments under a pillow in the President's

bedroom. Holding them out to him, she said, "Would you please shop around and see who belongs to this? It's not my size."[30] It is an amusing tale. Yet so obvious. Jackie was trying to be so clever, so sophisticated and so nonchalant on the outside, but it was harder than hell to swallow this deception in her everyday life with this man and his accomplices.

The most talked about affair of the President, within the beltway and in Hollywood, was the romance with Marilyn Monroe. She was everyone's favorite blonde. Women accepted her as an orphaned waif and men adored her as the universal sex symbol of all of the fantasies they could ever imagine. Jack and Marilyn first met at the Lawford's home in 1957 but saw little of each other until 1959 when their affair began in Palm Springs. As the affair continued, Marilyn began to confide to friends her dreams of marriage. Ridiculous as it might seem that anyone could believe that a Catholic President would divorce his popular wife to marry a three-times divorced movie star, the fact is that Marilyn's whole life had defied reality. "After all, what were the odds of this little girl from nowhere marrying the world's greatest athlete, Joe Dimaggio?" But she did, said producer Gene Allen. "And what were the chances of her marrying the world's greatest playwright, Arthur Miller?"[31]

Marilyn's appearance at the President's birthday party at Madison Square Garden was the straw that literally broke Jackie's back. Even jaded Hollywood-types were surprised when Marilyn's planned appearance at the Garden was trumpeted in the local trade papers. "This was deliberately bringing the rumors into the public," said screenwriter Nunnally Johnson. "Many of us felt that her appearance at Madison Square Garden would be like Marilyn making love to the President publicly after doing it privately all these months." Refusing to diminish her dignity, the First Lady went to great lengths to avoid any situation in which she would have to publicly tolerate the flirtation of other women with her husband. She dismissed the extravagant fund raising party held to celebrate the President's birthday as nothing more than a vulgar public display. When Jackie found out that Peter Lawford was arranging for Marilyn to sing "Happy Birthday" to the

President, Jackie refused to attend.[32]

As it turned out, Jackie was wise to stay away. She was the only one not there. The rest of Jack's loyal family attended the celebration. They gave him a quasi kind of respectability as the nation eagerly anticipated this public meeting of the two lovers. It was quite an event. When Marilyn slithered on stage in a dress that Adlai Stevenson said, "Looked like flesh with sequins sewed onto it," Kennedy was in his element. Marilyn gyrated on stage, oozed, undulated and purred, "Happy Birthday, Dear Mr. President." This high art of seduction sent orgasmic screams pulsating through the Garden as the mob shouted and screamed. A very pleased President hopped on stage and said, "I can now retire from politics after having had "Happy Birthday" sung to me by such a wholesome girl."[33]

Prior to this public copulation of spirits, Clare Boothe Luce had observed about Jackie, "She was not threatened, not even by Marilyn Monroe. But if somehow word had gotten out, it would have upset her terribly. She could not bear the thought of being publicly humiliated." Jackie was the daughter of Janet Lee Auchincloss and she would never recover from this devastating event.

As the elected leader of the most powerful nation in the world, Jack was now free to fully indulge himself in ways his father never dreamed of. According to British journalist, Glenys Roberts, "He seduced his own secretaries and baby-sitters who became pregnant by him and had to go to Puerto Rico for abortions. He ordered up prostitutes like most Americans ordered sandwiches." Things got even worse for Jackie after the debacle at Madison Square Garden. Jackie was now being confronted with Jack's affairs with Pamela Turnure, her secretary. "Jackie asked me if I knew he was having an affair with Pamela," said Betty Spalding. "It distressed her that there might be an ongoing affair with an employee she had to see every day. That seemed to bother her more than the fact that Jack was sleeping around."[34]

Then there was Mary Meyer who was the sister of Kennedy's dear friends, Ben and Tony Bradlee. She had known Kennedy from college and had taken long walks with Jackie when they were neighbors in Georgetown. According to a diary she kept, Mary's romance with Jack Kennedy began a year after he was in the White House. He first asked her to go to bed with him in December of 1961, but she refused because she was having an affair with someone else. When that affair ended, Mary began seeing Jack regularly at the White House two or three times a week for the rest of his Presidency, always when Jackie was away.[35] All of this secrecy was preposterous. Jackie had her own sources within the White House, and these few loyalists that she had kept her informed about everything going on while she was away.

The President and Mary seemed to be soul mates, much as Prince Charles and Camilla are in these times. Mary confided details of her affair to her close friend, James Truitt, who says that Mary and JFK smoked marijuana cigarettes together in the White House. She also told Truitt that she loved Kennedy but realized their liaison would be limited to brief encounters. Even though, she said, Jack felt no affection of a lasting kind for Jackie.[36]

It was with Mary that Jack traveled openly on a political swing through out the country on Air Force One. Their trip ending at her mother, Ruth Pinchot's home, on September 24th, just two short months before the assassination.

There are two devastating events which have not been publicized or even mentioned in all of the Kennedy-produced versions of the marriage, a marriage that supposedly was closer and better than ever just before the assassination. The fact was that earlier in their marriage Jackie had been treated with electro-shock therapy for her depression at Valleyhead, a private psychiatric clinic in Carlisle, Massachusetts. Her depression was caused by the miscarriages and Jack's constant womanizing. This therapy was kept secret in order to avoid any political embarrassment. Jackie's treatment was rarely referred to even within the family.[37] The true tragedy was that even though Jack was fully aware of his wife's delicate condition, he continued to blatantly womanize. He made no effort to consider how insensitive he was being to his wife. It was a most self-indulgent husband who would subject a fragile wife to such public humiliation.

The second fact is even more devastating, but it helps to explain Jackie's black moods and her exacerbated nerves. Paul Mathias noted, "She is not a happy person, she is erratic and so complicated, there are moments when she is out of control with herself."[38] Now who wouldn't be erratic, if your husband had slept with your own sister? While Jackie was in the hospital recovering from Caroline's birth, her sister Lee, and her husband Michael Canfield, arrived from London and moved in with the Kennedys at 270 Park Avenue. Like many men Jack's friend, Charlie Bartlett, considered Lee a walking sexpot. He was glad to hear from Jack that he had kept his hands off Lee. Jack even bragged to Charlie that he had passed this test of character. However, in the end, Jack failed the test of character. "Lee told me that she went to bed with Jack," said Nina Auchincloss. "The door to the bedroom was open, and Michael could hear them making love."[39]

Is it any wonder that Anita Fay said of Jackie, "From the first time I met Jackie I felt I was in the presence of a very great actress."[40] Oh yes, Jackie could act and no one would ever suspect that she knew about Jack and Lee until her final last will and testament was read.

Isn't there something about,

"Don't get mad, get even!"

SEVEN

Was divorce ever an option
for Jack and Jackie?

THE DIVORCE NEVER, MURDER IS BETTER

IN ANY MARRIAGE WHEN THERE ARE PROBLEMS thoughts of divorce occasionally occur. At various times, it did for both Jack and Jackie. It would, however, never be a possibility for them. As long as Jack's destiny was to be the President of the United States, then he and Jackie must remain together. They both knew it and their family and friends all knew it.

The problem for Jackie was to get through it all and retain some semblance of dignity. There was no question in anyone's mind that staying with Jack was the smart thing to do. Her value as wife of the President would be enormous. As a President's wife she would have great power.

If divorce were an option, her role as an ex-wife would put her on the lowest rung of the family pecking order. No one in the Kennedy family would approve of her ever leaving Jack. For that matter, there would be no support for her from anyone if she left him. She had to stay. Jackie was smart enough to know that by staying she could wield considerable power.

Jackie knew all of the Kennedy family's deepest secrets. She was, of course, indispensable since a divorce would end all hopes of Jack ever becoming President. As a Catholic, John F. Kennedy must present a perfect image of the happily married man. The Catholic church does not allow divorce. Nor would Jack's supporters ever be able to accept him as a man whose marriage had failed. Jack and Jackie had no real choice but to make things work. At least for the time being, they would be the perfect Catholic couple.

The "storybook wedding" climaxed the efforts by the Kennedys and Jacqueline Bouvier to re-invent themselves. The Kennedys were no longer strivers. They now set the standards. Jackie was no longer a poor, little rich girl humiliated by scandal and short on cash. On that September day, Jack and Jackie helped expand the American dream. The facade they constructed cloaked philandering, alcoholism and family strife. Jackie said they were two icebergs, "The public life above water, the private life submerged." The Kennedys fulfilled a social fantasy of money, power, fame and sex on such an overblown scale that when their cover was blown, faith in the politics of appearance would shatter. Many guests that day knew they were minor actors in a public charade.[1]

"As often happens in times of turmoil, Jack and Jackie's differences in outlook, interests and manner became more obtrusive," said Lem Billings, the President's best friend from college. "They both were bitter, disillusioned, withdrawn, silent as if afraid that conversation would deepen the wound. In that sense, they were both repressed, they couldn't talk directly to each other."[2]

Other areas of incompatibility made marriage hard for Jackie. While Jack thrived on large crowds of people and going to gaudy musicals, she preferred to give small but elaborate dinner parties at home. She would have occasion to use her elegant silver and china. Jackie liked to sip daiquiris and linger over the candlelit table, talking about foreign films or art. Kennedy preferred to drink beer and talk politics all night after a simple meal of steak and mashed potatoes.[3]

As their marriage struggled, the breach between Jack and Jackie widened. Rumors of an impending divorce began to circulate and eventually reached the gossip columns. Jack Kennedy sold Hickory Hill to his brother Bobby. Jackie went to New York to visit her sister, Lee, who had separated from her first husband the year before. "There was certainly talk of a divorce between Jack and Jackie," acknowledged Peter Lawford.[4]

During this time Jackie and Lee took a trip to Europe to sort things out. Jackie threw herself into a round of glamorous parties and shooting weekends in the English countryside. Word reached America of her extravagant lifestyle in England, and stories soon began to appear in the American press that she was behaving like an unattached woman. She and Jack appeared to be estranged. The first journalist to print such a report was Washington columnist, Drew Pearson. His item was picked up and expanded on by *Time* magazine.[5]

They were becoming the talk of the town and the word was spreading quickly. Jackie knew about her husband's compulsive womanizing endangering not simply the threadbare fabric of their marriage but his whole political future. She had grown so disgusted with Jack's behavior that she had begun to talk about it to her intimates. One Sunday in Washington, she was at a luncheon given by Walter and Marie Ridder, her dear friends. As usual, Jackie was by herself. "He's gone." Jackie shrugged, as she sat alone with Walter Ridder. "He's somewhere and I haven't heard from him. He's campaigning but I bet he's off with some dame. I've got to divorce him." "Well, Jackie" Ridder replied, as he later told his wife, "I can understand this, but do you want to really ruin his chance of being President?" "No," Jackie replied, making the choice that any of the other Kennedy women would have made.[6]

Others claim that the real problem for Jackie wasn't so much the other women but rather her hatred of politics. Peter Lawford recalled, "What truly distressed Jackie was Jack's career. She didn't care for politics. She had been brought up to think of most politicians as con men and crooks. She found that atmosphere of politics at odds with her own interest in literature and the arts. It's possible that had Jack not achieved his goal in 1960 that Jackie might either have pushed him into another career or left him and moved to Europe."[7]

The Kennedys exchanged many verbal outbursts. Outside the public eye, they both could give as well as take. Remember they both had Irish blood. One of their friends overheard them arguing. "You're too old for me," said Jackie. "You're too young for me," replied Jack.[8]

It is hard for people today to realize how difficult divorce was over forty years ago. It was considered by most to be the worst tragedy to happen to a Catholic family. For a Catholic political family, it was unthinkable. A divorce for any politician would be the end of his career. This was long before the time when Ronald Reagan would become President and his divorce from his first marriage was barely mentioned by the press or anyone else. The feeling back in the forties and fifties was that if a man couldn't keep his own marriage going how could he possibly run the country? It was still fresh in all Democrats' minds that Adlai Stevenson's divorce hindered him in his run for the Presidency in 1956. This was one mistake that the Democrats would not make again. With so many happily-married candidates to chose from, including the Kennedys, there would be an all-American couple up against the Nixons in the up-coming election.

As true as this all may be, it was essential to put all these divorce rumors to rest. It was critical for Jack and Jackie to put their best marital face forward, at least until after the election. So Joe Kennedy and Jack Bouvier huddled early on in the marriage and decided to talk some sense into their children. Basically, there was a meeting and a deal was struck between Joe and Jackie. Although the Kennedys have denied it, there are just too many reliable sources to collaborate this fact. First, there was Drew Pearson and then *Time* magazine. Neither of these sources ever recanted. The Kennedys chose to treat it as so totally ridiculous that they couldn't be bothered even commenting on such vicious rumors.

Designer Igor Cassini went on record to say, "Joe Kennedy told me he had offered Jackie a million dollars not to divorce Jack."[9] Then there is Peter Lawford's mother, Lady Mae Lawford, who relates in her book, "*Bitch*" that "A man tried to give me a picture of a man coming down the hall of a Beverly Hills whore-house. It was worth nothing to me. Why did I want it? Why should I pay money for a picture of my daughter-in-law's brother?" However, it did mean something to old Joe Kennedy. After he had obtained the picture of Jack Kennedy, he left it lying on the bed. When Jackie saw the picture lying on the bed, she became greatly upset and cried, "I won't stay with him, I refuse to remain with him anymore!" Whereupon old Joe Kennedy offered his daughter-in-law a check. The check was for a million dollars! The payoff..... to remain married to Jack. Jackie was a clever girl, such a good businesswoman. She said, "Make it tax free and it's a deal."Of course, Kennedy money always stayed in trust funds.

There are all sorts of accounts about the actual meeting between Joe and Jackie. My favorite comes from the book, *"All Too Human"*, by Edward Kline, in which he states that Joe, Sr., decided to take matters into his own hands. When Jackie returned from Europe to the states, he invited her to have lunch with him at Le Pavillon, the famous French restaurant in New York. Joe later described the conversation to Morton Downey in which he told Jackie, "Jack doesn't want to lose you. He knew that the relationship hadn't been too hot, but you have got to stick with Jack. He's going to be President." Jackie said that she did not care for politics or politicians and did not like being a campaign wife. She wanted more freedom.

Though she had always liked Joe personally, she felt that she was being suffocated by the Kennedy family. When they were at Hyannis Port or Palm Beach, she did not want to have dinner every night with the family. Joe did not have any problem with her demands.

The biggest problem would continue to be Jack's womanizing and the way he would flaunt it in Jackie's face. He would have to become more discreet if there was any chance for this marriage to survive. Frankly, Jackie was fed up with Jack rubbing her nose in it. He did not know the meaning of discretion. The closer he got to the Presidency the more reckless he became. It was almost a self-destruct mechanism within himself. He even told his Mafia connected mistress, Judith Campbell, "If I don't get this nomination, Jackie and I have arranged that we will separate. We will part. I want you to know that this has nothing to do with you."[11]

Some Kennedy loyalists steadfastly denied the whole thing. What pulled this marriage together at this time were the children. He would never have given them up. What he also knew was that his wife was strong enough to leave him. He knew that he may have been the President, but the public saw her as the movie star. Jackie's social-secretary, Letitia Baldridge, commented, "She was getting more and more fabulous, her popularity almost as great as his."[12]

Jackie did have her problems with the Kennedys when it came to finances. It turned out that the fabulously wealthy senator she had married turned out to be miserly with her. He did not want to offend the American voting public. Here she was in a marriage of convenience and not even getting the big bucks to go with it. Jackie was not happy about her financial situation.

As with so many other young couples, the Kennedys battled about money. The focus on her fashions emboldened Jackie to shop even more extravagantly. She spent over $100,000 in 1961 and 1962. She dismissed Jack's complaints by remarking, "The President seems more concerned with my budget than the budget of the United States.[13]

The President and First Lady established competing courts. Baldridge said there was a "civil war" between Jack's people in the West Wing and Jackie's people in the East Wing.[14] There was a gradual shift of power within the White House and within their marriage. As Jackie became more and more popular, she sensed that her time had arrived and she was eager to grasp the brass ring of life. Jack needed her and everyone knew it. She was indispensable to any future Presidential campaigns. She had now become a superstar.

When it came to talk of divorce, there was only one thing Jackie could do to help herself and that was to make herself indispensable to the Kennedy Presidency. Jackie Kennedy revolutionized the role of First Lady while insisting that she only wanted to be a good wife and mother. Rather than playing to American matrons, she played to the cameras and the masses. Herbert H. S. Feldman, a British attorney and author, described her as "hard, tough, self-serving with no great ambitions towards personal achievement but a great love for the limelight, publicity and applause. Her mouth betrays her. It is like that of a shark."[15]

People were beginning to become aware of the lack of affection between the Kennedys. Unlike other Presidents, Kennedy did not kiss his wife after the oath-taking ceremony. Instead he bounded exuberantly off the platform as if he had momentarily forgotten she was even there. In the rotunda of the capitol, when they met for the first time as President and First Lady, she tried to show her affection but was unable to express herself.[16] Ben Bradlee wrote, the Kennedys did not generate a sense of warmth or togetherness. Before one of their rare joint appearances, one aide reminded the Senator to 'turn to her with a gesture or smile'."[17]

These model parents, this glamorous couple, often worked at crossed purposes. Despite the unrelenting pressure for them to appear harmonious, deep fissures were often apparent. They led curiously separate lives, more typical of aristocrats than the suburbanites they purported to be. Shrewd observers could find hints of trouble even in the circumspect press of the times. Few pictures showed the two parents and the two children together. Even the Caroline Kennedy comic book illustrated the separate relationship each Kennedy parent had with the youngster. Of nearly sixty images in the comic book, only two pictured the Kennedys as a couple with their daughter.

The Kennedys did not work well together. Kennedy often made difficult decisions without his wife's encouragement. Jackie, in turn, made decisions about the children and household without Jack's help. The pressure to trumpet their union as a model marriage exacerbated tensions. Jack surrounded himself with sycophants; he prized loyalty. Jackie lashed out at him to prove her independence. Once, when the President was late on his way to church, secret service agents overheard the First Lady screaming, "Come on now, you 'Son of a Bitch'. You got yourself into this and you know your public demands it. So get your damned tie and coat on and let's go."[18]

She was an unhappy person and it was natural that she would eventually seek out someone to nurture her. Jack's affairs were talked about all over Washington. Jackie's affairs were kept very quiet and discreet. Jack was touring military bases in California when Jackie first sought comfort, solace and understanding in the company of one of his most trusted advisors. Black Jack Bouvier's daughter was always more comfortable in the company of men particularly more mature married men. At fifty-seven, Yale educated Roswell Gilpatric was a decade older than Jack and twenty-two years older than Jackie. While Jack was away, she invited Gilpatric to lunch alone with her at Camp David. "I loved my day in Maryland," Jackie later wrote to Gilpatric.

At one of their intimate White House dinners, Jackie had declared Gilpatric, whose sexual escapades were already known to Washington insiders, as "The second most attractive man in the Defense Department" next to McNamara. "Men can't understand his sex appeal," said Jackie. Angered by her husband's slavish devotion to Jackie, Madelin Gilpatric filed for divorce in 1970. Were her husband and Jackie having an affair while she was in the White House? "I have my own feelings about that," she said, "but I won't go into them. They were certainly very, very close. Just say it was a particularly close, warm, long-lasting friendship."

Gilpatric would not deny that, though for years he was less than forthcoming on his relationship with Jackie. "Both Jack Kennedy and Jackie told me things in confidence that I will never divulge," he said. He went on to concede that he and Jackie became "romantically involved" when she was First Lady. "We loved each other. She had certain needs, and I am afraid Jack was capable of only giving so much. I suppose I filled a void in her life."[19]

Later on, Jackie would again get even with Jack in her own way. On a trip to Italy with the Radziwills, Jackie met Gianni Agnelli, the heir to the Fiat automobile fortune. Gianni was a ruggedly handsome man with slickened-black hair. Soon he was seen escorting Jackie around Amafi. He scandalized Roman society by inviting Jackie on his 82-foot yacht. She was photographed by the paparazzi scuba diving and dancing barefoot on the deck of his boat. "George Griffin, the American Consular Officer, was disillusioned. Even the cynical secret service agents felt bad about it."

So did the CIA and the Deputy Secretary of State, George Ball, who also got into the act. "An agency official told me with some amusement that the CIA got a private message from Ravello to get Jackie's diaphragm," said Ball. "They were ordered to fetch it and sent it over to Italy by the next plane." Finally Jack could take no more and he sent Jackie a telegram, "A little more Caroline and less Agnelli."

"There was, I strongly suspect, a hidden drama being played out here, one that future biographers will explore at greater depth," said Margaret Truman. "Jackie was challenging Jack's attempts to control her....perhaps warning him that two could play the extramarital sex game." Worldly Italian aristocrats speculated that Jackie was carrying on an affair with Gianni as a way of getting back at Jack for all his years of womanizing. It must be true, they said, because Jackie could easily have stopped the gossip but had obviously chosen not to.[20]

So what is good for the gander is good for the goose. Jackie was testing the waters. Agnelli was no Onassis but they ran in the same circles and Ari was aware of this little indiscretion. Everyone was talking about it. The seeds may have been planted for a future romance with the President's wife.

No, divorce would never be an option for Jackie Kennedy. It would be easier and more fruitful for her to become Jack Kennedy's widow rather than his ex-wife. Her own mother had warned her on many occasions, "If you leave Jack, what will you become? A divorced Catholic woman!" How could Jackie cope without a husband? Where would she go? Who would support her?[21]

Aren't these bizarre questions coming from Janet Auchincloss who practically wrote the book on how to survive a messy divorce? If Jackie ever needed a role model, she would have to look no further than her own mother. She would do it with more style and class than Janet could even begin to imagine.

Jackie would never divorce, Jack. She would get her freedom in an other way. She may not have had it all figured out yet but she had high hopes for herself. She would go after the real money.

In the meantime, she would play her role perfectly. She was a great actress and she had been training for this role all her life. All it required was patience and timing.

Why be an ex-wife?

Jackie would not only survive,

she would thrive.

EIGHT

HOW DID THE POLITICAL LIFE AND CAMPAIGNING AFFECT THEM?

THE ENEMY NAMED POLITICS

*I*F JACQUELINE KENNEDY WERE TO BE ASKED TWO questions: What do you hate the most and what do you like the most, her answer would be that she hated politics more than anything else in her life. What she would like the most? After money.... her privacy would be the next most valuable thing to her!

These two issues were the major stumbling blocks in the Kennedy marriage. As much as Jack and the Kennedys loved and thrived on politics, Jackie truly despised every aspect of the political arena. Her hatred of public life came from her upbringing. Traditionally, it was only proper for a woman to have her name in the newspaper upon her marriage and her death. The old guard to which Janet Auchincloss aspired, abhorred any kind of publicity whatsoever. Both Janet and Hugh Auchincloss were shocked by the press coverage of their daughter's wedding.

The Kennedys invited most of the United States Senate. Jackie didn't want to have reporters at the wedding. Her mother was sensitive to having publicity of any kind. She thought it was demeaning and vulgar. Rose Kennedy recalled, "Mr. Kennedy said there will have to be reporters at the wedding because Jack is a public figure."[1]

This was something that Jackie would try to accept. She had a difficult time doing so. Jackie lived by her concept of the well-brought up young lady, being "a bit" interested in the arts, great wines, dinner parties, and riding to the hounds. Any participation in Jack's political career was a drudgery that sapped her energy and interest. Unlike her husband, she did not thrive on frenetic activity and saw no point in wearing herself out shaking hands with strangers and asking for their votes. Even posing for pictures seemed to weary her. She begged off as many media stories as possible, explaining in a letter to an editor how tiresome it was for her.[2]

At the very beginning of their marriage, the political situation became a problem. "I was alone almost every weekend while Jack traveled the country making speeches," says Jackie. "It was all wrong. Politics was sort of my enemy as far as seeing him was concerned, and we had no home life whatsoever." Jackie made no effort to take an active role in her husband's political planning. "Jack wouldn't, couldn't, just couldn't have a wife who shared the spotlight with him," she said, acknowledging her secondary position. Consequently, her political role became one of mere decor and then only under duress. "I show up and smile," she said of her campaign activities. Sometimes she would say a few words in whispery French or Spanish depending on which ethnic group the Kennedys were trying to impress.[3]

The Kennedy marriage was severely strained almost from the first when Jack was often away, and even when he was home the couple had difficulty communicating. By this time Jack's world was almost only politics, a subject that bored Jackie. "Asking Jackie to get interested in politics was like asking the boxer, Rocky Graziano, to play the piano," their friend, Betty Spalding, said. "She just didn't have any desire in the world to do it. She was smart enough, but it was out of her field. She didn't have the taste or stomach for it. Her nature was literary and artistic. Let's face it, he loved politics and she hated it." Reporters' wives watched her at parties, often sitting by herself. At one party when the subject of politics came up, "She literally took a chair, turned it towards a corner, and sat there for the entire evening without bothering to talk to anybody."[4]

Jackie herself sent mixed messages regarding her newly adopted role. Early in 1958, she said, "Politics is in my blood. I know that even if Jack changed professions I would miss politics. It's the most exciting life imaginable, always involved with the news of the moment, meeting and working with people who are enormously alive. Everyday you are caught up in something you really care about. It makes a lot of things seem less vital. You get used to the pressure that never lets up, and you learn to live with it as a fish lives in water."[5] This statement sounds like a Kennedy campaign release if ever there was one. Or perhaps, Jackie had just had a lobotomy and had become an earlier version of a Stepford wife, Kennedy style. Then again, maybe she did say all of the above but surely Joe Kennedy must have been listening close by.

When the mask slipped, it revealed an entirely different personality. One day a reporter saw the Kennedy car parked in front of a convent in Lowell, Mass. Jack was inside introducing himself to the nuns. Outside, sitting in the back of the car, Jackie looked tired and bored as she grimly flipped the pages of a fashion magazine. Then there were the many mornings that she simply refused to go campaigning for Jack and instead took long solo walks by herself.[6]

Jackie's hatred of the press took on a life of its own. She could not control her disdain for the fourth estate. Jackie conveniently forgot that she, herself, used to be a reporter.

The media was now her enemy and nothing could change her mind. If anything prevented Jackie from being a more enthusiastic campaigner, it was her inherent fear and distrust of the press. "Nothing disturbs me as much as interviewers. If you make your living in public office, you are the property of the public. Your whole life is an open book."[7] Now come on Jackie, what did you expect? This was no young vestal virgin who married Jack Kennedy. Jackie had been around the farm so to speak when it came to politics. Her one job should have prepared her for what her life as First Lady would be like. It all seems so totally fake and deceitful on Jackie's part. She knew from the moment that she accepted JFK's proposal what she was signing on for. She wanted the White House probably as much as Jack did. Perhaps the lady doth protest too much?

The truth is that Jackie hated the people, not the politics. "Jackie looked down her nose at the average person in politics. She didn't care for the "Irish Murphia" that surrounded Jack. They weren't good enough for her. She didn't care about people like that. She was a snob," said Mary Tierney, a reporter for the *Boston-Herald-Traveler* who covered Jackie during both the 1958 and 1960 campaign races. Jackie's disdain for the press was immediately evident to Tierney. "She was a little actress, but without her lines she was lost. She didn't go for full-fledged interviews unless she could control them."[8]

Tierney was right when she goes on to state, "Jackie was a very cold person. She didn't have a warm bone in her body."[9]

Early in their marriage, Jack had back surgery again and took a leave from his political duties while Jackie nursed him back to health. After seven month's absence, JFK resumed his senatorial duties. He would not use crutches in public, refused a wheelchair and walked unaided but still felt soreness in his back. Soon he felt up to throwing a gala at the Kennedy compound in Hyannis Port for some 400 State Legislators, State House officials and members of Congress, as well as their spouses. The affair served to announce Kennedy's return to office and hinted at bigger political events soon to come. Jackie played hostess, flashing her broad smile but feeling vaguely ill at ease. She resented her husband taking her by the arm and thrusting her forward with the words, "I want you to meet my wife...Jackie." She disliked political functions and particularly disliked the people who attended them. Mrs. John F. Kennedy took a decidedly snobbish view of politics. To her mind, the men were uncouth cigar-chomping jackals, their wives humdrum and predictable. They behaved as if they were on television, went through all the usual motions, said and did all the expected things. According to Jackie, the women talked about nothing but draperies and slipcovers, children and grandchildren, diets and cookbooks. They exchanged recipes and made simpering comments about "the good people back home," the masses whose collective vote determined whether their husbands returned to Washington.[10]

When it came to actually hitting the campaign trail, Jackie abhorred the idea completely. She hated helping Jack get out the vote. It makes one wonder what the Kennedys could have thought when they chose Jackie as material for a Presidential mate. It is so easy to image an Ethel or Eunice-type wife for Jack. A wife who would be right out there with him sharing the entire experience. Janet des Rosiers, the stewardess aboard the Kennedy family plane, the *Caroline*, felt that had Jackie done more campaigning with Jack, the opportunity and need for such dalliances with other women would have been greatly reduced. The trouble is that Jackie didn't enjoy campaigning," said des Rosiers. "She found the pace too hectic and didn't care to rub shoulders with Mr. and Mrs. John Doe. When she did campaign, she remained aloof, quiet, alone. She was very reserved. I think Jack might have tried to encourage her more. She represented a large part of the Kennedy image-making machine. It must have been disconcerting for him that she didn't accompany him more often. Nor did she generate great enthusiasm or buoyancy when she did accompany him.[11]

Not only the Kennedys were surprised by Jackie's lack of aptitude for politics. Her own relatives were baffled too. Amazingly Jackie, who had grown up on the outskirts of Washington, worked as a member of its press corps, and been involved with Jack Kennedy for two years before she married him, was unprepared for the task. "She hated politics and politicians. Jackie was accustomed to politics," Gore Vidal observed. "After all, she was brought up there. Jackie saw there was nothing glamorous about that world. To her it was just sleazy and boring."[12] She was a difficult political wife to gain access to and when it came to reporters Jackie was not gracious or friendly. She just liked the privileges, not the responsibilities.[13]

Whatever else Jackie might have been, she was controversial. She had as many supporters as she had critics. While some people felt she was much too stiff, formal and standoffish, others admired her and valued her character and her demeanor. Jackie's importance to JFK's campaign should never be underestimated. Always photogenic, mysterious and reserved, she made an undeniable impact on the American psyche. She was noticed more than any other Kennedy woman because she was different. She was refreshingly frank. She indicated that she campaigned with her husband because if she hadn't she never would have seen him.[14]

Gradually things began to change. At first it was very subtle. But then Jackie-mania began and it took the country by storm. Everyone within the campaign was taken by surprise, as Jackie emerged into the spotlight. Charles Peters, a campaign worker, shares his memories of the West Virginia campaign by telling us that he was vehemently opposed to Jackie going there. "I felt Jackie would compare unfavorably with Muriel Humphrey who was down to earth and much more like the West Virginians. I thought Jackie was too glitzy. I was in charge of Knawha County, the largest county in the state. I went out campaigning with Jackie twice. She seemed quite pleasant. You sensed a light restraint on her part but not much more. What amazed me most was the way people reacted to her. I first got the sense through Jackie's emerging popularity of what was happening in American society. There was no question that instead of identifying with the woman like them such as Muriel Humphrey, they identified with the princess. You could just tell they wanted Jackie. They had a wondrous look in their eyes when they saw her. After the dowdiness of Eleanor Roosevelt, Bess Truman and Mamie Eisenhower, they were looking for a new exciting image and the Kennedys did a superlative job of merchandising that aristocratic image. I think Jack Kennedy's motive for marrying Jackie was that she gave him class. At least there was the perception of class, since her background was actually the same as his."[15]

What struck JFK's entourage was Jackie's lack of post-victory exuberance. The night of the primary, Jack and Jackie went with their friends Ben and Toni Bradlee to see a "sexploitive" movie in Washington. When the film ended, the foursome returned home to Georgetown. Bobby called and told Jack he had won handily in West Virginia. They all flew there right away aboard their airplane, the *Caroline*. The victory celebration took place at the Kanawha Hotel. Champagne flowed and music played, Jackie slipped out a back door. She located the car that had brought them from the airport and crept into the back seat, and sat there alone, waiting for the return trip to Washington.

Jackie's malaise and ennui became apparent at other points in the campaign. Elizabeth Gatov, a Democratic party leader in California, noticed at once that, "Jackie really didn't like politics very much and she didn't like politicians or people connected with it. She wasn't comfortable with them and so when she was with JFK I'd try to find a couple of people—attractive, rather urbane men, to spend that period of time with her, and help make it as pleasant and as easy for her as possible."[16]

As the election year proceeded, Dorothy Schiff, then owner and publisher of the *New York Post*, remarked about Jack Kennedy's reactions to his wife by saying, "He was utterly cold in his remarks about her. I had a feeling he had very little interest in her except as she affected his campaign."[17]

On November 8, election day, Jack and Jacqueline went together to the polling section at the West End Library in Boston. They voted and then returned to Hyannis Port to await the results.

Early in the administration, Kennedy, who avoided confrontation with his wife, had sent Angier Biddle Duke, his Chief of Protocol, to talk to Mrs. Kennedy about the role of First Lady. "Tell her," the President had said, "the responsibility of the wife of the President in regard to visitors and things." "What do you want to do, Mrs. Kennedy?" Ambassador Duke had begun. "As little as possible," she said. "I'm a mother. I'm a wife. I'm not a public official."[18] Jacqueline Kennedy had a parallel obsession, a desire to give the Presidential experience style and elegance. She had been unhappy in her first days in the White House, comparing herself to a moth hanging on the windowpane of the presidency. She told a Kennedy family employee that she felt as though she lived in a fishbowl with all the fish on the outside. The role of presidential wife was bothersome, with its built-in expectations about decorum and protocol. "The one thing I do not want to be called is First Lady," said Jackie. "It sounds like a saddle horse." Much to Jack's irritation, Jackie was reclusive, refusing to appear at political events and fund raisers. Aside from intrusions into her privacy, she resented the Kennedy in-groupiness in the White House, the possessiveness with which they claimed the place.[19]

After Jackie moved into her own tastefully decorated bedroom, she issued a statement on what she expected her primary role to be, "I think the major role of the President's wife is to take care of the President and his children." Off the record she told Charlotte Curtis, her former dorm-mate at Vassar, that she didn't know if she could make it. "The White House is a snake pit. Jackie wore so many masks she was impossible to decipher," said Curtis. "With her elevation to the role of First Lady, she became ever more elusive, more secretive, more dramatic. Probably she felt very vulnerable. She was a stationary target for the press."[20]

To put it bluntly, Jackie was terrified when she entered the White House. Being a private person, she was very aware of the need to build a fortress around herself and her children. In such an environment, she also must have had moments when her very sanity would be threatened. The Presidency is so intimidating with all of the secret service protection and security everywhere. It would be a hard place to relax. Acutely aware that her privacy was at risk, Jackie forced members of the White House staff to sign a letter of agreement pledging never to write or talk about their years of employment with the Kennedys. The document had no true legal force and, in the end, only created resentment and negative publicity. Nor did it prevent staffers from writing of their experiences in the White House. If anything, it encouraged them.[21] How naive of Jackie to even begin to think this sort of request would be taken seriously. Perhaps she felt that if everyone could keep Jack's womanizing a secret all these years, then she was not asking too much of them after all.

Jackie's shyness and obsession about privacy became a central and controlling factor during her first year in the White House. She did her best to shun the White House press corps and ignored their pleas for personal interviews. She escaped the press and the pressure of the White House by spending as much time as possible away from Washington. When forced by her husband to respond to the press, she once said, "Poor Jack, he thinks if I ignore them he'll be impeached." Once when Jackie returned to the White House with a new German shepherd puppy, the press asked her what she would feed it? "Reporters," she shot back.[22]

After herself, Jackie's main concern was the privacy of her children. She expounded on her policy of secrecy in a lengthy memo to Pam Turnure, her press secretary and JFK's former flame, which began, "I feel strongly that publicity in this era had gotten completely out of hand, and you must protect me and my children, but not offend the press." She continued, "My press relations will be minimum information given with maximum politeness, I won't give any interviews, pose for any photographs, for the next four years."[23]

Is it any wonder that the press corps was out to get her. What a ridiculous statement to make as First Lady. Now the question would be, what will you want to do in four years? Will you cooperate when you and your husband wish to continue living in the White House? Oh yes, re-election time will change everything. The entire family will be available. What no one could know then, was that Jackie was serious. She would not be doing any of this eight years from now. She would see the press but it would be on her terms for the rest of her life.

Jackie was particularly rude to the women of the press. Perhaps she feared that other women would be able to see through her more easily. At a reception after the Bay of Pigs incident, reporter Ester Van Wagoner Tufty, recalled, "Jackie was doing her utmost to ignore us. The President noticed her giving us dirty looks. He went over and he marched her over to us and in his most charming way told her to say hello to us. What made it particularly difficult dealing with Jackie was her totally unpredictable nature. At times she proved quite thoughtful and other times she treated us like dirt. She repeatedly referred to the female members of the press as 'harpies'. In one memo I happened to see, she suggested, 'Keeping the harpies at bay by stationing a couple of guards with bayonets near them.' Frankly I could never figure out exactly what her problem was with the press. You know, if you don't want your privacy violated don't become the First Lady."[24]

Jackie's relations with the press were strained from the start, in part, because she made it clear she resented the spotlight. "I sympathize with all First Ladies when it comes to the press," veteran Washington columnist Betty Beale said, "Because you're damned if you do and damned if you don't." What Jackie did, she did well. But there were many times when she really goofed off. She had no intention of going to ladies' luncheons and doing the things a First Lady has always been expected to do. Jackie dismissed these traditional duties as "boring and a useless waste of my time. Why should I traipse around to hospitals playing lady bountiful when I have so much to do here to make this house livable? I'll just send some fruits and nuts and flowers."[25]

The truth was, Jackie chose to stay out of the limelight around the other women of the capitol. It was an embarrassing place for her. Most everyone in Washington knew what Jack was up to and they were laughing at Jackie behind her back. At least that's what Jackie thought. Many people were unaware of the details of Jack's sexual pursuits and some didn't even care. But what wife wouldn't be sensitive to this sort of ridicule. Jackie was a proud woman. Her position was not a comfortable one. No one envied her marriage to Jack Kennedy. Many felt sorry for her and that was even harder to take.

Jackie's other problem with privacy was centered around the secret service. During her years in the White House, they kept her in a constant state of agitation. She was told about kidnap plots against her children, assassination attempts on her husband, and various threats to her own person. They were there for her protection, too, but she didn't trust them or like them. Their loyalty was to her husband. They did such an outstanding job of keeping his affairs secret, it's easy to understand Jackie's feelings about them. "There was a lot of romantic swill about the secret service," she would later tell her friends. "Their finest hour was supposedly Jack's assassination, when they protected Lyndon Johnson who wasn't the target anyway, while Jack got killed."[26]

As for the children's privacy, there was a built-in conflict between the President and First Lady. JFK knew the children were invaluable to his popularity and he had no problem using them to his political advantage whenever possible. However Jackie was adamant that they were not to be exploited. "If Mrs. Kennedy had her way," Mr. West, the White House Head Usher believed, "the White House would be surrounded by high brick walls with a moat and crocodiles." When it came to press coverage of Caroline and John-John, spreads in magazines like *Life* and *Look* were fine as long as Jackie controlled the access and the circumstances. Glimpses into the lives of the first family were one thing, unauthorized shots by overzealous photographers were quite another.[27]

Not even the President had the courage to face his wife when the subject of the children and the press came up, so much of this subterfuge took place when she was out of town. Pierre Salinger, the President's Press Secretary, took most of the heat from Mrs. Kennedy regarding the children's exposure to the press. When Jackie would complain to him that yet another unauthorized photograph of the children had surfaced, he would explain that JFK had requested the picture be taken. "I don't give a damn, " Jackie replied. "He has no right to countermand my order regarding the children."[28]

Rightfully so, Jackie became very paranoid about the press. They truly were her enemies when it came to the children. "Jackie didn't want Caroline and John-John to be treated like stars," Tish Baldridge said. "But Jack knew the kids were a great asset for his administration. He was proud of them. He wanted to show them off." Jacques Lowe, a photographer, recalled, "It got to be a game between the two of them, with me stuck in the middle."[29]

To Jackie's way of thinking there was a big difference between showing the children off and using them. This difference of opinion between Jackie and JFK would be a problem during their entire time in the White House. It would also be one of the last things they would argue about before their trip to Dallas. While Jackie was on the cruise with Aristotle Onassis the month before the assassination, JFK used this opportunity to have a photographer come into the White House and shoot pictures of the children without Jackie's knowledge or permission. When she returned and found out, she went through the roof. This exploitation of her children must stop.

Aside from the issues of Jackie's hatred of politics and her lack of privacy, she did manage to make a big difference in the White House. Her restoration project was an achievement of great historical signifigance. "She changed the White House from a plastic to a crystal bowl," Letitia Baldridge said. Critics stopped calling the First Lady a "decorative bird in a gilded cage." Yet, despite all the excitement in her transformation of the White House, despite its new elegance and her enormous satisfaction, the White House still never meant home to Jacqueline Kennedy. The poking cameras waiting outside the gates, the inability to go out as often as she wished and the ever present secret service men were the things she could not escape. The phrase she used most often to her closest friends was, "It's like a prison." Jackie told journalist, Charlotte Curtis, her old friend that "The White House is such an artificial environment," she said. "If I don't take care of myself, I'll go mad."[30]

It was not just a prison as Jackie suspected, but it was worse than a prison. It was JFK's own secret little domain. A place where he was in charge and knew all. At the beginning not even Jackie realized the depth of her husband's deviousness.

By the summer of 1962, JFK had upgraded and expanded the taping system originally installed in the Oval Office by FDR. In a room beneath the Oval Office, a tape machine, installed at President Kennedy's direct request by secret service agent Robert I. Bouck, secretly recorded his meetings. According to journalist William Safire, the President was so pleased with the notion of being the only one in a meeting aware of being recorded that he extended the taping to telephone conversations. He touched a button that signaled his secretary, Evelyn Lincoln, to record on a dictabelt the calls he selected.

The first caller the President taped was his own wife. According to Safire, "This tape was later removed from the JFK library files, along with four numbered audiotapes of official meetings that Kennedy family members and their lawyers presumably felt showed embarrassing or illegal actions." None of those taped, from Jacqueline Kennedy to former presidents, friends and staff were aware that their conversations were being recorded.[31]

This act of secretly taping those closest to him shows a dark side of Jack Kennedy. It backfired on him. His secret taping impugns his character as much as any of his other affairs.

It also would make a wife very, very angry,

angry enough to get even!

NINE

WHAT WAS THE ACTUAL CRUISE LIKE AND
DID JACKIE AND ARI FALL IN LOVE
THEN AND MAKE THEIR SECRET PACT?

THE LOVE BOAT

*J*ACQUELINE KENNEDY AND ARISTOTLE ONASSIS fell in love on his yacht, the *Christina*, during their famous cruise in the fall of 1963. They agreed that in order to marry, Jackie must get out of her sham of a marriage. Unfortunately, divorce was not an option. Ari, in the throes of his desire to possess her, convinced her that by eliminating Jack Kennedy in such a way as to protect their involvement, their problems would be eliminated. The way Ari presented his plans for their future together, under the moonlight and stars, seemed so simple. Thus my theory that on this short cruise, they made a pact which was a simple exchange.....a murder for a marriage.

You may wonder what state of mind Jackie must have been in to even consider going on a cruise that could be a political disaster for her husband. No other Presidential wife had ever considered leaving her husband to take a luxurious cruise especially with one of the world's most notorious and wealthy men. In a pre-election year, it is impossible to think she would want to do it and incredible that her husband allowed her to go.

But when you look at events leading up to this adventure, Jackie indeed had quite a depressing year. Aside from all Jack's regular infidelities, there were so many other tragedies to deal with in 1963. First, there was the traumatic loss of their son, Patrick Bouvier Kennedy on August

9th, a loss that truly devastated Jackie and left her in a terrible state of mind. As she recuperated at Hyannis Port, JFK quickly dashed back to Washington to be with his mistress of the moment, Mary Meyer, the sister-in-law of Ben Bradlee, their dear friend from the Washington Post.

Jackie had been around long enough to know every move Jack made into or out of bed and with whom. She had her own sources and her own network of friends, staff and even domestic help to keep her informed of every move the President made. No one as calculating and realistic as Jackie could afford not to know since this very information gave her incredible power over all the Kennedys.

After their son's death for their tenth wedding anniversary on September 12th, Jackie gave her husband a money clip designed with a St. Christopher medal. The medal was to replace the one Jack had put into their baby's coffin. Replacing the medal was a poignant gesture. Putting it on a money clip was rather crass, especially since it was a well-known fact that Jack Kennedy never carried money. Even more symbolic was the President's gift to Jackie. He gave her a catalogue from J.J. Klejman, the New York antiquities dealer, and told her to select whatever she wanted.[1]

This wasn't a personal, warm gift chosen with deliberate care, but an easy expensive gift with no meaning or consolation attached to it. Jackie finally selected a simple coiled serpent bracelet that was very symbolic considering future events. A serpent ready to coil would most accurately describe Jackie's state of mind on this their tenth anniversary.

Then on September 24th, within days of their anniversary, JFK was parading Mary Meyer all over the country with him on Air Force One. He even visited Mary's mother, Ruth Pinchot, all of which was documented for the press corp and the entire world. As for discretion and secrecy right in her own home, Jackie could tune in every night to world news and see the President and his mistress on television right in her own living room.

No wonder Jackie jumped at the chance to go on a glamorous two week cruise on October 1,1963. All things considered the timing of this cruise couldn't have been more suited for the soon-to-be lover's future plans.

Oh yes, it was a traumatic time for the young Mrs. Kennedy.

August 9, 1963 - childbirth and the death of her son
One month later
September 12, 1963 their tenth wedding anniversary
Twelve days later
September 24, 1963-the President and Mary Meyer, his mistress, travel all over the country and even have their pictures taken with Mary's mother.
Six days later
October 1, 1963-Jackie escapes for the cruise into the waiting arms of Aristotle Onassis.
Seventeen days later
October 17, 1963-Jackie returns from the cruise a different woman, and agrees to go on first ever political stateside trip during JFK's Presidency.
One month later
November 23, 1963
JFK assassinated in Dallas, Texas, with Jackie at his side with the perfect alibi.

Obviously, all things considered, Jackie was very depressed and in need of a change of scenery and perhaps a little fun. So how did her path come to cross the path of Aristotle Onassis at this most difficult time of her life? Her sister, Lee Radziwill, brought them together in a roundabout way. During Aristotle Onassis's travels, he had the opportunity to meet Jackie's younger sister and they became fast friends. Of course the gossips insisted that it was much more than friendship. In those days it was only necessary for a woman to smile at Onassis to start tongues wagging and to supply juicy tidbits for the scandal sheets.[2]

Ari and Jackie had previously met and he had invited her on his yacht but she had declined. Now things were very different and Jackie could hardly wait to cruise with Onassis. Life as a Kennedy had become unbearable. Politics or no politics, she was out of there.

Early in 1963, Princess Radziwill told Onassis that things were not going smoothly between her sister and John F. Kennedy. In fact, as was widely rumored a few years earlier, the couple was on the brink of separation. Only pressure from Joe Kennedy, who understood that a break-up would permanently damage his son's political career, held them together. Supposedly, in the Kennedy version, Onassis thought that if he offered his hospitality to Jackie for a while it might enable the couple to make it through this difficult period.

It is hard to believe that Onassis would think that this cruise would help the Kennedy's marriage. It was a blatant ploy to entice Jackie to cruise with him hoping it might enable him to seduce the wife of the President. "Why not ask Jackie to join us on a two week cruise aboard the *Christina?*" Ari suggested. Lee thought it was an excellent idea and immediately relayed the invitation to her sister. Jackie was very enthusiastic about the trip, but she had a hard time getting Jack to agree. She insisted so strenuously that John Kennedy finally gave in.[3]

Is it any wonder that Jackie couldn't resist the opportunity to get away from Washington and cruise the romantic Greek islands? Here she had a husband who, within days of their tenth anniversary, was parading his current mistress all over the country. Jackie had good reason to be pissed off. There's no better revenge than the good life and what could be better than life with Onassis aboard his ship, the *Christina*. Even though she did not know it, it was her destiny. This cruise would not only change lives but would change history.

As for JFK not liking the idea of a long separation, even with the political consequences, he enjoyed getting Jackie out of the White House. It made it easier to cavort freely, without the presence of a wife near by. Things were different about this trip, an encounter that even the principals seemed unaware of. Nothing could stop or change a future that would hold death for one and a short life together for the other two.

As for Onassis, no one was richer, more powerful, more publicized or more outrageous than Aristotle. Combining shrewd cunning, extraordinary energy and amoral charm, the Greek Onassis rose from the back streets of Smyrna, Turkey, to create and control an international business empire. He controlled one of the world's largest shipping lines, owned an international airline, bought and sold the Bank of Monaco and had a reputation as one of the most ruthless deal makers of his age. He mingled freely with celebrities, artists and politicians. Until the time he acquired Jacqueline Kennedy, his most prized associations were with Prince Ranier of Monaco, and his adored Winston Churchill. He also numbered among his closest friends Greta Garbo, Eva Peron, Elizabeth Taylor and Richard Burton. He romanced Gloria Swanson and loved and abandoned opera diva, Maria Callas.[4] Although Ari had an unsavory past, all of these people were willing to overlook his past, in order to enjoy his incredible hospitality and charming personality. He had charisma and then some.

JFK finally agreed to the cruise for Jackie but he laid down the law. If Jackie insisted on going, Stas Radziwill, Jackie's brother-in-law would have to be included, as well as an additional chaperon for the sake of appearance, if for no other reason. It would hardly do for the First Lady and her married sister to be seen in close company with a divorced man renowned as a connoisseur of beautiful women. Jackie agreed and the President asked his friends, Franklin D. Roosevelt, Jr. and his then wife Suzanne, if they would be willing to act as chaperons.[5]

The President had reason to be concerned, especially with the "Golden Greek's" image not only as a foreigner but also a jetsetter. This was the worst possible combination from the point of view of the average American. In addition, Onassis had been the target of any number of criminal probes and investigations by the Justice Department. Onassis was the defendant in several legal skirmishes with the U. S. Maritime Commission. The most publicized of these involved his purchase of fourteen ships from the Commission with the understanding that they would sail under the American flag. Onassis had made more than $20 million by transferring them to foreign registry. He was indicted and forced to pay $7 million dollars to avoid criminal prosecution.[6]

In order to avoid publicity, it was announced that Onassis would not be aboard when the *Christina* sailed. However, Jackie with her reputation for good breeding, insisted that Ari accompany them on the cruise. Jackie stated the cruise would be "the dream of my life." As she was quoted at the time, "I can't possibly accept this man's hospitality and then not let him come along. It would be too cruel."[7] No one could argue this point since it was his ship.

Ari took precautions, however, not to show himself in port but spent the rest of the time happily with his guests. As usual, the press quickly discovered the truth. About a week into the cruise, an Italian photographer succeeded in taking a picture of Onassis with a telephoto lens. Thus it was disclosed once and for all that he was, in fact, aboard with the others. Who could have suspected at the time that the First Lady of the United States, like a simple peasant girl, was falling in love with Aristotle Onassis?

The first person to realize that Jackie was in love with Onassis, was Maria Callas. Maria didn't take it very seriously, since it seemed unlikely to her that Jackie would divorce the President. This was the first cruise in four years that did not include Maria on board. In a letter that quite a few people at the Kennedy White House read, Jackie described Onassis with such enthusiasm that John Kennedy asked her, by return mail, to come home as soon as possible. However, Jackie calmly continued her cruise all the way to Turkey.

At the time, the idea of a love affair or even a great friendship between Jackie and Ari seemed highly improbable. In spite of his hundreds of millions of dollars, they didn't belong to the same social class. Yet Ari's valet, Christian Cafarakis, who had been in his service for ten years tells us what many have known since 1968, and he himself guessed in 1964, that these two people were destined to one day become husband and wife. Even if John Kennedy hadn't been assassinated, Cafarakis states that, "I personally think Jackie would have divorced him and most certainly married Onassis."[8]

Speaking of revenge, Jackie had a few unsettled scores with Jack going all the way back to the 1956 convention in Chicago. After that convention, Jackie had been dismissed to Newport to await the arrival of their first child. Meanwhile Jack went on a Mediterranean cruise with his friends to recuperate from the stress of the convention. Alone, Jackie went into labor and gave birth to a baby girl who was born dead. By then Jack and his sailing companions had been at sea for three days and had time enough to turn their boat into a floating bordello. He was having so much fun that he decided there was no compelling reason to return home to Jackie. His decision to delay his return was a horrible lapse in judgment, and it would haunt him for years to come. It was one thing to be seen as a compulsive womanizer. It was something else to show his complete insensitivity to Jackie and his callous disregard for his wife in her moment of need.[9]

This was the kind of treatment that would understandably inspire payback time, and quell the vengeful feelings of a young wife. Although the cruise did not seem to be a proper way to mourn the loss of a child, the fact that Jackie went on it without her husband did not bode well for this marriage. It was especially hard for the American public to digest the fact that their beloved President's wife was going on a cruise with the world's wealthiest Greek playboy. No one could even begin to imagine that a President's wife would abandon him like this in a pre-election year. Can you imagine Mamie or Ladybird ever taking such a trip?

Why would JFK ever even consider letting his wife go on this trip? Well if the truth be known, he had to let her go. It was essential to keep her happy with the election coming up. Jackie had great potential to be a spoiler in the scenario of the President's life. Let's face it with her ongoing depressions, at any given moment she could go ballistic and reveal all the deep, dark, hidden secrets of JFK and all the other Kennedys. We must remember that all the Kennedys were aware that Jackie could be unpredictable.

The strains imposed on her by her husband's political career and the demands of his family tortured her. Early in the marriage tormented by her own wild extremes and deepening depression, Jackie finally sought help at Valleyhead, a private psychiatric clinic in Carlisle, Mass. that specialized in electro-shock therapy. In anticipation of a political scandal that might politically embarrass Jack Kennedy, his wife's therapy was a well-kept secret and rarely referred to even within the family.[10]

Jackie's attitude towards her husband was full of the most intricate paradoxes and contradictions. She had more in common now with Rose than perhaps she would ever admit, accepting her husband's sexual betrayals as much as her mother-in-law had Joe's. Yet on another level, she did not give in totally to this life. Evelyn Lincoln observed Jackie's disdain for all the obligations of the political wife, her extravagance, her parade of sophisticated, jet-set friends alien to the world of the Kennedys and her emotional disengagement from Jack. Lincoln had become convinced that the Kennedy's marriage had reached such a nadir she believed that after the election, there might be the first divorce in the Kennedy family.[11]

Although Jackie at times might have been unstable, she wasn't stupid. She knew she carried a big stick and revenge would be her eventual plan. It was all too much for any woman to bear. Besides the public infidelities, the real problem in her life was her total financial dependence. She would never be her own person until she had as much or more money as the Kennedys. It was as simple as that!

With her husband's reluctant approval Jackie departed for her rendezvous. The President's relations with his wife, complicated by her personal extravagances, her apparent lack of political sophistication and by his own recent infidelities, were delicate and complex. Jackie was not in good shape. Perhaps, after all, a cruise in the company of people with whom she would feel comfortable would be just the thing for her.[12]

The cruise was a success, marred only by periodic breakdowns in the *Christina's* telecommunications system which made it difficult for Jackie to speak to her husband.[13] This technical difficulty must have pleased Onassis immensely. The idea of having JFK's wife all to himself was the fulfillment of Ari's fantasy. It wouldn't be surprising if Ari, himself, made sure that communications with the President stayed unreliable throughout the trip.

The ostentatiously appointed *Christina*, with its barstools uphol-stered in whale scrotum and its gold plated bathroom fixtures, was hardly Jackie's style. But to the surprise of many the First Lady appeared happier than anyone had seen her in months. Even she had never been pampered to such an extent. But by the time they reached Onassis's private island of Skorpios, Lee was jealous of how surprisingly close Ari and Jackie had grown in such a short time. "Onassis fell for Jackie," said Evelyn Lincoln, JFK's private secretary. "Then it turned out that he became more than just a friend." Did Lincoln think Jackie had an affair with Onassis before the assassination? "I think so, yes. Jackie loved money. Onassis had money. That might have been what she saw in him. And she didn't like President Kennedy's political friends. She didn't like that kind of life.....Kennedy couldn't change his career because he was a politician."[14]

Ari entertained the First Lady with his rich lode of anecdotes and stories of life in Smyrna, the city of his birth. Ari talked of his early struggles, of how he had once been a telephone operator in Argentina for twenty-five cents an hour.[15]

On the cruise Jackie was excited by the superabundance of luxury, and she was fascinated by Ari who reminded her of her swarthy father. Ari's physical features were repulsive, his education rudimentary, his culti-vation practically nil. He thought that impressionists were people who wanted to impress people. But Jackie found him to be a fabulous raconteur.[16]

It was not all about history. On the *Christina*, the favorite games were those of sexual flirtation and assignation. Onassis may have had his barstools made from whale scrotum, but he played his sexual games with far more subtlety. Onassis may have looked more like a toad than a prince, but it was not simply his money that drew women to him. He was fasci-nated by women in a way that Jack Kennedy could never be. Ari lavished on Jackie all his attention, flattery and charm.[17] This was the very type of attention that Jackie was starved for.

Jackie insisted and he consented to be her guide. Retracing a path it had followed many times, the *Christina* touched at Delphi, at Lesbos, at Istanbul and circumnavigated the Peloponnesus. Anchored off Skorpios, the island he purchased the previous year that was still undeveloped, Onassis confided that he planned to build a 180-room replica of the Palace of Knossos on Crete. "Perhaps," he said to Jackie, "you'll advise me on redecorating Knossos when it is finished?" [18]

After her experience redecorating the White House, this invitation would be music to Jackie's ears. Imagine the thrill it would give her to decorate a palace without the financial constraints, she had to put up with on the White House restoration. And imagine working with a man whose funds were limitless, unlike her husband who was always haranguing her about her spending excesses.

As the *Christina* made its way across the Mediterranean, it occurred to Jackie that her sister might actually win Ari away from Maria Callas and claim all this luxury for herself. As Mrs. Aristotle Onassis, Lee would become a richer and more resplendent queen than Jackie, who, after all, would one day have to vacate the Kennedy White House. [19]

With this reality check, she began giving Ari the full Jackie treatment. She gazed at him adoringly with her widely spaced brown eyes. She punctuated her sentences with girlish words like "gosh" and "golly." She whispered to him at night as they sat together under the stars. She accompanied him to tea with Queen Fredricka. She danced with him to bouzouki music at nightclubs. She strolled with him through the streets of Smyrna. And she swam with him in the warm lagoons when the yacht anchored at eventide. A paparazzi with a telescope lens caught Jackie in a revealing bikini, a picture later seen all around the world. The others on board the *Christina* could not help but notice what was going on between Jackie and Ari. Every morning at breakfast there were feverish conversations among the passengers. Jackie had done everything but sleep with Ari…and a lot of people thought that she had done that too.

Robin Duke, the wife of Angier Biddle Duke, the Chief of Protocol and also on board, didn't think so. "The only way to keep Onassis interested in you was to drive him nearly mad with desire. You would not go to bed with him. Because once you did, you would be like everyone else. And believe me, Jackie wasn't like everybody else. She was not about to lose her mystique."[20]

On board, Onassis and Jackie sat together for hours alone on the deck, sharing their thoughts as they gazed up at the star-filled sky long after the others had gone to bed.[21] Realizing that they were falling madly in love, these confidential conversations were used to make their plans for a future together. It would be difficult but they were exceptional people and there was nothing ahead that they could not control. Their plan would be bold, daring, decisive and dangerous. Their new-found love would lead them to make a sacred, secret pact. My theory is based on the probability that they were motivated by lust or love whichever was closest to their true inner feelings at the time.

This love pact would be very simple. It would be a murder for a marriage. They both realized that the only impediment to their desire was the existence of her husband and he must be eliminated. There would be no other way to fulfill their destiny. It would be safe to assume that this decision was not discussed in great detail but rather in general terms. Ari would take care of everything leaving no trail back to either of them. Jackie had no need to know any of the specific details, only that it would take place soon. She might even safely assume that she would never be in any danger herself. For her alibi, she would have to be with him in order to play her designated role as wife of the martyred President. Most likely Aristotle knew that by not making her privy to his exact plans, there would be no need to worry that she might get cold feet or change her mind. Once their course was agreed upon, there would be no turning back. This was a deed that they would take to their graves.

Onassis's plan would be incredibly simple and brilliant, he would procure the world's best sharpshooters and hire them to commit the assassination. Even the assassins would never know who actually ordered this hit. He would protect their identity at all costs. It would be the perfect crime of the century.

By hiring professionals whose only motive would be money and the thrill of committing an unsolvable crime, there would never be a trail leading back to who hired these killers. Besides there were many other more likely suspects, since the President and his family had so many enemies. It is hard to even know where to begin when contemplating who might have killed Kennedy. This question, as we all know, would haunt our country and enable future generations to theorize about it even thirty-five years later.

It would be a brilliant plan and their pact would give each of them their hearts' desire. Jackie would have more money than she ever dreamed possible and Ari would possess the crown jewel in his collection of people. Is it any wonder that walking together along the water's edge Jackie told her host she wished her Greek idyll would never end.[22]

In Istanbul, Jackie was cheered by hordes of enthusiastic Turks as she came ashore to visit the Blue Mosque. "Come back," they yelled as she departed. "I will return when my husband is no longer President," she promised.[23] What a strange response. Most people would have expected her to say "Yes, I will return and bring my husband with me." However, her statement referring to a time, when JFK is no longer President, was almost prophetic in view of the near future events.

On the last night of the cruise, as was customary, Ari distributed gifts to his guests. Jackie received a diamond and ruby necklace easily worth in excess of fifty thousand dollars. He gave his other guests lesser baubles. "Ari has showered Jackie with so many presents, I can't stand it," Lee complained in a letter to the President. "All I've gotten is three dinky bracelets that Caroline wouldn't even wear to her own birthday party." Jackie surely was moving up in the world considering that at one time she didn't even own a piece of serious jewelry.

While Jackie was cruising aboard the *Christina*, Jack called Stanley Tretick, a *Look* photographer, and asked him to come to the Kennedy White House to take some pictures of John and Caroline. "I was surprised to get the call," Stanley said. "I knew that Jackie had been against me taking her kid's pictures for *Look*. She didn't view me as somebody artistic like Richard Avedon. She just viewed me as a press photographer. But Jack was getting ready for the Presidential campaign and he felt differently. He knew the value of *Look* magazine. "Things get kind of sticky around here when Mrs. Kennedy is around," Jack told Stanley. "But Mrs. Kennedy is away so now's the time to do some of those pictures you've been asking for of John and Caroline."[24] Welcome home, Jackie! You are just in time to see Jack exploiting your children for his own selfish political desire.

Although Jack had asked her to return home as soon as possible, when Jackie left the ship she was in a defiant and independent mood. She flew directly to Marrakesh to stay in the Casbah residence of the King of Morocco's cousin. Kennedy once asked his wife which country she would visit if she had a choice of Italy, Ireland or Morocco. "I know you want to go to Ireland more than anything in the world," she said, "but I would go to Morocco." And so she did!

Prior to the cruise, Jack had conveyed his wishes to Onassis to stay out of the U. S. until after the elections. One can't help but wonder at the reaction of a proud man who is good enough to wine and dine the President's wife all over the Mediterranean but yet is not welcome in the United States. It must have given Onassis great delight to sweep Jackie off her feet and make plans with her to rid them both of this ungrateful man.

When Jackie finally returned home to the United States, she knew she had yet a most serious admirer. This time, one who didn't leave her indifferent. Someone, in fact, she hoped to see again as soon as possible. Perhaps even within the next month or so.

On October 17th when the President's wife returned to the Kennedy White House, a member of the staff said, "Jackie has stars in her eyes— Greek stars."[25]

When she did get back, the First Lady invited Robin Douglas-Home, a close friend, to spend the afternoon with her at the country home she had built in Atoka, Virginia. "She was immensely more relaxed, more outwardly composed and happier than at any time in all our previous meetings," he said. "There was a new composure. Gone was much of the bewilderment, the repressed frustration, the acidity, and yes—even the bitchiness that had run through her previous conversations. To put it rather cruelly, I suppose one could say she had clearly grown up a lot, a batch of her pet illusions had been shed, she was learning to accept that her ideals were just not all one hundred percent attainable all of the time, the moods were less shifting, the wit less biting, the flares of aggression dimmed and deeper."[26]

Perhaps, Jackie had already begun the performance of her lifetime. She had the skills of a great actress and quite capable of fooling everyone with her new attitude. Although Jackie despised politics, she now willingly agreed to accompany her husband to Texas. She had made 13 trips abroad as First Lady, but she had refused to travel in the United States, never venturing farther west than her riding stable in Virginia. This would be her first political trip since the death of her child, except for the cruise.[27]

What could possibly have happened on her cruise with Onassis to make her come back to her husband with such a new attitude of cooperation towards his every wish and desire? It is as if she had been programmed to be the perfect political wife. The official story was that the loss of their child had suddenly brought them closer together. Everyone should forget the ongoing infidelities and her tremendously happy absences from the marriage. All of a sudden, the American public was to be spoon fed the newest versions of the perfect Presidential couple. Jackie was incredibly eager to help spread the word.

Could it be that all these changes were because someone new had come into her life, someone who could change her life for the better? Someone who could help her escape her degrading marriage.

All of a sudden, she would confide to others how close she and Jack had become since the loss of their child, a good cover story. But who in his or her right mind could believe this new-found closeness between a man who publicly traveled around with his mistress and a wife who eagerly rushed off on the most luxurious cruise two months before?

As for Ari's reaction to the cruise, he was immensely pleased. Jackie was to be the crown jewel of his collection. When he made the deal to acquire Jackie as his wife, he felt that he had finally arrived. By possessing the world's most sought-after woman, he would purchase the respect that he had long desired from the socially elite. He had bagged the biggest trophy wife of all time. Onassis felt that this marriage would provide him and his family with all sorts of powerful connections. He craved entry to the highest circles of power and prestige all over the world.

Now he must carefully make the arrangements.

This would be the ultimate business deal of his lifetime.

TEN

What actually happened in Dallas?

THE PERFECT ALIBI

*T*HIRTY-FIVE YEARS AFTER THE ASSASSINATION of
John F. Kennedy, the question remains: "Who killed Kennedy?"

No one really knows. There have been so many theories that it is
hard to keep them straight. Sorting through all of these theories is a mind
boggling exercise.

Even President Clinton is still trying to find out who did it. Webb
Hubbell relates in his recent book, *Friends In High Places*, that when
Clinton assigned him to the Justice Department soon after he took office he
said, "Webb, If I put you over at Justice, I want you to find the answers to
two questions for me. One, Who killed JFK? And two, Are there UFOs?
He was dead serious."[1]

Everyone is a suspect. The Kennedy's had so many enemies that
almost everyone involved in their lives is a suspect. Most people know by
now that it would have been impossible for Lee Harvey Oswald to do it
alone. It is unlikely that one man could have gotten off all those shots within
such a short time.

My own theory is that Aristotle Onassis, with the approval of
Jacqueline Kennedy, hired the best contract killers in the world to take out
Kennedy. To this day no one has a clue as to who they were. They were so

professional that they got away with the assassination without leaving a trail. To this day the identity of the killers is as much of a mystery as is the identity of whoever hired them. It is very likely that they didn't know who they were working for at the time of the murder. They wouldn't care. These are the type of assassins who work for big bucks with no questions asked. This is what they do for a living and the bigger the name, the bigger the payoff.

The last White House reception under President Kennedy took place on November 20, 1963, the night before his ill-fated departure for Texas. The evening marked Mrs. Kennedy's first official White House function since the death of her son, Patrick. The event was the annual reception for the Supreme Court Justices, their wives and other judicial officials, spouses and guests. As always, there was interest in how Mrs. Kennedy would look, how she would dress, how she had arranged the details of the reception.

White House correspondent, Jessie Stearns, recalled the elation of the press corps that day. "We had been invited to cover the reception, to take pictures and make written impressions to share with our readers. Such openness on the part of Jackie Kennedy was uncharacteristic. She had been nasty to us from the very beginning. I remember the details so clearly because the reception took place only a few days before the assassination. It was a period when JFK, though reportedly 'settling down' with Jackie, was still playing around with other women. There was ample evidence to support this notion, including actual sightings by some very reliable sources. That nobody reported these activities in the press was due to the fact that a President's personal sex life was then considered 'off limits.'

At this particular reception I was standing near the foot of the grand stairway down from which marched the honor guard carrying the Presidential flag and the Stars and Stripes, followed by the President, First Lady and guests of honor. They emerged to the marine band's playing of 'Hail To The Chief.' All of a sudden I heard this scuffling on the staircase, a kind of pushing and pulling. People were straining to look. But a moment later they came into sight. President Kennedy's hair was standing up on one side as though somebody had taken a clump and yanked it. He appeared momentarily ruffled and flustered. Jackie seemed quite upset. JFK began to pat down his hair, smoothing it back in place. As I recall, they then quickly moved us out of there. For obvious reasons they didn't want the press corps standing around asking questions."[2]

"What I imagined happened is that Jackie returned from her weekend home at Atoka, where she had been horseback riding, and either heard or saw something that irritated her. She arrived at about 1:30 in the afternoon, and the reception started at 6:30. I can fathom her just seething with anger for those five hours, and then he came over and she flew at him with words and whatever else. I'm willing to bet that they had it out again in their private quarters after the reception."[3]

Others recall that there were 700 assembled and waiting at the White House reception for the Judiciary, but the President and his wife were late. When the two came down the stairs to the East Room almost an hour late, observing reporters had some interesting notes. While the President's hair was never slicked back, "It now looked almost as if somebody had pulled it." His face had an expression one reporter described as "uneasy disgust." Reporter Helen Thomas said of the First Lady, "She looked as if she had been crying." The two moved quickly into the receiving line and the First Lady disappeared almost immediately afterwards.

Reconstructing the scene, some enterprising reporters discovered that the First Lady had provoked the President by arriving very late from Virginia. It had happened before. It would never happen again. The next day they were going to Texas.[4]

When Larry O'Brien was asked this same question his reply was, "I don't know if the Kennedys argued the night before we left. That's not the kind of information he would have shared with me. It's possible they had a Mr. And Mrs. Quarrel."[5] One other person recalls vividly the state of the Kennedy marriage prior to the trip to Dallas. The President's secretary, Evelyn Lincoln, recalled that JKF and his wife had an earlier argument. He had to persuade her to forgive him and come to Dallas as planned. "You can't tell people these things," said Lincoln, "because they don't want to believe you."[6]

Of course not, after the assassination rumors or recollections of marital discord would not fit with the official version of the Kennedy marriage. The Kennedy line would be the portrayal of a wonderful marriage and a devoted couple who were especially close since the death of their son. The world would be told that they were closer than ever. Jackie was very comfortable with this lie.

But Evelyn Lincoln, the President's secretary, held another view of the marriage. "No, I don't think the marriage improved at the end, that's what she wanted people to think. Before he got married he was the gay young bachelor and it was hard to change. I don't think they were compatible. They were both too independent and neither one wanted to give in. Besides, she was jealous of his celebrity. No, I really think that if he had another term, she would have left him at the end of it. He should have had a wife who was brought up in politics."[7]

The truth of the matter is that everyone was in shock that Jackie had agreed to go on this campaign trip. The general consensus was that Texas would be a tough trip. There had been much party in-fighting in Texas and Jack's mission was to heal some wounds. Jack was delighted that Jackie agreed to go and had freely offered to help him. A split in the Democratic party in Texas could have hurt him in the next election. It was a fence-mending operation, and Jackie was a pretty good carpenter.[8]

There is interesting speculation as to why Jackie actually did agree to this trip. Jack hated the pictures of Jackie in a scanty bikini aboard the *Christina* which appeared on front pages around the world. Those pictures were a political and personal embarrassment. For once Jack was getting a taste of his own medicine.

The press described several of the parties Onassis threw aboard his yacht, noisy soirees often lasting until dawn. "Does this sort of behavior seem fitting for a woman in mourning?" asked an editorial in the *Boston*

Globe Rep. Oliver Bolton of Ohio said in congress that, "The First Lady demonstrated poor judgement and perhaps impropriety in accepting the lavish hospitality of a man who has defrauded the American public." The Congressman raised some pertinent questions, chief among them, "Why doesn't the First Lady see more of her own country instead of gallivanting all over Europe?"[9]

Upon her return, Jackie remained only briefly at the White House, long enough to argue with her husband, before heading off to her weekend home at Atoka. However, after Jackie returned suntanned but rested, Jack did not say anything. Instead, he seized the opportunity to play on Jackie's guilt. "Maybe now you will come to Texas next month?" "Sure I will, Jack," she said, "I'll campaign with you wherever you want."[10]

This was an incredible statement coming from Jackie. She was not the type to feel guilty over anything considering all of Jack's fiascos. She had not once before during his Presidency campaigned anywhere in the United States. Previously she had only been available for the glamorous international trips overseas. She loved being the toast of Paris and other capitals of the world. Everyone knew she abhorred the campaign trail. What could possibly have made her agree to this trip and volunteer for others in the future?

Perhaps she already knew this would be the last trip she would ever take with Jack. Ari was not a patient man. Once she agreed to their deal, he would execute it as quickly as possible. There was no need to delay. Onassis could not risk that Jackie might change her mind.

Dallas would be a golden opportunity since it was a hotbed of controversy and hate. Kennedy had many enemies there. Some advisors had even warned him explicitly not to go. Both Senator Fulbright and Adlai Stevenson asked the President not to go to Texas. The mood in Dallas was ugly. A month before, U.N. Ambassador Stevenson had been booed, jeered, hit with signs, pelted with eggs and spat upon at the United Nations Day Rally.[11] The President even voiced his concerns to Senator George Smathers, "God, I hate to go out to Texas, and I'm gonna make Jackie go with me. I have a terrible feeling about going and I wish I could get out of it." Jackie was very nervous on the flight and there was an urgency with which she kept smoking throughout the flight.[12]

As shocking as the assassination of John F. Kennedy was, it is even more shocking to discover that he rehearsed the event just a few months earlier. During Labor Day weekend in 1963, the President, a James Bond fan, joined with friends to make an amateur film, in Newport, Rhode Island. The Presidential yacht, Honey Fitz, docked nearby, and a Navy photographer filmed the project. Jack came off the boat, walked down a long pier, then suddenly clutched his chest and fell over, flat across the pier. A beautiful woman, Countess Consuelo Crespi, and her young son emerged from the yacht and stepped over him as they walked to shore. Next Jackie came out and she, too, stepped over Jack's body. Finally his friend, Red Fay, came along and pretended to stumble over the body. As he did, he fell on top of Jack and red liquid spurted from Jack's mouth and all over his t-shirt.[13] It is hard to believe anyone would do this for amusement. It was in terrible taste. However, it did prepare Jackie for what she would soon experience within two months.

President Kennedy had often thought of his own mortality. He talked about death with his friend, Larry Newman. Newman recalled a mass they were attending one Sunday morning along with some reporters sitting just behind him. Just as the mass was starting, Kennedy turned to the reporters and said, "Did you ever stop to think, if anyone tried to take a shot at me, they'd get one of you guys first?"[14] Jack Kennedy had a certain fatalism about his own mortality and often expressed his view that nothing could keep a would-be assassin who was really determined from getting to him. He even predicted that a tall building would be where the shot would come from. He didn't seem to worry a lot about his own safety. He had sort of a what will be, will be attitude....*que sera, que sera!*

Kennedy talked a great deal about death and about the assassination of Lincoln. He joked that President Coolidge had said that any well-dressed man who is willing to die himself can kill the President. He talked about the deaths of Garfield and McKinley. He talked about the fact that for the last hundred years every President elected in a year divisible by twenty had died in office. "The poignancy of men dying young haunted him and one of his favorite poems was 'I Have A Rendezvous With Death'," recalled Jacqueline Kennedy.[15]

At San Antonio, their first stop that day, Jackie remained close to her husband as he presented a dedication speech honoring the Aerospace Medical Center at Brooks Air Force Base. Afterwards, they flew to Fort Worth, arriving at the hotel at one o'clock in the morning on Friday, November 22nd. Jackie later would recall bits and pieces of her last night with Jack. She told her husband that she couldn't stand John Connally stating, "That if a man's good-looking enough, it seems to be something ruinous, they almost get soft."

That night they occupied a three-room suite and slept in separate bedrooms. The President had injured his groin earlier in the month and he had cramps. Exhausted, they said goodnight and went to their separate rooms.

When they arose, Jack read the *Dallas Morning News.* A full-page, black-bordered ad denouncing him for signing the nuclear test-ban treaty calling him "Fifty Times A Fool," appeared in the paper. That Friday the *News Front* read, "President's visit seen as widening state Democratic split." Page 14 had a full-page advertisement, paid for by H.L. Hunt and other conservative businessmen, asking the President twelve questions, most notably, "Why has the foreign policy of the United States degenerated to the point that the CIA is arranging coups and having staunch anti communist allies of the U.S. bloodily exterminated?"[16]

The President handed the newspaper to Jackie. "Last night would have been a hell of a night to assassinate a President," he said, pacing back and forth in the hotel where he was waiting for the motorcade that would take him through the heart of Dallas. "I mean it. There was the rain, and the night, and we were all getting jostled. Suppose a man had a pistol in a briefcase. Then he could have dropped the gun and the briefcase, and melted away in the crowd. If someone wanted to shoot me from a window with a rifle, nobody can stop it."[17] "We're going into nut country today."[18]

After landing in Dallas, the motorcade departed Love Field airport at 12:55 p.m. First came the police motorcycle escort, then the Lincoln limousine carrying the President and Mrs. Kennedy and Governor Connally and his wife, Nellie. On the back seat, between the President and First Lady, there was a large bouquet of long-stemmed roses, a pleasant contrast to the strawberry pink wool suit and matching pillbox hat she had decided to wear for the Dallas procession. When she received the flowers at Love Field, Jackie noted that since arriving in Texas she had been presented only with bouquets of the state's more famous yellow rose. The red roses reminded her of the *Christina* and her trip to Greece.[19] Could these flowers possibly have been a pre-arranged signal? As the motorcade began, there was plenty of space in the limousine between the President and First Lady since each had to work the crowds on their side of the route.

Kennedy sat back and chatted with the Connallys. "Well," said Mrs. Connally, "you can't say Dallas isn't friendly to you." Kenny O'Donnell, a Presidential aide, was riding in a car right behind the President's when the assassins' bullets struck. "I saw the third shot hit. It was such a perfect shot. I remember I blessed myself." General McHugh, another passenger, riding in the same car as O'Donnell said, "We heard three shots as clearly as you talking to me. As we rode, bullets came over our head, one after another and I thought, 'My God, they're giving him a twenty-one gun salute'! Then we looked up and saw the President slumped over."[20]

The number of rounds remain as much a mystery today as they were then. Within a period of less than six seconds at least three shots were fired. The first bullet hit the President in the back of the neck, brushed his right lung, severed his windpipe, exited his throat. Another shot, believed to be the second of three, severely wounded governor John Connally, who was sitting on a jump seat directly in front of the President. The third shot struck the President in the back of his head, blowing away the right rear quadrant of his skull. The deed was done.

Acting on her own good judgement, Governor Connally's wife, Nellie, pulled her wounded husband into her lap and out of the line of fire bending over him with her own body.

Jackie later told the Warren Commission, trying to make them understand why she hadn't done the same for the President, "I was looking to the left, I used to think if I only had been looking to the right, I would have seen the first shot hit him, then I could have pulled him down and then the second shot would not have hit him."

The only problem with Jackie's explanation was the existence of the Zapruder film, which showed plainly that within an instant of the first shot Jackie was looking to the right, directly at her husband and, riveted to her seat, continued to stare at Jack for the next seven seconds without moving to his aid. When Jackie did move it was in an unexpected direction. She jumped up, scrambled out of her seat and onto the trunk of the car, accidentally kicking what was left of her husband's head in the process and began inching her way to the right rear of the vehicle. Her destination, a large mounted rubber handgrip at the very rear of the trunk, when if reached, could serve as a means of escape from the suddenly accelerating car. She had reacted not only to the finality of her husband's wounds but to Governor Connally's anguished cry of grief, "God! They are going to kill us all!"

Jackie panicked and, in her moment of truth, her instinct was self-preservation. The excuses she later offered for her abortive flight seemed to change with the seasons. She told the Warren Commission she had no recollection of ever having climbed onto the trunk of the car. She told William Manchester, the author, that she had crawled out to try to retrieve a portion of her husband's head. *Life* magazine had it that she was on the trunk of the car seeking help for her mate. Her momentary loss of courage was not featured by the media.[21]

Perhaps since she knew she would be close to the actual hit when it happened, it would be a normal reaction to try to escape. Or perhaps she did not know that it was the time and, being in shock, she reacted accordingly. These would have been professionals. Under no circumstances would Ari ever have endangered her life. Jackie knew this. Their alibi depended on her being right there. Her presence would forever keep her from being a possible suspect. She would not be the first wife to witness her husband's murder. All through history, unhappy wives have had their husbands eliminated with the help of willing lovers. There is nothing new under heaven and on earth.

Finally, at one o'clock, Jackie was told her husband was dead. She then did something that was out of the ordinary. Someone helped Jackie remove her bloody white gloves and she took off her wedding ring and slipped it on Jack's finger. Knowing she would have doubts about giving away her wedding ring, later Kenny O'Donnell removed it from JFK's finger at Bethesda Naval Hospital and returned the ring to Jackie.[22]

How can I say that it was unusual for a widow to take off her wedding ring? I too was a young widow. I was twenty-five when my husband was killed violently. I stood with two children under the ages of three behind a casket that held all that was left of my husband. It never ever occurred to me to take off my wedding ring. It was my husband's gift of love, given to me on our wedding day. I only removed it upon my remarriage, and then I had it reset and wear it now on my right hand.

The other strange thing about shedding her wedding ring immediately was that most widows would probably do exactly the opposite. They would take their husband's ring to keep. Jack, however, had not worn a wedding ring since the day of his marriage. Kenny O'Donnell was very perceptive to realize that Jackie's action would be misunderstood. Especially with so many people knowing about their argument the night before they left on this trip.

Now as Jackie returned to Washington, no longer the First Lady, her thoughts were already engrossed in planning her husband's state funeral. This would be her last time to perform as the President's wife and she was determined to do the best job possible. As the funeral began taking shape in her mind, Jackie vowed that she would make up to her husband in death what she did not give to him in life. Her final farewell to him would be a royal occasion, giving the nation an opportunity to mourn its slain leader. She wondered how Abraham Lincoln had been buried and decided she would follow the historical precedent of that day.[23]

This would be the performance of her life. The funeral pageant would set the tone for Jacqueline Bouvier Kennedy's place in history. It would prepare the way for Jackie to take her place as a historical figure of epic proportions. This would be the beginning of her legend. She knew too that someone would be staying at the White House who she wanted to impress.

He would be watching her every move and would be very important in her future.

·   As to.... Who killed Kennedy?

The answer is simple.

The best money could buy!

ELEVEN

WHAT DID THE FUNERAL ENTAIL FOR JACKIE AND ARI?

THE REQUIEM FOR A ROGUE

*O*N NOVEMBER 22, 1963 ARISTOTLE ONASSIS WAS in Hamburg for the launching of the Olympic Chivalry when he learned of Kennedy's assassination. He immediately telephoned Jackie's sister, Lee, at her home in London. She asked him to accompany her and her husband, Stas, to Washington for the funeral. He reminded her that he had been warned by Jack and Bobby Kennedy not to step foot inside America for at least a year. "I don't think that matters very much now," she told him. The following day he received an official invitation from Angier Biddle Duke, Chief of Protocol, not only to attend the funeral ceremony but to also be a guest at the White House during his stay in Washington. Although he was one of only half a dozen people outside the immediate family to be given this honor, his presence went almost unnoticed in the days of shock and mourning that gripped America.[1]

We know that neither Bobby Kennedy nor any of the other Kennedys would have invited Ari to such a private family gathering. The invitation could only have come from the mistress of the White House who was making all of the funeral decisions on her own. For some strange reason she had told Lee to bring Ari to the funeral with her. She would need him to be there for her. Jackie drew Onassis to her side, as close to her as she could without alienating Bobby.[2]

It seems odd that of all the people available to comfort her, she would choose to have Aristotle Onassis. So many others who were close to Jack would have been on hand to offer solace and be there for anything she might need. Jackie's twin Bouvier aunts and their husbands were also invited to the funeral, but they were not invited to stay at the White House.[3]

The world was deeply impressed with the way Jackie conducted herself during these days of national mourning. Only a very few people knew that Dr. Feelgood was quickly there for her. Max Jacobson, who flew down from New York, gave Jackie his elixir to help settle her nerves.[4]

When her sister and brother-in-law arrived from London, Stas Radziwill was struck by the regal atmosphere pervading the White House. "It's just like Versailles when the King died," he said. He would repeat that observation later when Jackie, imbued with the glory of France, insisted that an eternal flame be installed over her husband's grave, like the flame flickering over the tomb of the unknown soldier under the *Arc de Triomphe* in Paris. Robert Kennedy was stunned by this theatrical gesture. "I could understand a memorial, but she wanted a goddamned eternal flame", he muttered to the Secretary of Defense.[5]

Upstairs in the Presidential suite at the White House, obsessed with ceremonial details, Jackie made endless lists of everything she had to do. She dispatched memos around the White House. She wanted Bunny Mellon, her close friend, to arrange the flowers. She ordered a black veil to cover her face for the funeral. She designed black-bordered sympathy cards. She selected from the President's personal belongings certain things to give to his aides and friends and family as treasured mementos. These mementos she presented with personal letters. She wrote thank you notes to everyone on the White House staff. She even sent a note of condolence to Marie Tippit, the widow of the policeman shot by Oswald in Dallas. Jackie insisted that Luigi Vena, the tenor soloist at her wedding, sing the "Ave Maria" at her husband's funeral. She also stipulated that everyone walk with her from the White House to the cathedral in a solemn procession.[6]

Rising above her grief, Jackie resolved to impress her husband's and her own place in the consciousness of the American public. The funeral provided a means of demonstrating JKF's importance as a global leader, his historic links with Abraham Lincoln, Andrew Jackson and Franklin Roosevelt. A procession of international dignitaries would march to St. Matthews behind Jackie and other members of the family. The coffin would be drawn by the same caisson that had carried Franklin D. Roosevelt to his grave. A riderless horse with boots reversed in their stirrups, would follow the coffin, while muffled drum rolls marked the way.[7]

This funeral would be Jackie's shining moment and shine she would. She knew her own place in history would depend on this performance. She was determined to increase her own value to anyone who would be interested in collecting celebrities.

When Jackie learned that Charles de Gaulle would be arriving at the White House, she ordered the curator to remove all the Cezannes from the walls of the yellow oval room and hang Bennet and Cartwright prints. "I'm going to be receiving General de Gaulle in this room," she said, "and I want him to be aware of the heritage of the United States. These prints are scenes from our own history."[8]

Jackie supervised every detail of the vast state funeral. "I want everything done by the Navy," she said. She sent people to the Library of Congress, which was closed, and they used flashlights to check all the details of Abraham Lincoln's funeral. She duplicated that funeral as much as she could.

Cardinal Cushing had suggested that John Kennedy be buried in Boston and the family fully approved. But Jacqueline was firm, her husband would be buried in Arlington National Cemetery. He no longer belonged to Boston, he belonged to the Nation. Sargent Shriver softly suggested that some people might consider the eternal flame pretentious. "Let them," she said. Not only that, but she wanted to light the flame herself.[9]

The images generated over the next few days would be indelibly etched in the national psyche: Jackie's eyes swollen from crying and still wearing the suit stained with her husband's blood; Jackie standing next to Lyndon Johnson as he is sworn in on Air Force One; Lee Harvey Oswald clutching his stomach as he is shot by Jack Ruby; the world leaders from Haile Selassie to Charles de Gaulle marching in the funeral procession; the grieving widow behind the black veil; Jackie kneeling with Caroline in the Capitol Rotunda to kiss Daddy's flag-draped coffin; tiny, blue-coated John-John's heartbreaking final salute.[10]

First to last, Jackie made all the decisions for what would become the greatest pageant in American history. She had gotten her wish, she was overall director of the twentieth century. Her wish had been granted at the cost of her husband's life.[11]

"The cameras were frozen on the motionless widow," William Manchester, a Kennedy friend, wrote, "and omitting those who were reading newspaper accounts or talking to friends, nearly everyone in the United States was watching Mrs. Kennedy. Ninety-five percent of the adult population was peering at television or listening to radio accounts. To the Americans must be added all of Europe and those parts of Asia which were periodically reached by relay satellite. Even Russia had announced that the Soviet Union would televise the funeral, including the mass in St. Matthews. By Sunday noon, the USA and most of the civilized world had become a kind of closed-circuit hookup. Nothing existed except this one blinding spotlight. And that spotlight was focused on Jackie.[12]

Out of the spotlight, others in the Kennedy family were having a difficult time, particularly Bobby Kennedy. Bobby's private torment was that he felt some responsibility for his brother's death by pushing the assassination attempts against Castro, and that Castro might have, in revenge, engineered the death of the President. Or that his prosecution of the Mafia and corrupt labor leaders like Jimmy Hoffa might somehow have involved them in the murder plot.

Bobby's pain was visible, tangible, almost unbearable. It was easier for him to be angry than sad, anger gave him some opposing emotion to focus on. "The amazing thing was that he was still functional," said John

Seigenthaler, a close friend. Bob wore dark glasses to hide his red-rimmed eyes. He did most of the crying on his walks alone at home.[13] His pain was evident to all, as well as to Onassis inside the White House.

The body lay in state in the Rotunda of the nation's Capital. Two hundred and fifty thousand people lined up to see Kennedy's body. Moving slowly past the coffin, the line stretched for three miles, the crowd parted when they saw Jacqueline and Bobby arrive. Jackie put a letter in the coffin she had written to her husband the night before. There was no copy. Robert put in Jack's PT-boat tie clip and a silver rosary from Ethel. They both kneeled and prayed and then the coffin was closed. Bobby, Ted and Jacqueline said their private goodbyes at the casket before it was taken by the honor guard.

For the watching world, the highly formal historical pageant helped ease the pain. The caravan of cars, hundreds of them, carried the leaders of the world on a six-mile drive past a watching crowd of more than a million. "It was a mass movement," said Larry O'Brien, a Kennedy aide, "It was not a very orderly procession. There was dead silence, just the beat of the drums. To go up to that cathedral with the drums beating, to see people like de Gaulle, Haile Selassie and Prince Philip walk along the street and into the church, to look around and see these world leaders in every direction you looked, then on through the ceremony in Arlington, was overwhelming."

At the grave, a squadron of cadets from Ireland, whom the President had so admired, marched in drill formation. Cardinal Cushing made his blessing. The final twenty-one-gun salute was fired. Taps were played. The flag was taken from the coffin and given to Jacqueline. She was given the burning taper to light the eternal flame. She then gave it to Bobby, who put the end of it into the flame and passed it to Teddy. Ted seemed unsure of what to do with it until an army officer took it from his hand. The torch had been passed.[14]

After the ceremony at Arlington, Jackie met privately with Charles de Gaulle, Emperor Haile Selassie of Ethiopia, Ireland's President Eamon de Valera and Prince Philip who suggested that a receiving line would be a more efficient way of greeting the other foreign dignitaries than mingling. The queue—200 representatives from 102 nations, including eight chiefs of state and 11 heads of governments—stretched from the Red Room back through the Blue Room and the State Dining Room. John Davis, having flown from Italy to pay his respects, found his cousin in "an elevated mood. Finally she was running the White House. She loved being the center of attraction with all the world's dignitaries paying homage to her."

Davis further relates, "At the time he died I too was idealistic about JFK. Now whenever I see those old films of Kennedy on television, I have to stop myself from heaving. It's hard to believe that here was this absolute fake, this womanizer and opportunist, coming off like Euripides. All our dreams invested in that! What a disappointment."

Cecil Stoughton, who took the official photographs of Jackie in the receiving line greeting the visiting government officials, remembers thinking, "How can she stand to do this?" But on this day Jackie transcended rank, outdid herself. She remained serene, embracing some, reassuring others.[15]

Jackie gave the country and the world an unforgettable image of courage. Lynn Kotz, a writer, while interviewing White House Chief Usher, Mr. West, for his book told me that the Chief Usher wondered himself, "How could she plan the details of a funeral so carefully, so meticulously?" He did not, however, want these questions to ever appear in his memoirs. Could Jackie could have possibly given this funeral some pre-assassination thought? At the same time, it surely must have crossed her mind just what she would do if her husband ever was killed? She seemed so prepared for this event.

As for the official version of the marriage, Jackie's presence in the convertible united her with Jack closer in death than anything in life. The assassination and the dramatic public spectacle that followed, retroactively exorcised any public doubts about the Kennedys or their marriage. "The manner of the President and his wife to each other was always simple, courteous and loving, without trying," Katherine Anne Porter wrote in the *Ladies Home Journal*. She marveled at how their life was "lived hourly in love with joy, yet every duty done and every demand fulfilled." In this, the greatest performance of her life, Jackie acted instinctively and appropriately. Her breeding and hauteur paid off as she telegraphed her anguish while displaying self-control.

Television intensified Jack Kennedy's ties to the people during his life and intensified the trauma associated with his death. Jackie Kennedy starred in this modern mourning spectacle. "Mrs. Kennedy achieved on this tragic day something she had never quite achieved in the years she had been in the White House—a state of love, a state of rapport between herself and the people of this country," Ladybird Johnson noted. "Maybe it was a combination of great breeding, great discipline and great character." Jackie demonstrated the mores of her genteel, aristocratic upbringing on this most modern and vulgar medium. Her poise was a mark of her gentility. Her silence and grace confirmed the wisdom of a social circle that preferred self-discipline to self-indulgence. The matrons of America reconciled with Jackie that November. Yet even as she advertised its virtues, Jackie helped bury this traditional culture. The assassination would be seen as the end of American innocence.[16]

The thought that maybe Jackie was relieved to get out of an intolerable, humiliating and degrading marriage was never spoken, at least not publicly. Perhaps it was easy to give a performance when one knows that it is her last one. She would never have to play the game again. It truly would be her swan song.

The Kennedys, like their country, set a high standard that all would aspire to and none could achieve. Ultimately, they and their country produced such disillusionment that both the earnest efforts and the actual achievements would disappear along with the bright, shining and unrealistic image. Eventually the Kennedy's failures would make America doubt that the perfect couple could exist at all.

Just as late-twentieth-century Presidents would strive to do right by

Roosevelt in the Oval Office, all subsequent Presidential couples would strive to succeed as the Kennedys appeared to have done while in office. But those who followed would also be cursed by both the unrealistic standards the Kennedys set and the ensuing disappointment. First, the following Presidential couples and finally the nation would pay a high price for the lies that Jack and Jackie Kennedy lived.[17]

Such revelations would be routine twenty years later, making the Kennedys' apotheosis puzzling. How did the playboy and a debutante caught in a sham of a marriage seduce the nation? Apologists could justify the personal sins of Franklin Roosevelt or a Richard Nixon by pointing to political achievements such as social security or detente. But John Kennedy's greatest political achievements were personal. Americans loved the Kennedys for who they were or at least who they seemed to be. Yet Kennedy and his wife were nothing like their shining images.[18]

What do you think the inconspicuous visitor at the White House from Greece would think of this American way of handling grief? Remember Aristotle Onassis would be coming from a Greek background in which death was the ultimate tragedy. Greek sorrow has had a history of epic proportions when expressed by Ari's people.

First of all upon his arrival, no less astonishing was the sight that met his eyes when he encountered the party of mourners. Ted Kennedy was drunk and doing imitations. Robert Mc Namara, the Secretary of Defense, was wearing one of Ethel Kennedy's wigs. At some point they all piled into cars for a wild ride out to Arlington National Cemetery and back. Later they all laughed and sang and carried on with great hilarity.[19]

After dinner, Bobby Kennedy badgered the Greek ship-owner endlessly about his yacht and his wealth. During dinner Attorney General Robert Kennedy drew up a document in which Onassis agreed to give half his fortune to the poor of Latin America. Joining into what to him must have been the perplexing spirit of the occasion, he signed it in Greek.[20]

It is amusing to think about how the Kennedy children would have felt if anyone had ever badgered old Joe Kennedy about his wealth. Considering where it came from, he could have been presented with a formal document stipulating that Joe give half of his wealth to the moonshiners in the rural hills of Kentucky.

At the time Onassis's imposed role as jester to the soon to be mourning Court of Camelot was not deemed of any particular significance. It did establish his affability in a difficult social and emotional situation.[21] It was not a problem for Onassis to be so congenial. He knew that after all was said and done, he would have the last laugh, not the Kennedys.

His reason for being there was to be near Jackie during this difficult time. Obviously, Jackie was still in a state of shock from her close proximity to the actual murder which was understandable since the sharpshooters had not performed as expected. She was safe but the mere fact that John Connally wasn't, surely upset her. She needed to feel the close proximity of Aristotle Onassis to reassure her and make her feel safe and protected during these moments of national mourning. This was a woman who performed well in a crisis situation. She was a lady with a mission and her performance amazed and pleased Ari.

To this day people remember Jackie's dignity and unforgettable composure during the funeral and continue to marvel and admire her. It was quite a performance. There was a lot at stake for Jackie, approximately $5 million dollars that she and her children would receive upon her marriage to Onassis. This was money she would desperately need since by now she was aware that Jack had only left her $25,000 plus the income from the children's trust funds. Jackie had to give the performance of her lifetime right then or face the rest of her life as an indentured political servant to the Kennedys.

Now if Jackie and Jack had been passionately in love prior to the assassination, it would have been quite difficult for a widow like Jackie to carry on. However two months prior to this funeral, Jack was flying all over the country on Air Force One with his mistress Mary Meyer, one month prior to this funeral Jackie was returning from her cruise on Aristotle Onassis's ship with priceless jewels and precious promises.

This was a couple who not only led separate lives along with their separate bedrooms but didn't particularly even like each other

As she stood behind the casket holding the man who was never the great passion of her life, Jackie gave the country and the world an unforgettable image of courage. This was her time to ensure that the Kennedy Presidency would always be remembered with dignity and grace. Jacqueline was the self-anointed regal caretaker of the flame.

For Americans glued to their television sets this performance was the closest our country would get to the emotion other countries feel for their royal families. It was a gift to our country from Jacqueline Kennedy that we desperately needed to get through this national tragedy. You must remember that for the average American, John F. Kennedy was a beloved President. People in middle America didn't know a thing about his degenerate lifestyle. All the sordid facts about this Presidency were hidden from the public; consequently Americans were totally grief-stricken and very few even suspected that the Kennedys weren't the perfect couple we had come to love and adore. The American public needed the solace that Jackie gave to comfort them for the next thirty-five years.

Jackie did an incredible job of pulling herself together. She must have been very shaken by the actual assassination, for what was supposed to have been a very simple, clean hit turned out to be a disaster. No one could have anticipated Connally getting shot or the President's brains being splattered all over. Most people in shock react in unexpected ways. Once Jackie assimilated the fact that the act had really taken place and there would be no turning back for her, she rose to the occasion and then some.

Now, let us go forth!

If Onassis was pleased with Jackie during the week of the funeral, wait until he saw her version of the Kennedy Presidency and the Kennedy marriage.

This version would become known as Camelot,

a fairy tale to end all fairy tales!

TWELVE

What did Jackie do with the creation of Camelot?

THE FANTASY OF CAMELOT

*I*N CHILDHOOD GAMES, JACQUELINE BOUVIER always took on the role of the queen or princess while her sister, Lee, was a lady-in-waiting. Jackie even kept a crown on hand, part of a costume her father had bought her. According to her cousin Edie Beale, Jackie was always "an odd mixture of tomboy and princess. She never outgrew the princess role."[1] Jackie was an artistic child, highly sensitive to visual beauty. By the time she was eight, she was writing charming verse and drawing with crayon, pen and ink extremely well. These abilities would come together in a whimsical book she and her sister, Lee, wrote and illustrated in 1951 after a long summer trip through Europe which they titled 'One Special Summer.' In this book, Jacqueline unconsciously revealed her concept of her destiny in a montage entitled "dreams of glory," Jacqueline is depicted in a regal costume and a crown and is self-described as *"Jacqueline, fille naturelle de Charlemagne."*[2]

In 1940 when Jackie was only ten, her grandfather John Vernon Bouvier, Jr., self-published the remarkable Bouvier family history called *Our Forebears.* This book began with an epigraph from Lord MacCaulay, "A people which takes no pride in the noble achievements of remote ancestors will never achieve anything to be remembered, with pride, by remote descendants." Jackie's grandfather took great liberties in order to enhance the social status of his ancestors. One can imagine how a ten-year-old child would react to reading about such an ancestry. Most Americans are aware they are the descendants of penniless, uneducated, working-class proletarians who emigrated to America to escape poverty or political oppression. The Bouviers, according to grandfather, had been members of the French aristocracy before coming to America. One of them had been knighted by no less a potentate than the Sun King Louis XIV. This ancestry made the impressionable young Bouviers feel far different from most Americans, far more special. John Davis, Jackie's cousin, tells us that he believed this book gave all the cousins, especially Jacqueline, the illusion of a status far above that of the great mass of Americans. It formed the basis of the aristocratic demeanor Jackie came to display as she got older.[3]

With this background and upbringing, it's not surprising that Jackie's version of Camelot sprang up a week after her husband's murder in Dallas. No doubt that she preferred myth to history. Within a week of the assassination, Jackie gave her famous interview to journalist Theodore White at Hyannis Port in which she vehemently urged White to characterize the Kennedy White House years as resembling the mythical kingdom of Camelot. She did not want to take a chance and leave her story to the historians, those "bitter old men" as she called them, to write their history.[4]

It would be far better for everyone concerned if Jackie returned to her childhood fantasies and made her destiny come true. She had dreamed the dream, lived the life, and now she would write the history. This story must touch the hearts of the entire world and even in its great tragedy this story must give hope. It must also ennoble Jacqueline to such an extent that she would be beyond question or suspicion for the rest of her life. This enchanting tale would be the perfect footnote to her already perfect alibi.

As strange as it may seem, Jackie did not appear to care about who killed her husband. It was of no concern to her nor should it be to anyone else. It simply didn't matter. There was no need to speculate on various suspects. The less said about the killers the better. This lack of interest was such a clever part of Jackie and Ari's plan. Jack was gone. What counted for her was that his death be placed in some sort of story form to comfort the country and secure her place in every American's heart. She could do no wrong. Jackie quickly and boldly seized the opportunity of a lifetime. She would write her own history and she would come out a heroine for all the world to adore and worship.

Once the funeral was over, Jackie did not collapse or even retire from view. She began her discussions with the journalist, Teddy White. "A week after the assassination, I received a telephone call from Jackie inviting me up to Hyannis Port where she had gone to spend Thanksgiving," said White. "She knew I was writing a summation of the assassination for *Life* magazine and would I be willing to come up to have a talk with her?"

White quickly rented a car and driver to take him from New York. "Looking pale and drained, Jackie indicated she had left Washington to escape prying eyes. It was understandable considering that for four days an entire nation had entered the sorrow and private suffering of the widow of this fallen leader. She and I spoke for nearly four hours. She mentioned Patrick's death as a prelude to the assassination. It was an emotional event for both parents, and I think the President reached out to her as he hadn't done before. There weren't too many of these moments in their lives."[5]

This would not be the time to dwell on the arguments before Dallas, the President's current mistress, who was Jackie's friend, or the incredible cruise that Jackie had just returned from with Aristotle Onassis. These were all things that would be better left unsaid or even unthought. It was the time to create a new version of a sad, sorry marriage.

Now was the time for Jackie to become the adoring wife and Jack to become the devoted husband. Theirs would be a love story for the ages. Now she would actually be able to dictate the history of the Kennedy administration.

What an opportunity. She had lived their history one way but now she could change all of that and touch things up a bit for posterity.

Teddy White relates that upon his arrival, "Jackie regurgitated many of the details of the actual assassination. She remembered so much which she was eager to share. Her only solace was that Jack didn't suffer. He had made a special point of telling her on a number of occasions that he never wanted to end up like his father. He preferred death to permanent disability."

"We spoke about the political climate that had led to the assassination, the idea of a plot or even of government involvement in the event. Jackie couldn't have cared less about the many theories as to who might be behind the murder. What difference did it make whether he was killed by the CIA, the FBI, the Mafia or some lunatic."[6] Jack had so many enemies. There were those who were distrustful of his wealth, his family, his life style and his Catholic religion. Big business was more than unhappy about the reforms he had proposed. This civil rights stand had angered the south and some blacks felt he was too moderate.[7]

In a strange way, it was as if Jackie had already made peace with the fact that America would never know who had killed its President. She was much more interested in getting on with the healing of the country and getting her story out. How bizarre!! Not to even be curious about who had killed your husband? Especially when she had been sitting right next to him when it happened. It was unbelievable. Looking back now and realizing that she may have known who did it all along, helps to make sense of her actions then and her lack of anger or curiosity.

Jackie proceeded to tell Teddy White that, "Jack's life had more to do with myth, magic, legend, saga and story than with political theory or political science." That's when she came out with her Camelot theory. She believed, and John Kennedy shared the belief, that history belongs to heroes and heroes must not be forgotten. She didn't want Jack to be forgotten, or have his accomplishments cast in an unfavorable light. She wanted him to be remembered as a hero. She reported how at night he would often listen to Camelot on their phonograph, and how he personally identified with the words of the last song, 'Don't let it be forgot, that once there was a spot, for one brief shining moment that was known as Camelot.'"

"She put it so passionately that, seen in a certain light, it almost made sense. I realized it was a misreading of history, but I was taken with Jackie's ability to frame the tragedy in such human and romantic terms. There was something extremely compelling about her. At that moment she could have sold me anything from an Edsel to the Brooklyn bridge. Yet all she wanted was for me to hang this life epilogue on the Camelot conceit. It didn't seem like a hell of a lot to ask. So I said to myself, why not? If that's all she wants, let her have it. So the epitaph of the Kennedy administration became Camelot—a magic moment in American history when gallant men danced with beautiful women, when great deeds were done and when the White House became the center of the universe."[8]

The magic of Camelot never existed, except in Jacqueline Kennedy's imagination. Pierre Salinger, the President's press secretary, states that, "Camelot is a fraud, the word never came out during the administration, but only a week after in the interview with Theodore White. Now it has become the word. We are living in a world where the words Camelot and myth are attached to the Kennedy name. I constantly argue against this."[9]

Another observer, such as Arthur Schlesinger, agrees with Salinger. He recalls that "Camelot was, of course, unknown in Kennedy's lifetime. JFK himself would have regarded that with derision."[10] JFK's personal secretary, Evelyn Lincoln's comment was, "That story of hers about listening to the music of Camelot, he never listened to Camelot in his whole life! His favorite song was 'Bill Bailey, won't you please come home?'"[11]

Roger Hilsman tells us that, "Camelot was an invention of my good friend Teddy White, using Jackie's romanticism after the President's death. If Jack Kennedy had heard this stuff about Camelot, he would have vomited. It would have made him sick to his stomach. It was a journalistic invention."[12] Dean Rusk, who was Secretary of State, under Kennedy says that, "Kennedy would have kicked the idea of Camelot right out of the window. He was a very practical, hard-headed, down to earth kind of fellow who would not have indulged in the sentiment of Camelot when he was alive."[13]

Adam Yarmolinsky asks, "Why is Camelot associated with the Kennedy administration? Because it is a natural. But you've got to remember the last scene which is the key to the whole thing. It's just off the battlefield. The battle is about to begin and a young man runs onto the stage and says he wants to join the troops. King Arthur says, 'No, I want you to go tell our story.'"

It certainly seemed like Camelot at the time, and it seems like Camelot in retrospect. There is a bit of Oz in it too. If you went behind the scenes, you'd see somebody puffing and struggling and working the gears and levers. Kennedy was quoted as saying that, "Happiness consists in the fullest use of one's powers in the pursuit of excellence which is from a Greek anthology. There were more people who believed in the Kennedy administration than I have seen in any administration since. Pervading the administration was the sense that you could. There was a quality of youthful hope about this administration."[14]

William Sloane Coffin, Jr., tells us that, "The Camelot image was just that, there wasn't much substance behind it. It was glamorous. We love celebrities in this country. We don't have a king and suddenly here's a very young, bright, funny guy who could laugh at himself. His wife is gorgeous and there was a great family behind him."[15] As William Smith remembers, "There was a glamour about the White House at the time. The President looked good, his wife was attractive and they had a lot of money. They lived well and attracted interesting people around them. If you put it all together, there was a difference from any other Presidential style in this century."[16]

"Camelot is ridiculous, just a pop-culture myth." Norman Podhoretz tells us, "There was glamour surrounding the Kennedys, the glamour of cafe society combined with great political power. Many people were bought off. They were simply intoxicated. It was the merging of two very seductive worlds."[17] Lloyd Cutler says, "It's a romanticization of the fact that clean-cut young people-when I say clean cut I don't mean especially moral, but nice looking, vigorous people-were running the government."[18]

During the aftermath of the President's death, a wave of memorializing that verged on canonization would begin. As for Camelot's place in history, according to journalist, L. Fletcher Prouty, "The President did not love to listen to *Camelot*. This was not accurate. During the 1962-63 period, the U.S. Army had a contract study called Camelot under way in a think tank group associated with American University in Washington. Neither the President nor his Secretary of Defense, Robert S. McNamara, were popular with Army officials. Those who were members of the think tank used the word Camelot to characterize the administration in a derogatory sense."[19]

Now there was no turning back for Jackie, so she had better promote this Camelot myth quickly and stick with it while the iron of sympathy was still hot. Jackie was a survivor from her earliest days. She would survive again and this time on her own terms. At last she was free from a miserable excuse of a marriage, free of everyone laughing behind her back and free from the White House and the Kennedys. She was free to eventually marry the man who made her freedom possible, a man who adored and worshipped her.

But first Jacqueline must create a legend to frame her grief, this legend would showcase the life she had shared with President Kennedy. It would be a very selective presentation of history. This was a history lesson that Jackie sold, and the American public bought every word of it. Camelot was eagerly lapped up by everyone, here and abroad.

Jackie did not want JFK to be forgotten. Nor did she want his few accomplishments cast in an unfavorable light. She wanted him to shine. Now that he was out of the way, Jackie could make him into anything she chose. She would create the world's memory of Jack. She would walk with him in death as she had not done in life. Her gift to her children would be the image of their father as a great President and a great man. She knew his flaws and weaknesses but she would cover them up. Her Jack would be a youthful man who had sailed through life unsullied by the tawdry compromises and truths of adulthood.

In Jackie's version of their life , JFK took on the kingly mantle of King Arthur. She endowed him with a nobility that would never resemble the real life and affairs of the JFK everyone in Washington knew and remembered. In Jackie's revised version, she took on the role of King Arthur's Guinevere, a young Queen of incredible beauty and grace. From childhood on, Jackie had loved being the Queen. Now she would rewrite history in order to keep her Queenly persona for all time. Who better to be her Lancelot than Aristotle Onassis? He filled the role of ardent admirer and now he would be her rescuer. Although for the time being, nothing was said to remind anyone of the possible existence of a Sir Lancelot. He could wait in the wings. It was more important to establish the Camelot legend as a part of the Kennedy era.

Jackie's despised Irish "Murphia" now became her adored knights of the Kennedy round table. She turned to them every chance she got. They were eager and willing to do anything to ease her pain. Prior to the assassination, Jackie couldn't stand Jack's political cronies. She hated always having them around their home. She disliked their intrusion into her private life. Now things were different. She needed them and she made a tremendous effort to bond with all of them on the plane ride back to Washington. Jackie reached out to each and everyone of them and, in doing so, she secured their loyalty. No matter what the future would hold, they would always be there for her. They would never publicly question her motives or ever criticize anything she would do in the future. Their closeness to her would keep them close to Jack forever.

When it comes to ex-husbands, dead ones are the best ones. Jackie wanted their marriage to be remembered in a romantic way. Now it would be easy to build his legend and include herself with a regal aura. It did not behoove Jackie's image to tarnish anything about the Kennedy years. It would only reduce her value to Aristotle Onassis. She needed to be in a strong position of power to negotiate their future life together.

Thus Jackie became the professional grieving widow. She set an example of courageousness for everyone to follow and admire. It was her finest hour. As the entire world focused on her performance, no one watched more closely than her Sir Lancelot, Aristotle Onassis. She had invited him to be with her and share in her sorrow, but now he must wait patiently for her official year of mourning to end. He couldn't help but anticipate the joy that their eventual union would bring. She was the person he had been waiting for all of his life. It was written in the stars.

As a public relations campaign, the Camelot connection to the Kennedy Presidency was an unqualified success. It worked far beyond Jackie's highest hopes. This legend became a part of American history. To this day the mere mention of Camelot brings the Kennedys to the minds and hearts of millions of Americans. JFK will always be our great and noble King, and Jackie will always be our gracious and beautiful Queen.

The personality of John Kennedy had struck some deep emotional chord and had fulfilled some widespread human need. In the last analysis, it seemed that what the American people have always wanted in a President was not so much wisdom and competence, but glamour, charisma and a sense of hope and optimism which Kennedy projected. When all was said and done, they named all those landmarks after JFK not because of what he had done to deserve them, but because of what he had represented in the public imagination.[20]

Even if they had taken JFK's life, in return Jackie and Ari gave John Kennedy immortality. He will always be a legend and a national hero. Nothing in his short Presidency up to the time of his death would have been remembered other than just an ordinary presidency. In death, Jackie's last gift and farewell was the Camelot legend which made his Presidency quite extraordinary. Nothing he ever did could have equaled what Jackie made him in death. It was a farewell gift she not only gave to him and their children, but it also allowed her to easily escape from the scene of the crime.

Camelot became her alibi.

The Kennedys were the perfect couple. This charade was easy in the early years after the murder. The American public did not have a clue as to the type of man their President was. Thirty-five years later, the tabloids of the world have exposed all the sordid details of Jack and Jackie's life together. It is not a pretty picture. But a true one, since their lives have been in the public domain for so long. Everything is documented and most of their secrets have been exposed.

Along with the glorification of John F. Kennedy, there was also his continued idealization and sentimentalization. If the press had gushed over JFK before his death, now they became downright maudlin. The canonization had begun.[21]

Unfortunately, what proceeded was a monstrous distortion of truth, a myth created that could not possibly serve the interests of anyone but the Kennedy family. Jacqueline Kennedy's efforts to glorify her late husband inadvertently did much to cloud what might have been behind John F. Kennedy's assassination. The key elements in the myth-making process were the suppression of the truth about JFK's past, the discouragement of any serious inquiry into the circumstances of his assassination, the lifelong inclination of Jacqueline Kennedy to construct and try to dwell in fairy tales, and the concerted attempts by the Kennedys and their court historians to alter the truth.[22]

Everyone is quick to place the blame on the Kennedy family. It fitted into the master plan perfectly. The Kennedys relegated Jackie to her fairy-tale existence. This was fine. She did not want to be involved any further. It was time to distance herself from the actual crime.

Good-bye, Jack!

After all that this poor woman had been through, there wasn't a person in the world who could begrudge her anything. Everyone wanted Jackie to recover, to just get on with her life.

This Queen would not go quietly in the night off to a nunnery to disappear forever like poor Queen Guinevere. Jackie's reign was just beginning. Long live, Queen Jacqueline. . .

fille naturelle de Charlemagne!

THIRTEEN

WHAT WERE THE WARREN COMMISSION'S FINDINGS?

THE COVER-UP OF THE CENTURY

*F*ROM THE MOMENT PRESIDENT LYNDON JOHNSON appointed the prestigious Warren Commission to investigate the assassination of President John F. Kennedy, the American public anxiously awaited its conclusion. The hope was that this thorough investigation would answer all the many questions Americans had about the death of their President. Unfortunately we are still waiting.

It has been thirty-five years now and the waters are still as muddied as ever. Right from the beginning, it seemed apparent to almost everyone except the Kennedys that the assassination of JFK was not a one-man operation. How could anyone believe that Oswald, shooting from behind JFK, could hit him in the throat? The U.S. Attorney General, Robert Kennedy, was privy to all sorts of information which must have raised questions in his mind. Yet he seemed perfectly satisfied with the uncomplicated conclusions reached by the Warren Commission.

The Kennedys were non-committal about this murder because they had so much in their past to hide. The complete recklessness with which the Kennedys led their lives was astounding. This family took big risks and that meant suffering big losses. The President's files would reveal that Jack and Bobby Kennedy were more than merely informed about the CIA's assassination plotting against Fidel Castro of Cuba. They were its strongest advocates. White House files also dealt with three foreign leaders who were murdered during Kennedy's thousand days in the Presidency-Patrice Lumumba, of the Congo: Rafael Trujillo, of the Dominican Republic and Ngo Dinh Diem, of South Vietnam.[1]

JFK foolishly would sleep with anyone regardless of the circumstances. He had real charisma and great potential, but he was young and thought he was above harm. His personal recklessness is why the Kennedys never pushed the assassination investigation. The family didn't want to uncover the connection between the CIA, the Mafia and the President.

This all fit in perfectly with Ari's and Jackie's plans. Jackie's cousin, John Davis, even spoke to her about the assassination. In 1974, when he discussed it with her, she very quickly changed the subject. "That's characteristically how she dealt with anything unpleasant; she dismissed it by switching channels. By the time we discussed the assassination, she had gotten over it. She didn't want to be reminded of that period. She wasn't interested in the historical truth."[2]

Apparently no one else was interested in the truth either. The Warren Commission headed by Chief Justice Earl Warren would meet for nine months, conduct 25,000 FBI interviews, fill 26 volumes with evidence and conclude that Oswald acted alone. Sixteen years later, in 1979, the House Select Committee on Assassinations would again review what conspiracy theorists insist was altered evidence and conclude that there was evidence of conspiracy. This evidence was never developed.

Many very persuasive books were written and published and a motion picture was made in an effort to reopen the investigation. There still is no answer as to why important evidence continued to disappear from the National Archives, and why 21 witnesses scheduled to give testimony to the Warren Commission mysteriously died. Also there is Chief Justice Warren's assertion that all the facts would never be known in our lifetime, which left the door open to still more speculation and investigation, and both continue to this very moment.[3]

On July 3,1997, the nation's newspapers headlined that Gerald Ford's editing of a key sentence in the Warren Commission's report supported the final conclusion which was the single bullet theory. This ever so slightly altered sentence was to strengthen the Commission's finding that Lee Harvey Oswald was the sole gunman. "It was a small change," said Ford when it came to light. "One intended to clarify meaning, not alter history. My changes had nothing to do with a conspiracy theory." He said in a telephone interview, "My changes were only an attempt to be more precise."

Yet, his editing was seized upon by members of the conspiracy community which rejects the Commission's conclusion that Oswald acted alone. "This is the most significant lie in the whole Warren Commission report," said Robert D. Morningstar, who had studied the assassination since it occurred and has written an internet book about it. "The effect of President Ford's editing," said Morningstar, was to suggest that a bullet struck Kennedy in the neck, raising the wound two or three inches. Without the alteration, they could never have hoodwinked the public as to the true number of assassins. If the bullet had hit Kennedy in the back, it could not have struck Connally in the way the Commission said it did," wrote Morningstar. Conspiracy theorists reject the idea that a single bullet could have hit both Kennedy and Connally and done such damage. They argue that a second gunman must have been involved.

The only certainty that gripped the people in Dealey Plaza at 12:30 that ugly afternoon was the belief that President Kennedy, and perhaps others in his party were hit by gunfire in an ambush. Among the 266 known witnesses to the attack, there will forever be disagreement over the number of shots and their source. Of the witnesses officially interviewed, 32 placed the origins of the shots at the Texas school book depository, located on the northwest corner of Elm and Houston, above and behind President Kennedy's position. Fifty-one witnesses, including two secret service agents and a number of police officers, expressed the belief that the shots came from the area of a grassy knoll above and in front of President Kennedy. Many believe the shots came from both directions. Initially the disagreement was as strong among officials and police as it was among the spectators at large. Photographs show policemen and civilians running toward various spots. Depending upon where each thought the shots came from. Some scrambled up the grassy knoll, including Abraham Zapruder, whose home movies of the event became the assassination's most important record, related hair-raising accounts of hearing gunfire behind them. Some of these people who were directly in front of and below the grassy knoll, flattened themselves on the ground and covered their children in attempts to escape being hit.[4]

A major stumbling block for the investigation was the fact that many of the people called upon to testify had little knowledge of what was really going on within the United States government at that time. Dean Rusk who was then JFK's Secretary of State tells us, "I do have one reservation about my testimony before the Warren Commission. I was asked about whether we'd had any evidence of involvement of a foreign government, and I proceeded with a statement that we had not found any evidence of such. I then added a paragraph that I did not think that any foreign government had any motivation to be a participant in such a thing. Well, at the time, I did not know that the CIA was involved in various assassination attempts against Castro. Allen Dulles was sitting in on the Warren Commission and he did not take me aside and say, 'Wait a minute, there's something you ought to know about before you add that paragraph.' I have always been resentful that I was not informed about these CIA efforts to assassinate Castro in time to make a more straightforward presentation to the Warren Commission."[5]

It would appear that what happened at that time is what is still going on. No one, then or now, really wants to find out who killed Kennedy. It seems that most government officials at the beginning were also in a state of shock. They didn't know who to suspect which is why so many of them were eager to believe that Oswald did it. Making Oswald the lone, lunatic assassin would be easier on the country then telling the truth.

There are some who, even to this day, still believe the Warren

Commission's finding, yet their ranks are thinning out. There is Bobby Baker, former aide to Lyndon Johnson, who states, "I knew the people who served on the Warren Commission. If you were able to hoodwink that group of people, we're in terrible trouble. John and Nellie Connally were there. I have to take their view as to what happened." Also in agreement is Richard Bissell who said that, "I thought it was a very astute and proper thing to appoint a distinguished Commission like that. Allen Dulles was one of its members. I really never had any reason to doubt or question the Commission's conclusions. I am not one of those who thought the Commission did a poor job. As to a second assassin, I suppose you'd have to say that if there was one, it was indeed a failure of our intelligence, that the individual not only was never caught but that his existence has never even been officially admitted. There seems to be some hard evidence of the second man and the second gun.[6]

The truth was not going to be good for anybody. The insiders within the White House all knew that John F. Kennedy had many enemies who would be capable of killing him. Jacqueline Kennedy knew this was true, and she surely would have shared it with Aristotle Onassis when they conceivably made their plans in October of 1963. It is interesting to speculate on the reason that Jacqueline, despite her desire to glorify her husband's memory, did not take any apparent interest in the official investigation of her husband's murder. Possibly it could be because Robert Kennedy had not encouraged her for the same reason he had adopted the policy of withholding vital information from the Warren Commission. He did not want certain things to ever come to light. Jackie, in fact, in the immediate post-assassination period often appeared to her Bouvier relatives to be strangely withdrawn and inhibited in regard to the assassination.

This was a contrast to Martin Luther King, Jr.'s widow's attitude toward her husband's assassination four years later. She helped in the investigation in every way possible, exploring all conspiracies. In 1976 Mrs. King was instrumental in persuading congress to reopen the investigation of both her husband's and JFK's murders.[7]

Jackie's behavior was not typical and it certainly was not normal. Most women would demand an answer to who killed their husband. Instead Jackie became vague and preoccupied whenever this unpleasant topic was brought up. Obviously, Jackie presumed that someone was eventually going to kill her husband. It was just a matter of who and when. No one could go around planning assassinations on other world leaders, and not expect to be a target himself. At least now, with the assassination over, Jackie did not have to worry any more whenever she or her children went out in public with the President. They would no longer be sitting ducks just waiting for the President to be killed, and they along with him. At least she had the comfort of knowing that the ones that did it, knew that she was not to be a target under any circumstances. Unfortunately, Governor Connally had been injured but those things happen, and he had not been permanently harmed.

In retrospect, Jackie's attitude and lack of vengeance seems quite reasonable. If one already knew who was responsible and wished to protect his identity, what difference did it make who did it? It was quite an incredible reaction by a widow or for that matter any thinking person. It must have been comforting to Aristotle Onassis, with his own intelligence network, to know that even before the assassination there would never be an intensive investigation. There would never be a need for the truth to be pursued by any Kennedy, then or now.

As it turned out, Jack and Bobby were a couple of real boneheads in the Oval Office. They believed they could go around ordering hits on Castro and others and get away with it. The astonishing aspect of this lunacy is that they did it all on their own. They never bothered to brief people like the Secretary of State, Dean Rusk, or even the Vice-President, Lyndon Johnson. It was as if two little boys all on their own decided to play "gotcha last" with no regard at all for the country's integrity or honor.

It's no secret that JFK came from a long line of colossally stupid politicians. Admittedly, JFK was an attractive fellow but he was not a heavyweight when it came to intelligence or common sense. This lack of aptitude comes to him honestly from a long lineage of men born with the "stupid gene". First of all, there was his beloved grandfather, HoneyFitz, whose exit from the Boston political scene was rampant with rumors of indiscreet affairs all over the city. Then old man Joe Kennedy, who truly fancied the presidency for himself, blew himself out of the water when he went to the Court of St. James. It wasn't bad enough that he stupidly advocated isolationism when it was so blatantly self-serving, in order to save his own sons. Then he foolishly tore Eleanor Roosevelt apart. He claimed it was all off the record and a big misunderstanding, but it was the end of his dreams for himself. Then there was poor Joe, Jr., who volunteered for an impossible combat mission only to blow up trying to upstage his younger brother Jack's heroism in the Pacific. It probably wasn't the smartest mission to volunteer for at the time. True, he was a hero. But being dead didn't help his Presidential plans.

After Jack's death, the family's poor political instincts continued with Bobby's self-destructive quest for the Presidency in 1968. It was almost as if he were on a suicide mission just to atone for what had happened to Jack, and the part he had played in his brother's death. The self-destructiveness continued with Teddy's involvement in the death of Mary Jo Kopechne. This was followed by Teddy's futile attempts to run for the Presidency through the years. Even the younger generations seem not to be immune with all of their public disasters including rape trials, molestations, divorces, drug abuse, etc., etc. The modern day male Kennedys are what the tabloids live for and the Kennedys do not disappoint their public.

"Even Lyndon Johnson was astonished at how brazenly the Kennedys had carried on within the Oval Office. Right after the assassination, Johnson asked the CIA and FBI for information on the plots to kill Castro, which he had apparently known nothing about. The following day, aghast at what he had learned, Lyndon Johnson met with CIA director, Richard Helms, who briefed him on the CIA-MAFIA plots and sketchily on the AM/LASH operation, a sabotage and assassination plot against Castro. Johnson then ordered Helms to have the CIA's Inspector General prepare a full report on all the CIA plots to murder Castro. On May 23, 1964 Helms personally brought the report to Johnson and briefed him orally on the contents. It was after this meeting that a deeply shocked Johnson became firmly convinced that President Kennedy had been murdered in retaliation for his plots to kill others."[8]

Now the real cover-up would begin. It would not cover-up who killed Kennedy, still important, but not as important. The real cover-up would be why Kennedy was killed! President Lyndon Johnson felt that it would irrevocably damage this country's reputation and honor, if it were to be known that our President and his Attorney General brother were murderers trying to solve world problems with assassinations rather than diplomacy. It was a sad and tragic commentary on our country, and one that must be kept secret. It was a time of shame and so the charade began and continues to this day.

At the time, no one quite understood why Robert Kennedy showed a strange passivity in the investigation. None of his close associates in the Attorney General's office ever heard him discuss the case. No one ever saw him bang his fist in anguish or anger, vowing revenge. He even limited the Warren Commission's access to autopsy photographs, keeping them and his brother's brains in his personal custody.

His deputy, Nicholas Katzenbach, said that Robert Kennedy, "Never really wanted any investigation." Ted Sorensen recalled that, "I had one conspiracy theorist who claimed to have all sorts of evidence, and when I spoke to Bobby, he said, 'I don't want to hear it. I can't be involved in that.'" Bobby's reluctance to dig too deeply into the assassination was believed to be because he was fearful of all the sexual dirt that would be uncovered and all the convoluted relations with the Mafia that would be so difficult for the public to understand. It would not only hurt his brother's image but would destroy any political future for himself and Ted.

At the very beginning, Robert Kennedy privately suspected that the CIA was implicated. Within hours after the assassination in what must have been an incredibly dramatic confrontation, Robert Kennedy asked John

McCone, former director of the CIA, did you kill my brother?" Kennedy later related the incident to Walter Sheridan, a close friend, as follows, "You know at the time I asked McCone, if they had killed my brother and I asked him in a way that he couldn't lie to me, and they hadn't."[9] Bobby was satisfied and there would be no need for him to ask any further questions. In his heart, he already knew the painful answer.

Arthur Schlesinger, the historian, recorded a long session with Robert Kennedy. "As we talked until two-thirty in the morning in New York City, RFK wondered how long he could continue to avoid comment on the report. It is evident that he believes it was a poor job and will not endorse it. However, he is unwilling to criticize it and reopen the whole tragic business."[10]

It would be far better for all the Kennedys to get on with the business of politics and put all of this behind them. It would be comforting to the real killers to be aware of this family's particularly strange mind set. It is often said, "Where there is no question asked there will never be any answer given."

Apparently Teddy was not in the loop as to what had been going on at the White House. After reading all the various reports, Senator Ted Kennedy had his own team of investigators check the various stories. He was not privy to all the damaging connections that Bobby knew of and he felt the need to know more. Ted then appeared behind a closed session of the Senate Select Committee on Intelligence Activities, where the Senator said, "He had seen no evidence to cast doubt on the Warren Commission's findings." There is no written record of Bob and Ted discussing this. In a bitter comment, historian, H. A. Fairlie noted that the Lincoln assassination industry had remained viable for more than fifty years. He recommended the Kennedy assassination industry as "one of the most promising fields for the young to enter."[11]

If you were picking the ideal and easiest public figure in the world to assassinate, John F. Kennedy would be your perfect choice. Former CIA official, Ray Cline tells us now that, "The Oliver Stone movie is crazy. The idea that the CIA and FBI and the military could all cooperate together is nutty, no bureaucracies ever cooperate together. If the CIA had been trying to assassinate Kennedy, I would have known it."[12] So now let us speculate as to who might have been hired to kill Kennedy.

In 1992 a book by Bill Sloan and Jean Hill called *JFK, The Last Dissenting Witness* was published and it gives us some interesting insights to what actually happened so long ago. As Jean Hill tells us, "I'm just an ordinary person who fate happened to place in a certain spot at a certain time. I'm not a political person or a theorist. The only thing I'm 100% sure of is what I saw and heard on November 22, 1963, in Dealey Plaza at 12:30 p.m. I know what I saw but I will have to leave the explanations for who the killers were and why it happened to somebody else."

Jean's basic beliefs about the physical act of murdering President Kennedy can be summed up in five points. Each of which stand in total contradiction to official government conclusions.

1. At least four-probably six shots were fired.
2. At least two-and possibly three-gunmen were involved.
3. At least one gunman was positioned behind the fence atop the grassy knoll and fired at least one shot from that location.
4. The fatal head shot which exploded the President's skull came from the right front (the direction of the knoll), not from the direction of the school depository.
5. Some of the shots, including the one that hit Kennedy in the throat, did come from the direction of the depository.[13]

In early 1977, Mary Farrell, the renowned Dallas archivist of assassination material, was making her way through a new carton of documents forced from the CIA by a suit brought under the Freedom of Information Act. Thousands of pages faced her, many of them so illegible that a casual observer would consider them hopeless to decipher. One of the hundreds of pages she studied that afternoon was CIA document 632-796. It appeared to be a simple request from the French government to the U.S. Government inquiring about the whereabouts of an individual. The document dated April 1, 1964, reported that the French intelligence service wanted help in locating one Jean Souetre, a French OAS (Organization Algerian Separatists) terrorist considered a threat to the safety of President Charles de Gaulle. In fact, Souetre had been convicted in one instance for participation in an assassination attempt. The French had approached the FBI's legal attache in Paris to ascertain from U.S. authorities the last known whereabouts of Souetre in order to assure the safety of de Gaulle. Subsequent released documents would show that Souetre had been a suspect in an earlier assassination attempt on President de Gaulle.

Why should the French believe that U.S. Intelligence would know the whereabouts of Souetre? The answer to that question is absolutely astounding. The document asserts that Jean Souetre was in Fort Worth, Texas on the morning of November 22, 1963. That morning President Kennedy also was in Fort Worth, where he made his first speech of the day in a parking lot outside his hotel. A few hours later, John F. Kennedy was in Dallas, where at 12:30 p.m. Jean Souetre was also in Dallas that afternoon.

Within 48 hours of Kennedy's death, according to the query from the French, Jean Souetre was picked up by U.S. authorities in Texas. He was immediately expelled from the United States. French intelligence wanted to ascertain whether he was expelled to Canada or Mexico. The French also wanted to know why the U.S. authorities had expelled Souetre. The simple purpose was to ensure the safety of President de Gaulle on his pending trip to Mexico. One would expect that the U.S. officials who reportedly picked up Souetre in Dallas following the assassination might have an interest in a man of his reputation. A court document later described Souetre "as a trained and experienced terrorist and perfectly capable of murder."

Evidently there was considerable interest by certain officials, but it was carefully concealed from the Warren Commission and ,of course, the public. There is no reason to believe the matter ever would have come to light were it not for the routine query from French intelligence. It seems highly unlikely that the CIA officer charged with deciding the release of secret papers in 1976 had even an inkling of the revelations contained in this particular document. The contents possibly would never have been known if the document had not fallen under the sharp eyes of Mary Farrell, archivist of the Warren Commission.

The precise manner of U.S. Response to the presence of a French assassin in Dallas on November 22, 1963, is officially unknown. The CIA document asserts that the FBI told the CIA that it had nothing in its files on the subject. The accuracy of that assertion seems questionable.[14] Nothing official is known about why U.S. authorities were prompted to pick up Jean Souetre following the assassination except that he was a known French terrorist.

Even more startling to contemplate is that someone, representing some authority in Washington, apparently authorized the pickup and deportation of a known French terrorist on the day of the assassination. That authorization could have come from the CIA, the FBI, the State Department, or the Immigration and Naturalization Service. The documentation regarding this deportation has never surfaced. All these years later, with few slender exceptions, it is likely that the information remains entombed in the vaults of U.S. intelligence.[15] Basically, take your pick, any one of the above agencies could have been the prime exit vehicle for assassins in a hurry to leave Dallas, Texas, and the United States.

It doesn't matter whether one, two, or three Frenchmen were in Dallas on November 22. More important is the fact that the U.S. authorities knew at least one was there and yet they concealed the information from the Warren Commission. One of the few certainties supported by documents about the assassination is that both the CIA and the FBI were aware of the French presence long before the Warren Commission wrapped up it's work.[16]

A brief, filed in connection with a Freedom of Information Act suit, documents this matter as to why a French OAS terrorist would be a logical suspect in the assassination of President Kennedy. The Algerian Civil War ended in 1962, when President de Gaulle granted independence to Algeria. It was granted over the most violent terrorist opposition of the OAS, which consisted largely of military deserters who opposed de Gaulle giving away their country. They were trained for all kinds of mayhem and made more than 30 attempts on de Gaulle's life. These were 2,000-3,000 well-trained and available-for-hire killers. In 1963, they were the pool from which one would hire a competent assassin.

From his earliest days as a United States Senator, John F. Kennedy was publicly and passionately in favor of Algerian independence. Kennedy was vocal in his opposition to all OAS activities. Clearly the OAS possessed the classic ingredients necessary for murder. Next to de Gaulle, the OAS hated Kennedy the most.[17] If more than thirty attempts could be made against de Gaulle, the argument goes, why not one against Kennedy?

This act would be an assassin's dream come true. Not only would he be paid an incredible amount of money to eliminate someone, but that person would also happen to be his mortal enemy. It's no wonder that this deed was very easy to accomplish with eager volunteers on the available list.

The point is that Jean Souetre was in Fort Worth and Dallas at the same time President Kennedy was in those cities on the very same day as the assassination. Indications are that the United States picked up a man believed to be Souetre in Dallas that day and kicked him out of the country. No government agency had admitted to having dealt with Souetre on the given day.[18]

This theory isn't saying the hit-men were French terrorists but rather this is one possibility among many. There is not much belief in the Warren Commission's findings nor is there much hope of ever getting to the real truth of the murder since LBJ ordered the government's files on the assassination to remain classified until 2039. There will be no one alive at the time that the files are opened who will be able to contradict them. It is your basic well done cover-up.

The investigation must have been very difficult for Lyndon Johnson to carry out. As much as he may have wished to deflate the Kennedy legacy and keep the growing legend in check, there was no way to do so without publicly revealing everything he had so carefully hidden for the sake of the country and his inherited Presidency.

Johnson knew how he could puncture this process of enhancing "the image of the Kennedy family and the Kennedy name." It would be easy to leak what he knew of operation Mongoose, the CIA-MAFIA plots against Castro, and the Kennedy-Campbell-Giancana affair. But he was afraid of being too overt in his hostility and therefore he limited himself to occasionally leaking little bits and pieces of what he knew, thus alluding perhaps to the Trujillo assassination and the murders of Diem and his brother, or the attempts on Castro. He confided to Pierre Salinger that what had happened to John F. Kennedy, "May have been divine retribution." By and large Johnson held his tongue, and the American public in the mid-sixties never learned the darkest secrets of the Kennedy administration.[19]

The entire post-assassination series of events has been a calculated, contrived, emotional build-up, not for the sake of paying honest respect and homage to John F, Kennedy, but to enhance the image of the Kennedy family and the Kennedy name. All of which would never have taken place without the efforts of Jacqueline Bouvier Kennedy. Despite the Warren Commission and various investigations, the American people were ready, willing and eager to accept the Camelot version of the Kennedy years. This lie would find fertile soil in which to grow and thrive throughout the coming years.

In 1963, it was easy to just accept the government's version of events. Even though some things just didn't make sense, it was almost un-American to question the authorities. If the Warren Commission's flawed explanations were good enough for the Kennedy family, then certainly the rest of the country should go along with the one assassin conclusion. It also helped that Lee Harvey Oswald was conveniently murdered, which made it easy to quickly close the investigation. It was all best forgotten and our country eagerly embraced the soothing mystique of Camelot.

How perfect,

how predictable,

how easy,

to get away with murder!

FOURTEEN

WHAT WAS JACKIE'S WIDOWHOOD LIKE?

THE BLACK WIDOW

ON JANUARY 14, 1964, JACQUELINE KENNEDY
appeared on television to thank America for the eight hundred thousand
condolence letters she received. Dressed in black with a simple hairdo,
flanked by Teddy and Bobby Kennedy, she emphasized her husband's two
greatest assets, his popularity and his charisma. "The knowledge of the
affection in which my husband was held by all of you has sustained me,
and the warmth of these tributes is something that I shall never forget," she
said. "All his bright light is gone from the world."[1]

Now the big job would begin. Jack Kennedy must be protected
from the historians. The truth about his life and his administration must be
kept from the American public. By making him a saint and their marriage
sacred, Jackie would be creating the biggest and best alibi in the history of
the world. This would be a very difficult undertaking. Jackie would need
much help in accomplishing the canonization of her cheating husband.

There would be many from the Kennedy camp who would willingly jump on board to give credence to and help sustain the Kennedy
legend. In 1965 Arthur M. Schlesinger, the historian, finished his ode to
the fallen leader, *A Thousand Days*. "Now no one will ever be able to hurt
Jack because your book is a testament against them and for all that he could

not finish." Jackie wrote.[2]

Jackie's widowhood had made her the primary keeper of the Kennedy flame and she would indeed be a vigilant guardian. After the funeral, a British journalist wrote for his paper, "Jacqueline Kennedy has today given her country the one thing it has always lacked and that is majesty." Jackie wrote to President Johnson the day after the funeral, "But more than that we were friends, all four of us. All you did for me as a friend and the happy times we had." Jackie stayed in the White House for eleven days after the assassination. She had a plaque mounted in their bedroom, that read, "In this room lived John Fitzgerald Kennedy with his wife Jacqueline during the two years, ten months, and two days he was President of the United States."[3] The only other commemorative plaque in the room was to Abraham Lincoln. Eventually Pat Nixon removed the Kennedy plaque.

In her closing days in the White House, Jackie gave gifts of JFK's small possessions to household staff and political aides and cleaned out the Oval Office. She successfully lobbied the new President to change the name of the space center from Cape Canaveral to Cape Kennedy.[4] It was almost as if she knew that this particular Presidency would not have much to put in the history books. She didn't want people to remember his tenure from the Bay of Pigs, so it was her mission to rename important sites after JFK. One way or another, Jackie was determined to give this Presidency a bigger sense of accomplishment than it ever deserved.

Throughout the spring of 1964, planning proposed official memorials for JFK became an outlet for Jackie's creative energy and executive ability. She even approved a Dallas plan to build a memorial plaza near the site of the assassination. It was, however, her vision for the John F. Kennedy Presidential Library that made her days as busy as they had been with the White House restoration.[5]

President Johnson asked congress to rename the national cultural center in Washington the John F. Kennedy Center for the Performing Arts. He sent a bill to congress for $17.5 million to help finance the enterprise. He and Ladybird even made a substantial personal contribution to the JFK

Memorial Library.[6]

After leaving the White House Jackie and her children moved to a house in Georgetown, loaned to her by a sympathetic couple. At this home Jackie got a taste of things to come and it was not a good omen. Everywhere she went in Washington she was besieged by mobs of tourists and curiosity-seekers. There was absolutely no privacy to be found for Jackie or her children. Within a short time, she decided to move to New York City to escape the oppressive atmosphere of Washington. The family moved to a suite at the Carlyle Hotel until they found the fifteen-room apartment at 1040 Fifth Avenue where Jackie would live until her death. Jackie grew to love New York because there she felt that she could get lost in the crowd. She hoped that she and her children would gradually be able to lead a somewhat normal life there.

Financially her first years of widowhood were not going to be easy for Jackie. Most people assumed that JFK's widow inherited millions. Actually she only received a lump sum payment of $25,000 and all her husband's personal effects. In terms of capital, she received less than $70,000. Although John Kennedy was one of the wealthiest men to ever occupy the White House, his taxable assets only totaled around $1.8 million. The two trust funds he established for his wife and children were estimated at $10 million. Jackie's share as a widow was limited to yearly payments from the principal of one trust. Basically Jack left her an income but not capital.[7] Her worst fears about her husband's generosity had come true. Fortunately Jackie had a great backup plan in place. All she would have to do would be to continue in her role as a grieving widow until her ship, rather I should say, tanker came in!

While she waited to be rescued, Jackie threw herself into obtaining funds for the John F. Kennedy Memorial Library. In order to raise funds, she organized a mammoth assault at home and abroad. She mounted a one-woman telephone campaign that rivaled her efforts on behalf of the White House renovation. Without her direct solicitation, the French government would never have given a $100,000 contribution. Jackie's old stand-by,

Gianni Agnelli, likewise donated $100,000, and the financier, Andre Meyer gave $250,000. Although he surely would have contributed, Jackie curiously refrained from asking Aristotle Onassis to make a contribution to the Kennedy Memorial Library. In hindsight, it does seem strange that Jackie would not ask Ari to make a donation. After all they were close friends and she had spent time on his yacht just one month prior to the assassination. Ari had flown right to Washington as soon as he heard the news of JFK's death, and he was discreetly there for Jackie in the White House during the funeral. Perhaps they both felt that they didn't want to call attention to their relationship so soon after the assassination. They would not want anyone to ever suspect their connection or their future plans. If they had nothing to hide, why would she refrain from asking Ari of all people?

During this period, Jackie began to have trouble controlling the Kennedy legend that she wished to present as an actual history for the American people. Her biggest problem would be with William F. Manchester and his book, *The Death of the President*. Originally Manchester had been Jackie's first choice to tell their story. She was very eager to get the word out and she was happy to do everything she could to cooperate. Everything went along swimmingly until the book was finished. Prior to this, Manchester had signed a contract with the Kennedys giving them full right of review and revision before publication. So the Kennedys were not worried. The author had also promised that all royalties from the book would go to the JFK Library. "Jackie felt these clauses were necessary because she wanted to avoid commercialism and sensationalism" said a Kennedy aide. "But when she found out that *Life* magazine was paying Manchester $665,000 for serialization rights, she began to raise hell. She said that, "Manchester was just cashing in on her husband's death and she would take him to court in order to stop him."[8] It was all right for Jackie to allocate the money from this book for the Kennedy Library. But she felt that if it didn't go into her project, Manchester had no right to any profit himself. Basically, she didn't approve of his making money from the serialization of his own book.

And so began the battle of the book. In the Manchester book, Jackie objected to the personal references to her vanity such as searching the mirror for wrinkles in her face and her sleeping arrangements with the President their last night in Dallas. She also wanted to delete the description of how she slipped her wedding ring on his finger. She wanted no mention of her chain-smoking or her drinking. Although she had given the author ten hours of taped recorded interviews, she now insisted that he not use any of the taped material in his book. She demanded that the tapes be locked up in the Kennedy Library for 50 years. She also insisted that the letters that she had written from the Onassis yacht not be quoted in the book. No one realized at the time just how serious Jackie was about her objections.[9]

The former First Lady who had now taken on the role of the woeful widow was into re-writing history to suit her own purposes. She was also practicing censorship. Jackie was very firm about what she wanted told and how it was to be told to the American public. Her official version of life with Jack was to be spoon-fed to her adoring public by her chosen authors. It came as quite a shock to Jackie when her chosen few did not adhere to her wishes. Still reeling from the tragedy in Dallas, the country revered JFK's widow, yet they had no idea of the imperiousness which lay behind that black veil.[10]

Nobody would feel the brunt of her anger like William Manchester in light of her unreasonable objections to the publication of his book, *The Death of The President.* Jackie had already been difficult with other Kennedy books. When Maude Shaw, the childrens' nannie, wrote *White House Nannie* Jackie had threatened to sue. When Red Fay, Jack's close friend, penned *The Pleasure of His Company* she insisted on many changes and deletions. Fay agreed to everything Jackie wanted deleted, but she was still mad at him for writing the book in the first place. Fay sent her a $3,000 check from the royalties for the Kennedy Library. Jackie returned it. He was one of Jack's closest friends, but she never spoke to him again.

Jackie cooperated with Ted Sorensen and Arthur Schlesinger, Jr., on their Kennedy books, but she insisted that she be referred to only as "Jacqueline or Mrs. Kennedy and never as Jackie," said an aide. "You'll notice in both books that her marriage to JFK is described in loving terms, and never do they hint at the painful truth behind the relationship. Nor, God help us, are any of Jack's other women ever mentioned in these books."[11]

The entire episode was so unreasonable on Jackie's part. The fact remains that William Manchester had personally been approached by Jackie to write his account of JFK's assassination. According to Manchester, "Jackie had called and said that Jim Bishop, whom she couldn't abide, was about to write the official book on the events of November 22. Would I be willing to write the official account of the assassination? How could I refuse Jacqueline Kennedy? After nearly three years of back breaking research and writing, she decided she did not want it to appear, or wanted it to appear in some unrecognizable form."[12]

Jackie's rationale, as expressed in her oral history for the Lyndon Baines Johnson Library, was that she had been locked in a shell of grief and it was hard to stop talking once the floodgates opened. What Jackie did not say in her oral history was that while doing her own interviews with Manchester, she had been drinking heavily and continually. It was the only way she could get through her reminiscences, and it helped account for the highly personal nature and tone in parts of the book.[13]

As things progressed, the entire situation became impossible, since Jackie was determined to allow only her version of this historical event to reach the public. When Gardiner Cowles, of *Look* magazine, went up to Hyannis Port to try to settle his publication's differences with Jackie and pave the way for serialization, he was figuratively mugged. "Mrs. Kennedy became very abusive," said William Atwood in an oral history he did for Columbia University. "She called Cowles a son-of-a-bitch and a bastard. She became verbally violent, to the point that Gardiner came back amazed that the great lady of the funeral and all that could talk like that." "Mrs. Kennedy by that time had become really out of control so far as the rest of the family was concerned. She'd become an embarrassment to Bob Kennedy, who still had his own political future in mind. This kind of sordid battle over the memoirs was not something RFK wanted to be involved in since all the other newspapers and magazines were on Manchester's side in the affair."[14]

Jackie told Manchester that she was prepared to fight and she was going to win. "Anybody who is against me will look like a rat, unless I run off with Eddie Fisher."[15]

As for William Manchester, the experience was one that he never would recover from and left him shaken. "Why she cooperated with the venture, read the manuscript, apparently liked it and then told the press I had written a tasteless and terrible book I will never know," said Manchester. "I spoke with that woman for many hours, shared some of her deepest, darkest thoughts, wrote the authorized account of President Kennedy's assassination, but I don't have the faintest idea what Jackie Kennedy Onassis is really like. That's a question I will take to my grave."[16]

Perhaps without knowing it, William Manchester had answered his own question once he referred to her as Jackie Onassis. It would not be proper or beneficial for the future Mrs. Aristotle Onassis to have shared any of her deepest, darkest secrets regarding JFK with anyone let alone a writer. Commissioning this book to be written was one of Jackie's biggest mistakes. Of itself, the book was a brilliant idea, but trying to control and censor a man like Manchester would prove to be impossible. He was not one of the loyal Irish Mafia who would give out only the official sanitized version of the Kennedy legend. Well, so much for writing history; Jackie had tried and failed. It wasn't really a problem because everyone still loved and worshipped her. She could do no wrong and the country was very sympathetic to her every wish and desire. After all that this woman had been through, she was not to be denied anything. The country lay prostrate at her feet. She was our sad lady and we longed to see her smile again. If only she could find happiness, then perhaps we would all regain our health. It was our hope and prayer for her future and our own.

Once the final period of mourning passed, Jackie shed her widow's weeds. For the rest of the year her every move was chronicled in the society pages. Every time she set foot out of her Fifth Avenue apartment her photograph appeared in newspapers around the world. To everyone it would appeared that Jackie's main mission was to heal herself and to gradually rejoin the land of the living. What no one realized, was that Jackie and Ari had quite different objectives in mind. For the moment, the most important goal on their agenda was to keep their involvement a total secret. In order to accomplish this, Jackie must go forth into the world and create all sorts of interesting possibilities for the world to focus on.

"Jackie Kennedy was the tease, the temptress of her age," said Paul Mathias. "She perfected the art, she invented it. She was Miss Narcissist, perpetually searching mirrors for worry wrinkles and strands of prematurely gray hair. She didn't worry about growing old, she worried about looking old. Within 18 months of JFK's assassination she had two dozen of the world's most brilliant and important men dangling like marionettes, dancing at her fingertips, most of them very married, very old, or very queer." Mathias's outspoken assessment contained barbs of truth.[17]

In the years immediately following the President's death, a number of renowned gentlemen pursued Jackie. There was Adlai Stevenson who in his own self-deprecating fashion demonstrated more than a passing interest. Jackie was also paid homage by the poet Robert Lowell. After the death of his wife, Lord Harlech, a family friend had been prominently mentioned as a possible future husband. During this period Jackie had relationships with some very married men such as Roswell Gilpatric, a Kennedy aide, and Andre Meyer, the financier. As much as the press loved these involvements and tried to magnify their significance into romance, the truth was that all these men were merely covers. Jackie was cleverly toying with these men in order to keep them interested in her. Jacqueline Kennedy was a coquette, someone who gives you hope, who lights the match.

Jackie's natural flirtatiousness was bound to create interest everywhere she went, and she was very much into making her presence known on the social scene. Helene Gaillet, a professional photographer, spoke of Jackie during this time. "Being an unattached and single woman once again, Jackie also represented a tremendous threat to all the married women in her social circle. With her personality, fame and beauty, she only had to enter into a room full of couples and all conversation came to a dead halt. She had the kind of electrifying aura that brought the room to a stop, and four men would immediately dash over to her. Or they were afraid to approach her because they were intimidated. She intimidated men. It took a certain type of man to become involved with someone as famous as Jackie."[18]

The basic game for Jackie after the first year of mourning was to keep busy and to keep an incredible schedule. Her pace was unbelievable. In January, she refused to fly to Washington to participate in the Johnson inaugural. In February, she flew to Mexico to get away. Then in March, she went to Florida with the children.

In April, Jackie refused an invitation from the Johnsons for the dedication of the White House Rose Garden in her honor. She sent her mother, Janet Auchincloss, to take her place at the ceremony. In May, Jackie took the children with her to London for Queen Elizabeth's dedication of Runnymeade in memory of her late husband. True to form Jackie always did prefer international events over domestic politics.

In October of 1964, Jackie threw her own party in honor of John Kenneth Galbraith, President Kennedy's former Ambassador to India. All the guests were in some way connected with the Kennedy administration, and they represented the fading facade of Camelot. Their common bond was their worship of the memory of JFK. Lyndon Johnson was ridiculed and they poked fun at his Secretary of State, Dean Rusk. They feasted on French pastries and pate, danced the frug and toasted the dowager, Queen Jackie.

There was one guest, however, who only stayed a few minutes. Again just as he had done at the funeral, Ari remained quietly in the background. He would stay discreetly near to her at all times. There would be no need to fear their exposure. Aristotle Onassis did not linger. He became very good at being patient. It was enough for him to admire her from afar while everyone else drank and danced till the wee hours of the morning.[19]

Ari was willing to wait until the proper moment. Jacqueline was being presented to the world as the glorious, glamorous widow of the slain President. He had no need to worry about Jackie's supposed romances. They were all carefully staged to deflect any interest as to the real romance in her life. Their secret was safe and it would remain safe.

Rumors continued to fly about Jackie and the men she was seeing, she frequently borrowed other women's husbands for escorts, and men like Franklin D. Roosevelt, Jr., Richard Goodwin, Robert Mc Namara, and John Galbraith were glad to take her to the theater or the ballet. The other men she was seeing-Mike Nichols, Chuck Spalding, Michael Forrestal, William Walton, Arthur Schlesinger, Jr., Truman Capote-were all connected in some way to the Kennedy administration. Some were single. Some were gay. All were safe.[20]

Jackie continued her relationship with Roswell Gilpatric and just as Onassis was stringing Maria Callas along to create a smoke screen for his affair with Jackie, so too, did Jackie with Roswell, her lover from the White House years. Jackie even invited him along with her on a trip to Mexico. Roswell related that, "The trip was very romantic, and Jackie surprised me by being so open about us." Something else surprised him. "Even at the most romantic moments," he said, "she kept mentioning Aristotle Onassis's name. What did I think of him? Was he as rich as they said he was? Was he, as some people said, a 'pirate'? She also said she felt he was very protective toward her, that he cared about the children and their welfare. She was weighing the pros and cons, and it became very clear very fast that Onassis was the man who most intrigued her."[21] This is the only recorded slip made by Jackie revealing her true feelings during this time of deception. Poor Roswell Gilpatric, who was planning on divorcing his wife in order to eventually marry the widow Kennedy, was so obviously being used by Jackie. At least Jackie was decent enough to send him a "Dear John" letter while on her honeymoon with Ari with sweet sentiments to sooth his devastated ego. This gentleman in turn got his revenge in

1970 when he conveniently leaked to the press this letter and four other highly personal and lucrative ones written by Jackie to him validating their affair.

But the only one who truly mattered was Aristotle Onassis. Of course for this reason, they did not go out in public during this time. The lovers did see much of each other as possible but only in controlled circumstances that could not jeopardize their relationship. Ari and Jackie had all the time in the world. They had come so far together from their cruise on the *Christina* back in October of 1963 when they had most likely made their initial plans and pledged their love. It had been quite a journey and they were now slowly approaching the time when they would expose themselves and their love to the world.

It would be a difficult time for them, and it would turn out to be much harder than they ever anticipated. No one could possibly prepare them for the hostility that their announcement of love would create in others.

Theirs was not to be a popular union. It would take the world by storm and would scandalize just about everyone. How could the beautiful princess marry the old toad? This relationship was incomprehensible to most of Jackie's admirers.

No one wanted to see this as the ending for Jackie and her children.

However, all of this would be in their future.

Now, secrecy was their main objective.

FIFTEEN

WHAT WAS THE COURTSHIP LIKE?

THE NOT SO SECRET LOVE

*A*LTHOUGH ARI AND JACKIE DID NOT PUBLICIZE their romance until the 1968 announcement of it by Janet Auchincloss, they had been seeing quite a bit of each other right from 1964 the year following the assassination of JFK. Most books and accounts of Jackie's life barely mention Onassis until the surprise announcement of their marriage took the world by storm. Their relationship prior to the marriage was very subdued and underplayed. They were very good at keeping a low profile when it came to each other. There was no reason to go public with their relationship until Jackie had observed a proper, respectful period of mourning.

However it did not keep the lovers from seeing as much of each other as they possibly could since they were very secretive. People might have noticed their attraction to each other but since they were so discreet, their relationship did not become public till 1968. However, Ari's onetime valet, Christian Cafarkais wrote an interesting but overlooked book about *The Fabulous Onassis* in 1972. It is a behind-the-scene story of the life and loves of Aristotle Onassis, told to us by a person who served him for ten years as a Man Friday. In his book, he told the details of Ari's clandestine courtship of Jacqueline. To most persons, the idea of a love affair or a great friendship between Jackie and Onassis seemed improbable. Despite his millions, he simply did not belong to the same social class as Jackie. Yet as Cafarakis tells us, and what many others had known since 1968 and as he had guessed in 1964, these two people were destined to one day become husband and wife.

The valet tells us, that even if John Kennedy had not been assassinated, he personally thought that Jackie would have divorced him and most likely married Onassis.[1]

What most people didn't realize was Ari and Jackie had been in love since the cruise in 1963 just one month before JFK's death. The first person who realized that Jackie was in love with Onassis, aside from Maria Callas, his long time mistress who was excluded from the famous cruise, was John Kennedy himself. Maria did not take it very seriously, since it seemed unlikely to her that Jackie would divorce the President.

JFK was not pleased with his wife's new friendship. In a letter that many people at the White House saw at the time, Jackie described Onassis with such uncharacteristic enthusiasm that John Kennedy asked his wife to come home as soon as possible. Jackie calmly continued her cruise all the way to Turkey, but took care not to mention Onassis in subsequent letters to her husband.[2]

When Jackie returned to the United States, she knew she had yet another serious admirer, this time, one who didn't leave her indifferent. Someone whom she hoped to see again as soon as possible.[3] As Carfarkis continues in his narrative, he retired from the service of Aristotle Onassis in 1968 when he came into an inheritance that he wasn't expecting. He suddenly found himself in possession of a fortune. He bought a house in Monte Carlo and with his healthy bank account enjoyed a life of relative luxury for the rest of his life. With time on his hands and many exciting memories, he decided to write a biography of his ex-boss.[4]

The one thing he felt lucky about was that he had never had to be in the service of Jacqueline Onassis. He then relates that Onassis married Jackie on October 20, 1968. What very few people know is that Jackie had been planning this marriage for over five years. She felt that only one man was worthy of becoming her second husband, Aristotle Onassis. Very few people are aware that between 1963 and 1968, the couple saw each other very frequently.

A week before Christmas in 1964, Onassis was in Paris. He summoned his servants George and Helene and told them that a very important person was scheduled to visit him on December 21th. Since the guest had to remain anonymous at all costs, it would be necessary for them to organize their work so that neither of them would see the visitor.

George and Helene were used to their employer's wild flights of fancy, but this time he seemed to be asking for the impossible. They racked their brains to think of some way to wait on his friend without ever seeing him or her. Was someone going to blindfold them and guide them in and out of the room? Eventually, they reported back to their boss to tell him they were stymied. After long thought, Onassis found a solution. He had a revolving table placed in the corridor between the kitchen and the dining room. Helene could put out the meals, course by course, and Onassis himself would serve them. Next Helene was to clean the bedroom reserved for the VIP and make the bed while the guest was in the bathroom. The bathroom could then be cleaned after the guest had returned to the bedroom. Both servants were then to remain in the kitchen for the rest of the day.

However, there was a third servant who couldn't help but see this mystery guest, Rozas, the chauffeur. On December 21, 1964 at exactly eleven o'clock in the morning, he picked up Onassis in the Rolls-Royce and drove him to Orly. At the airport, he was instructed to drive right onto the runway toward an Olympic Airways jet that had just landed. It was a regularly scheduled flight, but only one passenger was aboard...Jackie Kennedy. She was ushered into the car with Onassis, and Rozas headed straight back to Paris. The formality of clearing customs had been waived.

Jackie stayed in his apartment from December 21th to 23rd. Everything went according to plan and the service was discreet as possible. Of course, George and Helene knew perfectly well who was visiting their employer.

Whenever Onassis took Jackie out, they never went anywhere they might be recognized. For the most part, they spent their time in one of the living rooms in front of the fireplace.

Jackie returned three months later and the same procedures were followed. Only this time Onassis decided to invite a third person to one of their intimate lunches at the apartment, his son Alexander. The young man was quite surprised to find himself in the presence of the former First Lady of the United States. But he was accustomed by then to expect almost anything from his father and made an effort to be sociable. The lunch went off very well. Later, he asked George and Helene, "What the hell is my Father doing with Jackie Kennedy?"[5]

Considering that Jackie came from the United States especially to see Onassis on these two occasions, one naturally wonders exactly how far the relationship had progressed at that point only one year since JFK's murder. It was something of an enigma to those few who were aware of Jackie's secret visits. Did Onassis have some ulterior business motive in getting to know her because of her valuable contacts? Were they simply good friends? Or were they lovers?

Counting her trips to Paris and Onassis' visits to the states, they had seen each other at least thirty times since the death of John Kennedy.[6]

Obviously their discretion and reserved reunions kept anyone on Onassis' staff from seriously considering if they had a romantic commitment to each other. Since Maria Callas was still very much on the scene, she provided a perfect cover. No one would think Ari was anything other than a very good friend to Jackie. Ari was very careful not to tell Maria any details of his visits from Jackie. Poor Maria did not even have a clue that she was being used in such a devious way by Onassis. Right up to his actual marriage to Jackie, Ari would pretend that he wanted to marry Maria very much.

Maria and Ari had been lovers since 1959 when they had slipped away together on the *Christina* for a romantic interlude. On their return, they found that their respective spouses had filed for divorces against them. Did Onassis love Callas? Some acute observers were inclined to think not, and these may have included Callas herself. "I only wish it were a romance," she later told the press when denying it. It may be significant that not once in the next nine years during which Onassis and Callas were regular companions did either publicly proclaim that they were in love or intended marriage. Maria's husband, Giovanni Meneghini, had said that Onassis would marry Callas, but in the understandable heat of the moment he had failed to appreciate the Greek distinction between a wife, a legendary business property and a kindred spirit. Onassis felt a deep affinity with Callas, but there is no evidence that he ever considered her a potential wife. Onassis always maintained that they were "just good friends," and it is possible that for once this hackneyed phrase conveyed the essence of a relationship.[7]

One can only feel sorry for Maria Callas. There is no doubt that Aristotle Onassis was the love of her life. She gave up everything to be with him and she was always there for him all the days of his life.

It was cruel the way he kept Maria as a cover right up until he married Jackie. The next time he "officially" saw Jackie again was five years after their romantic cruise in 1963 on another cruise that took place in the Bahamas. Again Lee and Maria were aboard, as well as their two servants, and Onassis' sister and brother-in-law, Mr. and Mrs. Garoufalides. This time the situation was a little more obvious. Just as he had five years earlier, Onassis flirted openly with one of his guests, not Maria, but Jackie. His attraction to her was so blatant that Maria, outraged, took a plane from the Bahamas to New York then left the same day for Paris.

After Maria was gone, everyone joked about Onassis' true feelings and even organized a "truth" game in order to find out his real sentiments about Jackie. They were anxious to know if he might eventually be tempted to marry the young widow. When Jackie was asked by Lee and Mrs. Garoufalides about why she didn't marry Onassis, Jackie replied simply, "He hasn't asked me."[8]

The timing wasn't quite right for Jackie and Ari to go public with their love. After so much concealment, it was hard to know when the right time would be to expose themselves as lovers to the world. How could they be sure they would be accepted? How could they be sure that no one would suspect the origins of their romance and the bond that committed them to each other for life? It was risky business. For these shrewd people, it was a most difficult time.

So difficult that after Maria left the ship in the Bahamas at the beginning of February 1968, Ari spent two further days with Jackie. Then he left to be with Maria again. He deserted his guests on the ship and followed Maria to Paris. Once there they made a very serious decision and decided to marry. Maria had insisted that he marry her. Among other things, she told him it would soon be too late for her to have children, a long cherished dream she didn't intend to sacrifice. Onassis replied without hesitation, "All right, let's get married." Maria had won.[9] Maria was still bitter over the abortion Ari had forced her to have years before. Her wish, to bear his child, was still her life's desire. The wedding was scheduled to take place in London. Just as it was about to take place, the bride and bridegroom had a violent argument that caused them to break up forever. Onassis immediately left and took a plane to Athens. Maria sadly returned to Paris.[10] Now who do you think might have started the argument?

Ari left quickly and in Greece he promptly went to see his family and consulted with them about the possibility of marrying Jackie Kennedy. His family advised him to go ahead. He left for New York, met with Jackie and asked for her hand in marriage. The wedding was to take place four months later, in July. But the tragedy in Los Angeles that cost Bobby Kennedy his life caused it to be postponed until October.[11]

It is hard to believe that Ari would ask his family's permission to marry Jackie. It would be more likely that he told them his plans and if they did not approve, it wouldn't matter to him. He was not to be denied the person he had risked everything for, and he had already waited much too long to possess her. His treatment of Maria Callas was brutally cruel. This was not a particularly nice man to deal with and this was what attracted Jackie to him. He would literally slay dragons for her.

During the secret courtship, other people were aware of the attention Ari paid to Jackie. But few others besides his valet actually realized the depth and extent of his devotion to the young widow. After his invitation to the funeral and his stay in the White House, in the months and years that followed, he became her sympathetic and attentive friend. The press was not informed and did not detect him on his visits to her cooperative apartment at 1040 Fifth Avenue in New York, discreetly bringing presents for the children and Jackie, too. The presents were lavish ones, such as the roses he presented one day with their stems clasped in a diamond bracelet. Onassis knew Jackie well enough to keep her happy until their marriage could take place.

Lee was quietly told not to talk about them in public or to embarrass her sister in any way. Once the mourning period was over, Onassis was not among her public escorts who were frequently mentioned as possible candidates for her hand. Onassis was indeed biding his time and waiting for his moment. He did it well. Not even his closest friends suspected that something might be afoot. When the opportunity arose and he might be successful, he would have achieved the social coup of a lifetime. His trophy wife would do his children no end of good, bringing class and sophistication into a family that, even he had to admit, was sorely lacking in both.[12]

Of course, all of these actions could have been a part of a well planned cover up from day one of their secret pact. Things had played out just as they had hoped. It had taken much patience but they had the time and could not afford to do anything rash or impetuous which would jeopardize their future together.

The first time Jackie and Onassis were publicly seen together was at the 1967 dedication of the aircraft carrier John F. Kennedy in Newport News, Virginia. After the ceremony, as friends gathered around her, Jackie was surprised when she suddenly glimpsed him and then called out, "Ari, I didn't know you were here!" She was impressed that he had come from

New York without having made his presence known to her, or even intending to be able to speak to her.[13] Now if this wasn't testing the waters of approval nothing was, and Jackie's surprise was conveniently noticed by all those present. It was some surprise and some great acting by Ari and Jackie taking place in such a public arena.

As Jackie's ties to Ari began to become public, they grew stronger each month. She had visited him publicly now, not only at Skorpios, but also at his Avenue Foch apartment in Paris. In New York they were seen at El Morocco and "21" with Rudolf Nureyev and Margot Fonteyn, and at Dionysius and Mykonos, two plain but authentic Greek restaurants. Often they were trailed by an American photographer named Ron Galella, whose candid shots of Jackie in restaurants, at nightclubs, walking along the street created a brisk market. But even the photographs of Ari and Jackie together did little to arouse public curiosity. The prospect of a union between them seemed too remote to even be taken seriously. It was too bizarre to even consider.

In March 1968, several days after Robert Kennedy had announced his candidacy for President, Onassis was interviewed at a cocktail party at the George V Hotel in Paris. Asked his opinion of Jacqueline Kennedy, he said, "She is a totally misunderstood woman. Perhaps she misunderstands herself. She's being held up as a model of propriety, consistency and of so many boring American virtues. She's now utterly devoid of mystery. She needs a small scandal to bring her alive such as a peccadillo or an indiscretion. Something should happen to her to win our fresh compassion. The world loves to pity fallen grandeur."

Bobby Kennedy found the statement disconcerting. Confronting his sister-in-law, he was told that she and Onassis had discussed marriage but had reached no decisions. Several days later Jackie received a visit from Ethel and Joan Kennedy. They begged her not to marry Onassis. Such an action with all the negative publicity attached to it would irrevocably damage the family name and Bobby's chances for the Presidency.[14]

At this time Rose Kennedy was getting very tired of paying for

Jackie's exorbitant expenses. The Kennedy Matriarch played a distinct role in giving Jackie reason to marry Onassis quickly. Rose was continually telling Jackie's mother that her daughter was going to have to cut back on her expenditures, including her personal staff. "This cannot go on," Rose said to Janet Auchincloss. "Now that Jack isn't here to provide for her, Jackie's going to have to learn to survive on less. My husband's office cannot continue to finance every whim of hers."

To others at the time, Onassis represented a means of escape for Jackie as well as the financial independence she had so long craved. She needed security and she adored luxury and Onassis offered both. She wanted a strong male figure in her young son's life, and she wanted to evade what she described as America's "oppressive obsession" with her and her children.[15]

Jackie couldn't have helped but be thankful that she and Ari had made their pact. She must have been sick of the Kennedys making political demands on her and asking her to deprive herself of happiness so they could protect their precious image and win another campaign. As for Rose complaining to her mother about Jackie's spending habits, it was the same as when Jack was alive. The Kennedy's only liked spending Joe's money on themselves. They could be so thoughtless and selfish.

These were the same issues that a young woman could have taken into consideration years before on a cruise under the stars. Possibly during this cruise a pact was made that she would try to keep as soon as possible.

In April 1968, Bobby persuaded Jackie to attend the funeral of Martin Luther King, Jr., in Atlanta with him. She would have preferred to have visited the family alone after the funeral, but she acceded to her brother-in-law's request.

Jackie and Coretta were in the same boat. Coretta resented her husband for all of his womanizing but modeled herself instantly after Jackie. Her performance at the funeral was right on cue. Both women played the martyr role to perfection. In both cases, their performance served a national purpose. Neither one of them was as distraught as they appeared.

The only difference is that Mrs. King didn't turn around and have Aristotle Onassis to get married to.[16]

At Easter Jackie and the children flew to Palm Beach in an effort for Ari to get to know the children better and win them over. Jackie spent the summer shuttling between Newport and Hyannis Port, where she was soon joined by Aristotle Onassis. She wanted the children to become better acquainted with him, and she hoped to introduce him to members of the Auchincloss and Kennedy families. He made a promising start with Caroline and John arriving at the compound weighted down with presents. Larry Newman, Jackie's neighbor on the cape, saw her and Onassis, "Go up the street together, holding hands, dancing, doing ballet steps, playing like kids. I would see them eating their lunch of hot fish and cold champagne, they seemed extremely happy together." I said to myself, "Isn't it tremendous that at last she has found someone to be with? We all heard so much about the money she received for marrying Onassis, but it looked to me as though they were very much in love. He seemed like an attractive fellow, a guy who knew how to handle the romance question."[17]

As for the families, Auchincloss and Kennedy, they both were caught completely off guard and were opposed to the idea of this union, never realizing that none of them could prevent what was already written in the stars. All that summer Jackie continued her mission to elevate Ari's credibility with her crowd and her families. He had a lot to learn. Although he had lived close to her world for a long time, it would never be his world. While many of her friends and relatives accepted his presence, few genuinely welcomed him. He was "Not one of us," said a member of their caste. Although it was apparent to many that an affair was in the air, their different backgrounds would still have demanded a quantum leap of the imagination to contemplate anything more profound.

That the Kennedys continued to have interests of their own that ran counter to hers as a woman no longer deterred Jackie. Jackie took Ari to visit Joe and Rose Kennedy.[18] Rose Kennedy did voice concern over the religious question since Onassis was both divorced and a member of the

Greek Orthodox Church. She found their guest charming and entertaining. Rose's feeling was not shared by Jackie's mother. Jonathan Tapper, a major domo for Janet Auchincloss, reported that Janet "Didn't particularly care for Aristotle Onassis. She considered him vulgar, both in appearance and manner. She would talk negatively about him. She felt he didn't have the air of elegance Jackie deserved."

Bobby was the next one to speak to Jackie and try to persuade her not to announce her decision until after the election in order to avoid damage to his image. Jackie agreed to compromise, to go along with the Kennedys, for the moment at any rate. After the election she would decide. Bobby said he hoped she would decide against it.

Although Jackie and Ari had already decided to wed in July, no one knew of their plans which were changed immediately upon the assassination of Robert Kennedy on June 5, 1968 in Los Angeles. As soon as Jackie learned the news, she immediately flew to Los Angeles to be with the family. In London, shortly after the announcement in California that the Senator was dead, Ari telephoned his friend, Gratos. "She's free of the Kennedys, the last link just broke," he said. He showed no hint of regret, no trace of surprise, merely "a sort of satisfaction that his biggest headache had been eliminated," said a London aide. Gratos was shocked by the killing; he was not surprised by Ari's reaction to it.

The night they buried Bobby by candlelight along side his brother in Arlington Cemetery, Ari said to Andre Meyer, "I guess the kid had everything but the luck." The man who had been a guest at the White House for the funeral of John F. Kennedy found his name conspicuously absent from the guest list of those invited to St. Patrick's Cathedral on June 8. "In the circumstances his presence would have been in bad taste," David Harlech, one of the ten pallbearers, said later.[19]

Although J. Edgar Hoover's own reaction to RFK's assassination was comparably cold-blooded, for a short time he considered Aristotle Onassis a possible suspect in this murder. Those closest to Ari shared Costa Gratos's belief that Onassis "had always taken what he wanted, and for the first time in his life he had come up against a younger man who was as tough and determined as he was. And now he was dead." [20] Isn't it amazing that Hoover would consider even for a brief moment Onassis as a suspect in this murder, yet not in the preceeding JFK murder?

Immediately after the funeral, Jackie summoned Aristotle Onassis to be with her at her mother's home, Hammersmith Farms. Ari brought along his daughter, Christina, with him. However it was a mistake to introduce Onassis to the Auchinclosses so soon after Bobby's funeral. Now more than ever Jackie wanted seclusion, and there was no one better than Ari to see that she got it. She began a campaign to convince her family and friends that Ari was not a monster, but a man of sympathy and dimension. [21]

Now that Bobby was dead, Jackie could proceed full speed ahead and her perfect reason would be Bobby's assassination. Her intention could not have been more blatant had she placed a marriage announcement on the front page of the *New York Times*. "I hate this country," she lamented the day after Bobby's burial. "I despise America and I don't want my children to live here anymore. If they're killing Kennedys, my kids are the number one targets . . .I want to get out of this country." [22] It made sense, to every American who read her words. It was understandable that this poor woman would need to escape. But where to? Who could protect her and care for her?

These questions were soon to be answered.

If you are wondering at this point why Ari and Jackie would even care about having a good relationship with the Kennedys, there are two very good answers. One, for the sake of Caroline and John, it would be important for them to be close to their father's family. Secondly, it would be a key element in their cover up. It would not behoove the future Mr. and Mrs. Onassis to have anyone in the future to suspect that there may have been some hanky panky going on between them for a very long time. It would be much smarter to stay on good terms with everyone. This way they would be protected from angry people making ridiculous accusations in the future.

In August, Jackie and Teddy traveled to Skorpios. Jackie and Ari felt that to keep appearances up, it would be appropriate for Teddy to represent Jackie in the prenuptial negotiations. This trip aroused no suspicions in the States. As for taking Teddy along, it seems unlikely that Jackie would let anyone represent her when it came to money and her future. Ted Kennedy was just a cover. It would be safe to assume the financial aspects had been taken care of by Ari and Jackie years ago. As for the prenuptial contract, Jackie and Ari wrote it and Teddy just thought he did it for Jackie. It made for a great story and one that would appear good to their public.

Senator Kennedy told Onassis that, "We love Jackie and want her to have a happy and secure future." "So do I," replied Onassis. "If she remarries she will lose her income from the Kennedy trust," warned Teddy. "How much?" Ari asked. "Approximately $175,000 a year," said Kennedy. Onassis, having previously explored the matter with Jackie, knew of her situation and thought it was odd that one of America's wealthiest families would place her on such a limited budget. Her total income was paltry for a person of supposed means. Although he said nothing about it to Teddy, he told Jackie that she was being kept a political prisoner by the Kennedys.[23] This was exactly why Jackie had decided to cast her lot with Ari. The pact she had made with him would surely reap her more financial security than she ever would have had as a Kennedy.

The secret of the marriage was already known by too many people to be contained much longer. On October 15th, the *Boston Herald Traveler* ran a front page story predicting a marriage in the near future between John F. Kennedy's widow and Aristotle Onassis. The story ran without any official confirmation from the Kennedy family, but Cardinal Cushing, refusing to lie, did not deny the story.

That day Jackie called Onassis in Athens to tell him the story was out and they should get married as soon as possible. Ari agreed with Jackie and eagerly dropped everything to begin making the necessary arrangements in Greece.

Next Jackie called her mother in Virginia. "Hi, are you free?" She asked. "No, I'm not," replied Janet Auchincloss. "I want you to announce my engagement to marry Ari, and then we'll leave from New York with the children for Athens and get married on Sunday." "Oh, my God, Jackie. You can't mean that," screamed her mother. "Sorry, Mummy. It's too late."

Unaware until then of her daughter's plans, Mrs. Auchincloss was stunned by the phone call. Jackie's half-brother, Jamie Auchincloss recalled, "Mummy was hysterical. She did everything she possibly could to talk Jackie out of that marriage. She was incensed. But it was no use." Mummy kept saying, "She's getting back at me for divorcing her father. That's what she's doing. I just know it."[24]

Isn't it interesting that Janet who had taught Jackie from early on to marry for money, big money, was now against the biggest money marriage ever? Janet seemed to be more concerned with status now. She loved being the mother-in-law of the country's dearly departed President.

Since Janet's husband had provided generously for her, she didn't feel concerned about her daughter's financial problems any more. The sad part is this selfish woman knew from Rose Kennedy all about their harassment of Jackie over money. This had been going on since the beginning of her marriage to Jack. It was no secret. It isn't surprising that Jackie knew from the get go that she would always have to take care of herself and her children. Thus, she surely spent a large amount of time on her prenuptial contract with Ari. She had been burned in the past and it would never happen again to her. When it came to money, Jackie would be the one calling all of the shots.

At 3:30 P.M. October 17, 1968, Nancy Tuckerman made the announcement in New York to the press. "Mrs. Hugh D. Auchincloss has asked me to tell you that her daughter, Mrs. John F. Kennedy, is planning to marry Aristotle Onassis sometime next week. No place or date has been set for the moment." She said. The statement was intentionally vague because Jackie wanted to keep the place and date a secret to avoid the avalanche of reporters and photographers.

Two hours later she walked out of her Fifth Avenue apartment, wearing a gray jersey dress, holding the hands of her two children. Accompanied by her good friend Bunny Mellon and a group of secret service men, she entered a waiting limousine which whisked her to the airport.

There she met her mother and stepfather, Jean Kennedy Smith, Pat Kennedy Lawford and her daughter. Onassis had arranged for the wedding party to fly on his airline, Olympic Airways, and bumped all scheduled passengers in order to give them complete privacy during the eight-and-a-half hour flight to Greece.[25]

Nothing, not even his children, could divert Onassis from what he had come to believe was his manifest destiny. Society photographer, Jerome Zerbe said, "It was the most expensive mistake he ever made. It was indicative of a greater failing on his part. He believed money was a more powerful force than morality. The person Onassis wanted to marry he couldn't. We all know who that was—Queen Elizabeth. She would have been the top.

But he couldn't have her.

So he settled for Jackie."[26]

SIXTEEN

WHAT WAS THE MARRIAGE LIKE?

THE MONEY MARRIAGE

*T*HE ANNOUNCEMENT OF THE MARRIAGE OF Jacqueline Bouvier Kennedy to Aristotle Onassis caught the world by surprise and created an incredible reaction that was mostly negative. To the world at large, it made no sense at all. It was widely regarded as some sort of catastrophic disaster.

On October 18, 1968, the announcement was made which so deflated the Kennedy image that it has never recovered. Jacqueline announced that she was going to marry the divorced Greek shipowner and multimillionaire, Aristotle Onassis. He was a man who was twenty-nine years older than Jackie with an unsavory reputation. Onassis was so unlike the late John F. Kennedy in looks, manners and values that her marriage to him suddenly raised disturbing questions about her first marriage to JFK. Had that union also been just for money and power?[1]

Ari and Jackie had waited so patiently to make this announcement and they must have been horrified at the intensity of the public's reaction to their news. This worldwide rejection of their union stunned them. The world's press banned together and each headline became worse than the one before. "Jackie-how can you?" headlined the *London Tabloid*. "America has lost a saint," headlined the West German *Bild-Zeitung*, adding in subtitle, "All the world is indignant." Then there was the classic headline, "John Kennedy dies today for a second time," from Rome's *Il Messagero*.

Not everybody was shocked by the Kennedy-Onassis marriage. Those who knew Jackie best saw nothing especially unusual about it. Those members of the Bouvier family, for example, were surprised by the marriage but hardly shocked. Her cousin John Davis tells us that, "Those of us who had grown up with Jackie felt that Onassis was precisely the type of man we thought she would marry. She had always liked older men, much older men, even as a teenager. We all knew that her mother and her father had relentlessly coached her to marry a very rich man. Furthermore, Onassis was a man very much like Jackie's father, whom she adored. Like BlackJack Bouvier, Onassis was a very masculine, protective man who loved to indulge women. Both men were totally materialistic. They both were very "worldly" and each man had a way of making a woman feel very appreciated and secure."[2]

The bottom line was that Ari was everything Jackie was looking for in a man and a husband. She knew this from the moment they had decided to enter into their pact. They both were tired of waiting. They had been patient enough and now it would be their time. Finally Jackie could realize her childhood "dream of glory." With a sixty-eight-year-old shipping emperor by her side, she could finally be *"la fille naturelle de Charlemagne,"* with Camelot replaced by a new fairyland on the enchanted Greek island of Skorpios.[3]

After the assassination of Robert Kennedy, the timing would be ideal for Jackie to exit the Kennedy nightmare. What more sublime escape could there be than a shimmering island in the Aegean Sea with one of the most luxurious yachts in the world just waiting for her arrival? After all that she had gone through, the beauty and serenity of Skorpios and her new life with Ari would be heaven on earth.

There is no question that had Jack Bouvier lived to see this marriage he would have been thrilled to see Jackie acquire such a wealthy husband. Repeatedly he had drummed it into Jackie's ears that she should marry a very rich man. Janet had also urged Jackie to do the very same thing over and over again. By entering into this union Jackie was doing the very thing she had been raised to do. This brings up the question of money, or more specifically Jackie's lack of it with the Kennedys. By marrying Ari, Jackie was finally able to break free from her financial dependence on Jack's family. She could finally indulge her very extravagant tastes which was, for the Bouvier family, reason enough for her to wed Onassis.

Some of her various relatives' quotes express their feelings rather well, such as Louis Auchincloss who said, "Well we assume that she needs the money. After all, how can she live on $250,000 a year." Then there was Gore Vidal's famous line, "I can only give you two words....highly suitable." George Smathers said what everyone else was thinking, "I think she did it just so she'd never have to be beholden to the Kennedys again." My own favorite comments came from, first, Joan Rivers who said, "Come on, tell the truth. Would you sleep with Onassis? Do you believe she does? Well she had to do something, you can't stay in Bergdorf's shopping all day." My second other favorite comment was given by Bob Hope when he said, "Nixon has a Greek running mate. Now everyone wants one."[4]

Still Jackie's reputation suffered grievously from the marriage, especially in Europe where Onassis was emphatically not liked. People could not believe that this paragon of American womanhood would marry a disreputable old man. A man who seemed to have no ideals whatsoever. His only interest was in piling up enormous sums of money and collecting yachts filled with celebrities.[5] Little did the world realize that this was all Jackie ever really wanted out of life

On the face of it, the only obvious thing Onassis and Jackie had in common was their heavy smoking. Yet, they had important complementary qualities. At the simplest and most obvious level, this could be reduced to the fact that Jackie was one of the world's most expensive women and Onassis had one of the world's largest personal fortunes. In 1968 his worth in money and assets was reckoned to be $500 million. That does not imply that Jackie desired Onassis for his money, rather that marriage to someone who was not exceptionally, perhaps excessively, rich was simply not a feasible option for Jackie.

The frankest public defense of the marriage came from her sister Lee Radziwill who said, "Americans can't understand a man like Onassis. If my sister's new husband had been blond, young, rich, and Anglo-Saxon, most Americans would have been much happier. Onassis is an outstanding man. Not only as a financier, but also as a person . . . active, great vitality, very brilliant, up-to-date . . . amusing . . . a fascinating way with women. He surrounds them with attention. He makes sure that they feel admired and desired. He takes note of their slightest whim. My sister needs a man who can protect her from the curiosity of the world. I think she is rather tired of being a public personality and a part of the political life. Politics had never been her dominant interest. She did it proudly and with honor. But it isn't fair that she should have to continue to force her nature. Had she married just anybody, she'd probably have remained exposed to the curiosity of the world. She loves Onassis. Onassis is rich enough to offer her a good life and powerful enough to protect her privacy."[6]

This entire statement from beginning to end surely would have made BlackJack so proud. One daughter was doing exactly as he would have wished and the other daughter was in total agreement and publicly supportive, just as he would have been himself. There was no doubt that this would be the most brilliant marriage to ever occur in the Bouvier family.

Janet Auchincloss would not feel the same way. When Jackie had married Jack Kennedy, Janet looked down upon the Kennedys and felt that Jackie was marrying beneath herself in terms of her social standing. It was overlooked though due to the financial benefits Jackie would gain by becoming a Kennedy herself. Janet had grown quite comfortable with being the mother-in-law of the President and socially the presidency elevated Janet's family to a much higher level of social prominence not only within this country but the entire world. Janet immensely enjoyed the reflected glow of her eldest daughter's prominence as a national treasure. Even though Janet was aware of Jackie's dire financial condition as a widow of a Kennedy, she still was opposed to Jackie marrying Onassis. Recalled Jamie Auchincloss, "She did everything she possibly could to talk Jackie out of that marriage. She was just incensed. But it was no use. Jackie had made up her mind and there was nothing anyone could do about it." As usual, Janet was still only thinking of herself and the diminishing prestige of the Auchincloss family. Needless to say, her mother's reactions did not affect Jackie's plans. Here was Jackie's chance to go for the really big bucks and now Janet was opting for status over security for her daughter. So much for motherly love.

The disparity in their ages appears to have been an advantage rather than a hindrance. It had not been an obstacle as far as the marriage of Jackie's sister to Prince Radziwill was concerned since Stas was twenty-two years older than Lee. It is entirely reasonable to assume the two sister's relationship with their father was an explanation for their predilection for older men. Onassis was everything that BlackJack had wanted to be but never quite became. Of all of Jackie's suitors, Ari best evinced her father's quality of elusive attraction. He also could combine it with something her father never could provide, the promise of security. The irrepressible Doris Lilly made a similar observation when she wrote, with refreshing disregard for psychological jargon, "Jackie . . . always seemed to have been attracted to older men, possibly because you don't have to shoot them in the legs to keep them home at night."[7]

Jackie and Ari were so well suited to each other because their ideas were in harmony. Jackie had been imprisoned in the political mythology of the Kennedys. Yet she hated politics. She was very much like Onassis who was apolitical. Jackie valued her position as First Lady for the degree of privilege it conferred. She could be both prominent and yet secure from unwanted intrusions. Whereas Onassis's archaic kingdom, with its island stronghold and its fiefs on the sea and air, seemed capable of offering comparable prerogatives. If the transition from Camelot to Skorpios re-quired a leap of faith and imagination, the route linking the two kingdoms was plain to see for Jackie.[8]

What so many people who were outraged about this marriage failed or refused to see was that these two people were in love and desperately wished to spend their life together. No matter what or how they came to be together, their love for one another was genuine and sincere at the time of the marriage. They had cast their lot together and come what may they were prepared to face the future.

Of course, there is the issue of the famous marriage contract. This was supposedly negotiated for Jackie by Ted Kennedy before the marriage took place which is ridiculous. Ted's participation was just superficial. Teddy could no more handle a complicated prenuptial agreement than he could handle finding poor Mary Jo in the water at Chappaquidick years later. Anyone who knows Jackie well would know that she would personally handle her own financial arrangements.

She had been duped by the Kennedys with their interest only trust funds for widows when her own financial security was at stake, and she would never let that happen again. Who can blame her? Ari would be most understanding about her concerns. He would do everything possible to ease her financial burdens and make this marriage as easy as possible for her. Ari set out his proposals precisely since he had hatched the deal in his head many months ago when he and Jackie had pledged their love.

Along with the obvious age discrepancy, there were other problems to be faced. There was the religious issue that would create a spiritual struggle for Jackie, but not much of one. Jackie would fall back on the words of her recently departed husband, Jack Kennedy who said, "When the chips are down, money counts more than religion." This remark was more than enough to resolve Jackie's theological dilemma, if she ever had one. More than an excuse, it was a reason, a whole philosophy.[9]

As for all of the various problems confronting the lovers, it was just speculation in the press. It gave everyone something to talk about. There were no problems between Ari and Jackie. Everything had been settled between them long ago.

The official version given to the press at the time of the marriage announcement was that they had always been very good friends. Ari would have occasionally taken Jackie to ballets, concerts and dinners over the last three years. Gradually their friendship became much more and slowly they realized their love for each other.

To clear the way for his upcoming marriage to Jackie, Ari had broken off his ten year relationship with opera singer Maria Callas. Callas complained publicly that Onassis was only furthering his collection of famous beautiful women. Sadly Maria had been used by Onassis for over ten years, right up to his marriage to Jackie. His romance with Maria was a great cover for what was really going on between Ari and Jackie since the cruise in 1963.

Jackie did have Aristotle agree to a three-million-dollar cash payment before the marriage. He had no problem at all with this gift to Jackie that he felt would give her a feeling of security. Her own view of the marriage was supposedly so innocent when she told friends, "You don't know how lonely I've been."[10]

While most of the world accused her of marrying Ari for his money, Jackie did not do so. She did receive the $3 million and $1 million for each of her children. However, what most people ignore or do not realize is that Jackie upon her marriage gave up all claims to the Onassis estate. Realistically under Greek law, Jackie as a wife would be entitled to much more than the mere $5 million that Ari had settled upon her and her children. However, both Ari and Jackie knew that the secret pact they had made between them would keep them together and be more binding than any premarital contract. Money would never be an issue for them. What united them was a crime so heinous that nothing in the world would ever be able to come between them or turn them against each other. To betray the other would be to betray one's own self. Their marriage would be for all time and eternity. As we will see in the future, even though Ari contemplated divorce it would never be an option for either Ari or Jackie. Neither one would ever completely leave or desert the other one.

To seal their engagement, Ari had given his bride-to-be a $1.25 million engagement ring, a heart-shaped ruby the size of an egg surrounded by one-carat diamonds. It was just the beginning of a long list of fabulous baubles that Ari took great pleasure in giving Jackie. Naturally, she adored the gifts and the spirit in which they were given to her. It was truly one of the happiest times in Jackie's life. This was what she had been born for and it was wonderful to finally be were she belonged. It had been a struggle to get here but well worth the effort.

Meanwhile, some two hundred fifty journalists, all eager to cover the "wedding of the century" were converging on this little island of Skorpios. Onassis spared no effort in protecting his bride's privacy. He hired helicopters with bullhorns to guard the island. A security force of 200 men held back the mobs of journalists and photographers. Jackie released a statement pleading for privacy and promising to pose for pictures once the ceremony was over. "We know and understand that even though people may be well known," she said. "They still hold in their hearts the emotions of a simple person for the moments that are the most important of those we know on earth—birth, marriage and death. We wish our wedding to be a private moment in the little chapel among the cypresses of Skorpios with only members of the family present, five of them little children. If you will give us those moments, we will so gladly give you all the cooperation possible for you to take the pictures you need."[11]

An agreement was reached with the press that allowed four newspapermen to attend the ceremony. The marriage took place at 5:15 p.m. on October 20th. It was described by Mario Modiano of the *Times* of London, "The tiny chapel set among bougainvillea and jasmin was packed with relatives from both sides. It was raining which is always considered a good sign at any Greek wedding. Jackie looked drawn and concerned. She wore a long-sleeved lace dress with an ivory ribbon in her hair. The groom looked slightly off-key in a blue suit, white shirt and red tie. Artemis, Onassis' sister, was sponsor. She placed on the heads of the couple delicate wreaths shaped as branches with lemon buds connected with white ribbon.

As the priest chanted, the rings were placed on their fingers and exchanged three times. They both drank from a goblet of red wine. The priest translated parts of the ceremony into English for Jackie's benefit. They did Esiash's dance around the altar three times with the priest. Upon leaving the chapel, they were showered with petals and returned to the yacht. The pool of journalists were invited for a champagne toast."[12]

Returning to the yacht, the guests retired to their suites to prepare for the wedding feast. Jackie spent an hour alone with Onassis in their private quarters while her personal maid readied the children for the evening. The children changed into their pajamas and went downstairs to join the adults in the living room. Jackie was radiant in a floor length white skirt and black blouse and the gold bejeweled caftan belt the King of Morocco had given her while she was First Lady. What she wore on her third finger of her left hand stopped everyone. Gone was the gold wedding band from JFK and in its place was the huge cabochon ruby the size of an Easter egg, surrounded by diamonds. Transfixed by Jackie's $1,200,000 display of jewelry, no one said a word. Ari gave Jackie ruby earrings framed in diamonds to match her ring, and a solid gold bracelet studded with rubies in the shape of a ram's head.

No guest ever left the *Christina* without a precious memento from the host, and this evening Onassis presented treasures of fabulous jewelry for the women and watches for the men. Then getting down on his hands and knees, the tycoon began tumbling around with the youngsters. Jackie watched them lovingly and everyone watched Jackie.

The guests were then ushered into the dining room and seated for the wedding dinner. Onassis rose and toasted the seven sisters assembled around his table saying, "This was a good omen for a family now united by love and marriage." Then Jackie stood and lifted her glass. "I wish to make a toast to the only brother at this table," she said referring to her new stepson, Alexander. By the time the wedding cake was served there was not one dry eye at the table. Onassis's sisters smiled through their tears as they watched Ari enjoying himself. Jackie and Ari cut their cake and after everyone was served, the children were hugged and sent to bed. The adults enjoyed after dinner drinks and dancing. Jackie and Ari sat together holding hands. They looked at each other occasionally and smiled secretly, as if sharing a special bit of knowledge the rest of the world would never know.[13]

They had made it and no one suspected a thing. They had actually pulled off the crime of the century. It must have been the most sublime moment in their lives. Their love for each other had triumphed and now they would be together forever. No matter what the world may have thought, they loved each other and their wedding day would be by far one of the happiest days they would ever spend together.

Ari and Jackie both went into this marriage with great expectations of happiness. There were early signs of tenderness. Jackie gave him her own special name, Telis. He even tried to stop her from chain smoking, snatching away her L & M's the moment she would reach for them. Within days of their wedding, Jackie summoned Billy Baldwin to Skorpios to redesign her house. An old friend who had decorated her Washington and New York homes, Baldwin had never seen Jackie so "free" she appeared relaxed and radiant, in almost hoydenish high spirits. There was no sign of any disappointment over the world's coolness towards the wedding. Ari gave him a free hand, "This house I want to be a total surprise. I trust you and I trust Jackie." He had only one request, a long sofa by the fireside, "So I can lie and read and nap while I watch the flames." It was a nice idea and clearly part of the fantasy life he envisioned for himself now that he had acquired Jackie.[14]

Their life together was predictably unpredictable with both of them traveling much of the time. As for Ari, he pretty much continued to lead his life just as he always had and it would be Jackie's task to fit herself into his routine and his schedule. Asked if marriage had changed his way of life, he replied, "Not at all . . . What do you expect me to do?" Even so he was obviously elated at the exclusive social occasions he attended with his wife. Gardiner Cowles, the publisher of *Look* magazine, attended a dinner in

Manhattan given by David Rockerfeller in honor of the newlyweds. Onassis's manner was unusually muted. "He was happy to stay in the background, basking in his wife's social radiance," recalled Cowles. "One had the sense of a man who felt he had accomplished something prodigious and was proud of it."[15]

They were both very excited about each other. The marriage was a good one since each met the other's deepest emotional needs. Ari gave Jackie the security and stability she wanted in her troubled life. She showed her feelings by her actions and words. She told a friend in Athens, "It's a delightful feeling to be in love." Ari confessed to all his friends, "I love that woman. I truly love her." Jackie gave him the emotional satisfaction of having won what he yearned for most, the ultimate crown jewel.

Jackie and Ari had a great deal in common. According to Pearl Buck who had close ties to friends of both, "He loved beauty, she loved art, and he had the money to indulge her tastes . . . and he loves children. He has a natural ability to communicate with them. He loves Jackie with maturity and compassion."[16] Jackie felt especially fortunate to be his chosen one. It was said of Ari, "He pays absolutely mad, dedicated constant court when he is attracted to a woman, literally sweeping her off her feet. He is known for the sheer, driving force of his personal passions as well as his business maneuvers." It is little wonder that such a man could get a woman such as Jacqueline to fall in love with him.[17]

Letitia Baldridge described Ari in such a way that any woman could see the attraction when she said, "Ari was a diamond in the rough who enjoyed the power of his extraordinary money and the convenience of ships and an airline. He offered Jackie just about anything she could want. That's terrific if you've been through hell, and you come back to your apartment, and somebody had flown over from Greece to be there to comfort you."[18]

It was such an exciting time in her life and many were able to watch and enjoy the change in Jackie that was taking place before their very eyes. Gore Vidal pronounced on the early stages of "the marriage of the century" in uncharacteristically glowing terms, "Onassis is dynamic and pro-

tective, and I think that is what Jackie needs. Not so much physical protection, but a certain kind of warm fatherly affection. Though she's independent, she's very brittle. She needs someone who will give her a thicker
lining. I think Onassis is doing this for her. Jackie is very happy with
Onassis-perhaps more so than with her first husband . . . John Kennedy
was wrapped up in himself and his career. She was like another room at
the White House, almost a prisoner. Can an omnivorous, rich businessman
of sixty-four find happiness with an attractive woman of forty? The answer
is yes!"[19]

Another attractive and quite successfully married woman herself,
Pamela Harriman was very supportive of Jackie. "Her marriage to Jack
was different from her marriage to Onassis. One didn't have anything to do
with the other. Her first marriage was in innocent youth. By the time she
married Onassis, the years had gone by with much sadness. In a sense,
although he was Greek, he was really isolated from the whole world. He
roamed the seas of the earth, a lord unto himself. Imagine being able to slip
into that, away from the real world after so much sadness."[20]   Little did
clever Pamela, with her brilliant and financially successful marriage to
Averall Harriman, suspect that Jackie was just as clever a girl with her
alliance. Pamela, of all people, would be able to appreciate the obstacles
that these two lovers had overcome.

The first year of their marriage was spent finally being alone and
getting to really know each other. They swam, they sunbathed, took long
walks and went fishing together. Onassis amused himself from time to time
by boasting to his business associates as well as to friends of his wife about
his sexual life with Jackie. Over the telephone he told his friend, Gratos,
one morning that he had performed five times the night before, and twice
again that morning.[21] Ari was incredibly devoted to Jackie and her children
in the beginning of this union. A solicitous husband, he catered to her
whims and wishes. He did everything he could to make her happy; most
important to Jackie was the attention he paid to her children.

Once, while both were reading on the deck of the *Christina*, Jackie suddenly rose from her chair, walked over to him and kissed him. Surprised, he asked, "What's that for?" "That's because of last night," she said. Ari had stayed up all night long because young John had a stomach ache. "I just thought about it," Jackie said, and she kissed him again. Ari grinned. A minute later, he rose, went to her and kissed her passionately. "What's that for?" she asked. "I just remembered," he said, "that a couple of months ago I was ill and you stayed up with me." They both laughed and kissed again.

He was the most considerate of husbands. Jackie told friends that, "His constant attention and ingenuity are wonderful. Last Thursday he told me that I looked pale and needed a bit of a change. He suggested that we fly to Paris and have dinner at Maxim's. He's always doing things like that. He notices things others fail to see. He has such a brilliant mind and can pick up things and analyze them and be right." Then came the frank, artless admission that she was in love with him.[22]

They were extremely affectionate in public and very relaxed and comfortable in each other's company. Lee Guthrie recalls seeing them as, "They sat close together all evening or rather well into the morning. Ari had his arm around her and they whispered together and kissed each other like two high-school kids in the throes of first love." Ari made a tremendous effort to be a good father and even though his work required that he travel frequently, he made a valiant effort on the children's behalf. He brought them gifts, was unfailingly cordial to their friends, and would take them fishing, sailing, and water-skiing on their trips to Skorpios.[23]

After the onslaught of public rebuke, Jackie began to get support from unexpected sources. One telegram she received stated, "All the happiness in the world magnificent Jacqueline. Wish my name were Aristotle Onassis instead of Maurice Chevalier." Ladybird Johnson wrote that, "This complete break with the past might be good."[24]

The transition from being Mrs. Kennedy to Mrs. Onassis became easier for Jackie as she arranged dinners where Ari could get to know her friends. Gloria Steinem recalled, "I remember going to a dinner when

Jackie was married to Onassis. She insisted that I sit next to him because she said, 'No one else will argue with him except you. He won't be bored.' So we fervently argued. But she wanted him to be a part of things, amused, stimulated. She said, 'If you knew him, you would like him very much.'"[25]

Jackie assimilated herself into Ari's life when she embraced everything Greek. Ever since her visit in 1961, she had loved its culture and studied its history and mythology. The Greeks seemed to understand Jackie better than Americans who still felt betrayed by her marriage to Onassis. Jackie immersed herself in every aspect of Greek life. She became familiar with the corners of the small country, searching Athens for antiques and old books on Greek art. She relished sharing her pleasure in being in Greece with her friends and family, inviting them to Skorpios.

Skorpios captivated Jackie the most. It was an absolutely fantastic place. The warm water was a color that is often mentioned in Greek mythology as wine colored, a deep purple that wasn't blue, the clearest, most beautiful water. It was like a lake. There were various places on the island where you could swim or have tea or eat dinner or lunch. Each site was perfect at a different time of day. The sun was everywhere, the setting sun, the rising sun, shining on the other islands in the distance. The place was covered with beautiful flowers. There was a whole part of the island set aside for a marvelous variety of fruits and vegetables. Jackie imported cherry tomato plants. In the mornings she clipped orchids, roses and tulips making dozens of flower bouquets for the house. She took long hikes through the hills heavily forested with pine trees. She decorated the main house primarily with native wicker. Jackie embraced Greek customs, speaking Greek, dancing the surtaki, even preparing stuffed grape leaves. Karl Katz, who was a friend of both Ari and Jackie, tells us that Onassis was a proud Greek. As a result, Jackie became tremendously interested in educating herself in everything Greek.[26]

As for Ari's take on their marriage of distances, he said, "Jackie loves traveling, sight-seeing, long walks, mountain climbing, skiing and literally hundreds of things that are just not to my liking. If we were together, she would probably get nervous always seeing me bringing up the rear! I know that Jackie would eventually give up her activities to please me and just stay with me, but then, that wouldn't really be Jackie. I don't want that to happen. When I do see her, she enthusiastically tells me what she has been doing. I have found that the longer the separation between us, the happier we are to meet again."[27]

For all of their differences, their first year of marriage went incredibly well considering all the obstacles that they had to overcome. Alexis Miotis, director of the Greek National Theater, who had known Ari since 1922 and Jackie from 1952 tells us of their harmonious relationship. "After Ari married Jackie I accompanied them on several excursions aboard the *Christina*. Jackie is a sweet person, very noble. Her behavior sets a standard for those around her. Obviously many people thought the marriage might be a sham, but I saw nothing wrong with it. Ari had a sense of glory about everything. He paid a good deal of attention to the 'glorious people'. He admired Jackie because she was First Lady, not only in the White House but First Lady of the land. Ari wanted to be emperor of the seas and wanted a Cleopatra to sit by his side. For Jackie, it was his charm combined with his money. He had money, yes, but he also had charisma. He was a domineering personality. He was the one man she could marry who would never become Mr. Jackie Kennedy."[28]

Theirs was a union born of out of their destiny to be with each other. It was written in the stars and these star-crossed lovers were not to be denied their season in the sun. As they settled into their life on Skorpoios and sailed the seas together, their bond of love became so much more. This pact of murder for a marriage that they had made so long ago bound them together in such a way that nothing could ever separate them.

He gave her everything she needed.

She in turn gave him her love and loyalty.

SEVENTEEN

HOW TO FIGHT DEPRESSION FOR ONLY $1.25 MILLION A YEAR?

THE SHOP TILL YOU DESTRUCT MARRIAGE

JACQUELINE BOUVIER KENNEDY ONASSIS WAS the original material girl. When it came to shopping, Jackie was in a class by herself. No one could touch her. She gave meaning to the term "Shop Till You Drop"! But she never did drop like the rest of us mere mortals. When it came to spending money, Jackie was a black belt.

This talent is not something a woman is born with. It is an art that must be developed and nurtured over the course of a lifetime. Jackie took it upon herself to inspire an entire generation of women. She gave other women something to strive for. No one could ever reach her or out spend her but just trying would be enough for most.

Jackie got her start early in life. While still in her teens, her father warned her about her overspending. He implored her to try to live within their means. It was hopeless even then. When Jackie made up her mind to possess something, there was no stopping her until she got it.

It became apparent to everyone who loved her that Jackie would have to marry into wealth to maintain the lifestyle she so adored. So it was not a problem when the dashing young Senator, John F. Kennedy, asked for her hand in marriage. He was heaven sent, along with his fabulously wealthy family, and Jackie was thrilled to become a member. All she had to do was to make sure that all her bills were sent to the Kennedy office at the Mart, their headquarters in Chicago. Everything was paid for and, just as in a fairy tale, everyone was supposed to live happily ever after.

Unfortunately, when it came to money and Jack Kennedy the perfect fairy tale didn't come true. Jackie's extravagance was well known within the Kennedy circle. "That Jackie," President Kennedy once yelled in the presence of Senator George Smathers of Florida, "she's unbelievable. She absolutely does not know the value of money. Thinks she can go on spending it forever. God, she's driving me crazy, absolutely crazy. If the taxpayers ever found out what she's spending, they'd drive me out of office." Another time in a calmer mood, he asked if there was such a thing as shoppers anonymous. He even brought in Carmine Belluno, an expert at cracking the secrets of Mafia bookkeeping, to bring her accounts under control. Not even Belluno was equal to the task. In 1962 alone, Jackie disposed of an estimated $121,000 or roughly $700,000 in 1996 money.[1]

According to Ben Bradlee, a *Newsweek* correspondent and Kennedy confidant, JFK was as angry about the purposes for which Jackie spent money as the actual amounts involved. The Kennedys had never skimped where their political ambitions were concerned. But Jackie's inability to explain such expenses as $40,000 on department stores was a different matter. According to her former secretary, Mary B. Gallagher, Jackie spent more than the President's annual salary on family expenses in 1962.[2]

Bruce Gould, then editor of *Ladies Home Journal*, recalled that "When Jackie became First Lady, the President raised hell with her because of all the money she spent on her clothes. Very likely that's why she eventually married Onassis. She was mad about clothes and one way or another was determined to get them."

Jackie's fashion splurges apparently started long before she reached the White House. She had a fetish for expensive clothes, and also for household furnishings. Nothing was more important to her than having a nice home. It was practically pathological, and probably dated to her childhood when she was shuffled from one household to another and not allowed to take root.[3]

Jackie admitted spending money on clothes, not the $30,000 per year that *Women's Wear Daily* claimed she spent, "I couldn't spend that much unless I wore sable underwear." She confessed to having purchased several Givenchey and Balenciaga creations and to frequenting a number of other European couturiers. She was different from other first ladies not only in manner, but in her appearance. In the middle of one of their campaigns, her mother said to her, "Why can't you look more like Muriel Humphrey or Pat Nixon?"[4] It is an amazing comment when one is able to look into the future and see that Jackie's uniqueness is what made her so incredibly appealing to the American public. Muriel and Pat were middle America. Jackie was someone special. She was enchantingly fresh and her style inspired the women of America. She became the role model for the sixties and her worshippers copied everything she wore. Jackie was well on the way to becoming an icon. This mystic aura would stay with her throughout her life and survive her death. She was the ultimate in taste, glamour and style.

Jackie's greatest assets were her intelligence, insight and curiosity, enhanced by her position and connections. She was a good listener, receptive and seemingly sensitive, although given to excess and a life-style reserved for the very rich. She was marked by an attraction to material objects such as horses, antiques, clothes, homes and furnishings. Finances had always been a problem area for Jacqueline, probably because she had never had the kind of money at her disposal she would have liked.[5]

Jackie's compulsive spending and her passion for shopping were certainly the expressions of a deeper problem within her own psyche. It was as if her need was so great, nothing could fulfill her. She collected everything she saw such as clothes, jewelry, art objects or other ambiences. It was impossible to fill her closets or her soul. She would never have enough of what she needed to make things right for her. This need was central to her character and would determine how she would live her life.

This great need to possess things even when she didn't need them would affect her choice of a second husband. Ari would be the answer to her prayers especially after the Kennedys had nickled and dimed her during her recent widowhood. Fred Sparks, a Pulitzer prize winning reporter, estimated that Jackie and Ari disposed of $20 million during the first year of their marriage. Sparks figures were at times conjectural and fanciful, but he may not have been far wrong if the houses, servants, airplanes and the yacht were included in the total.

In New York, *Women's Wear Daily* called her "the retailer's best friend," a title that was earned, not merely bestowed. These retailers estimated that Jackie spent $1.25 million in clothes the first year of her marriage to Onassis.[6] This marriage experience was going to be wonderfully different from her years under the Kennedy scrutiny. Jackie felt like the proverbial bird in the gilded cage who was at last set free into the gilded world of Aristotle Onassis. For the first time in her life Jackie could spend and buy without accounting to anybody for anything, and she didn't have to bother with cash. Her face was her charge plate. The bills were sent directly to the Onassis office, where they were paid by an indulgent tycoon who delighted in pleasing his wife. He could afford her compulsion to shop, her obsession to redecorate and her passion to accumulate. "God knows Jackie has had her years of sorrow," her husband was quoted as saying. "If she enjoys it, let her buy to her heart's content."

He showered her with trips and vacation cruises around the world, with first-class accommodations, with suites filled with flowers, fruits and champagne. He summoned perfumed tribes of national celebrities to entertain her, chauffeur-driven Rolls-Royces to transport her, bodyguards to protect her and private planes to fly her wherever she wanted to go. All that money could buy rained down on Jackie the day she became Mrs. Aristotle Onassis.[7]

For Jackie, her marriage to Onassis was definitely therapeutic. It was also good for the morale of the entire female species as we watched her spend her way to happiness. It was an incredible performance, the likes of which we will probably never see again. The fashion papers reported her every move. "Jackie-0 continues to fill her bottomless closets." Ari professed to find it all very normal. "She is making Daddy-O's bills bigger than ever with her latest shopping sprees. She is buying in the carload lots." Onassis said, "There is nothing strange in the fact that my wife spends large sums of money. Think how people would react if Mrs. Onassis wore the same dresses for two years, or went to second class beauty salons. They would immediately say that I am on the verge of bankruptcy and that my wife will soon be forced to work for a living." In his more euphoric moments, it must have seemed like a fairly even trade-off. Business was good, he could afford to indulge her, his name was on the social register at last. For once he had all the publicity he wanted.[8]

Jackie set high standards on her shopping expeditions all over New York. She was the talk of the town. She was a speed shopper who could be in and out of any store in the world in ten minutes or less, having run through $100,000 or more. She didn't bother with prices, just pointed. She bought anything and everything, music boxes, antique clocks, fur coats, furniture and shoes. She loved hitting the international fashion shows and buying the entire collection. And Ari encouraged it. In addition to giving her a portfolio of credit cards, he loved leaving little presents for her on her silver breakfast tray.[9] They both felt that money was meant to be enjoyed and spread around. Although she would not be on a level with Mother Teresa's good works, Jackie would spend enough to help out local economies everywhere she went. The money she spent surely helped out the merchants and working people in the fashion industry. Also Jackie's extravagance prompted others to join in and spend since it was the "In" thing to do.

Initially Jackie satisfied the protective and possessive side of Onassis' nature. "She is like a diamond," he explained revealingly, "cool and sharp on the edges, fiery and hot beneath the surface." The nature of the comtract between himself and Jackie was the essence of simplicity. "Jackie is like a little bird that needs its freedom and its security," he said, "and she gets them both from me."[10]

Under Onassis' watchful eye, Jackie eagerly tested the limits of his love. His unconditional generosity was proof of his love. This she could accept since this was what she had been seeking all her life. The little child of divorce was finally able to put away all her insecurities and shine brilliantly for her benefactor.

Her appetite for good things increased. The upper east side of Manhattan, with its department stores and boutiques, is something more than the world's most elaborate consumer center. It enforces the taste of urban America. Jackie's expenses the first year were incredible. The $1.25 million figure is based on nothing more precise than the sums quoted by the owners themselves so it is open to suspicion.

Yet there can be no doubt of the scale and seriousness of her shopping expeditions. Her visit to a store often produced among the staff and other shoppers a reaction verging on hysteria. This reaction was intensified by the speed and variety of her purchases. What was different about this phase of her acquisitiveness was that it seemed compulsive, exceeding even the lavish standards of the wealthy circles in which she moved. She bought dresses and jewels by the dozens. If a designer had a little blouse she fancied, she would order it in every color it was made in. It seemed unlikely that she ever wore many of the clothes she bought.[11]

It is truly a loss to posterity that no one ever wrote a book about Jackie's clothes and her closets. It makes one wonder how she ever organized all her clothes and how did she ever keep track of what she wore or where or with whom? All of this was pre-Imelda shoe closet time, but Jackie's personal maid sure missed out on a great opportunity considering everyone else who worked for the Onassis' wrote books about them.

This shopping madness was so out of control that it almost seemed like a sickness. Although he took genuine pleasure in giving people things, Onassis' gifts were rarely in the spirit of undiluted generosity. He usually expected something in return. As for Jackie she was a possession he took great pleasure in displaying. In one sense, her capacity to adorn his name and person was in itself a sufficient source of satisfaction. Jackie did not appear to be a giver. She shopped just for herself. Occasionally she would purchase gifts for Onassis, but basically she preferred receiving rather than giving.

Truman Capote recalls one expedition with Jackie. "It was the last full year of my friendship with Jackie, and I accompanied her on one of those Shop-Till-You-Drop sprees. She would walk into a store, order two dozen silk blouses in different shades, give them an address and walk out. She seemed in a daze, hypnotized."[12]

All of this came about with the encouragement of Onassis. He reveled in the emergence of Jackie, the super-spender. During his courtship he had showered her with bracelets and rings. For their wedding, he had given her a million dollars worth of rubies. For her fortieth birthday, he gave her a forty-carat diamond with a matching ensemble, a diamond necklace and bracelet worth another million dollars.

Together their expenses were enormous and to be fair to Jackie, a large amount of her expenditures were just for the basic maintenance and everyday expenses of your average millionaire couple. Now remember all of these amounts are quoted from thirty years ago so some of them will seem almost reasonable until you factor in that they would be doubled and some tripled by current 1998 costs. Jackie received $5,000 a month for her children. Then there was $10,000 a month for all the expenses of her New York apartment which covered the essentials like taxes, staff, bills and cars. There were her own personal expenses of $7,000 to pay for masseurs, hairdressers, pedicurists, and so on. Plus add in an additional $10,000 a month for clothes and $6,000 for her bodyguards.

Airfares on Olympic Airlines were free whenever she traveled, first class, of course. Basically, Jackie cost Onassis approximately $450,000 a year which didn't take into account all of the extravagant presents he gave her. Nor did any of this amount cover the expenses of their daily life together, whether they happened to be in New York, Greece or Paris. Remember these are all 1968 amounts. To acquire a logical perspective about some of their other major expenses, the *Christina* alone costs $420,000 a year for maintenance, salaries and cruises. The island of Skorpios costs $365,000 a year.[13]

But even Onassis had his limits. Eventually when he looked into his wife's spending, it was with great distress that he discovered some double dipping. In addition to her huge monthly allowance, Jackie regularly bought up the fanciest fashions in New York and Paris. She'd walk through the town with her husband's credit cards charging clothes. That was only a part of the operation. After buying the clothes, she'd sell them at Encore and other stores and then stash the cash.[4] Onassis would wonder what she could be doing with all the extra cash? It was an unanswered question. Knowing Jackie's life long fear of financial ruin, I can't help but think that she probably just kept the money for a "rainy day." The thought of not having total, complete control of her own finances would be anathema to her. She had to have her own money. No matter how much money Ari had already given her, it would never be enough.

Ari often wondered what became of all the clothes she bought, since most of the time she wore only jeans. Ari became outraged to discover that on 23 occasions Jackie had taken Olympic Airways planes and helicopters out of service for her personal use. He complained ceaselessly about the $5,000 she spent for messengers to deliver the gifts and letters she preferred not to mail.[15] Gradually Onassis brought Jackie's expenditures under a degree of control by insisting that she follow his own practice of charging everything to the Onassis offices in New York, where she could be audited. He then cut her allowance from $30,000 a month to $20,000 and moved her account to Monte Carlo, where his people could keep a closer eye on it. She complained that she was short of cash. Ari acidly suggested that she sell her jewelry. Suddenly, Jackie's continuous spending was causing a rift in the relationship.

It was at this time that Jackie sued Ron Galella, a free-lance photographer, who made an estimated $50,000 a year by peddling pictures taken without her permission. Jackie's lawyers won the case, Galella was suitably enjoined, and Onassis was presented with the bill on the lawsuit. It was a legitimate bill and Jackie was his wife so he paid out $235,000. "Everyone is happy now," he said.

Ari also bailed out Jackie's Aunt Edith Beale and Edith's daughter when the Suffolk County health department threatened to condemn their twenty-eight room mansion, a relatively inexpensive episode for only $50,000, but the gratitude of the rest of the family was not conspicuous. Nor was the gratitude particularly abundant closer to home as Jackie complained openly to her friends about Ari's lack of taste.[16]

Things were going rapidly downhill as Jackie was managing to spend herself out of her relationship with Onassis. This problem would contribute to the downfall of her relationship with the one man in the world she had put her trust in. It was a very confusing time for both of them. During the first year of their marriage, a mathematically inclined observer calculated that she and her husband were together 225 days and apart 140, although that was in part Ari's own doing. "He did not like having her around, but he couldn't be without her for long either," said one of his aides. "If he didn't see her for more than ten days in three months, life would be hell in the office. Then if he spent more than a month with her, he got fed up."[17]

"Ari maintained that Jackie's travels and the distances that separated them were the less of his complaints, and that her spending was his bigger beef. 'I am an enormously wealthy man,' he said, 'but I still find it hard to understand why I should receive a bill for 200 pair of shoes. It isn't as if I don't provide her with a generous expense account. What's more, the shoes are only one item. She orders handbags, dresses, gowns and coats by the dozen, more than enough to stock a Fifth Avenue specialty shop. This woman has no conception of when to stop squandering my money.'"[18]

"There was a looming matrimonial problem between the Onassis'," said Roy Cohn, Ari's lawyer. "It was predicated on her, quote, overspending, number one and number two, on the fact that she was always where he wasn't. She was never where he wanted her to be. According to him, she considered him nothing more than a money machine."[19] Jackie couldn't help herself and it certainly seemed as though she wasn't even trying. In her more desperate moments, Jackie tried to forget how she really felt by going on wild spending sprees clocked at $3,000 a minute.[20]

Although Jackie was not in therapy at the time, she was spending far more than any reputable therapist could have ever charged. There was no point in Jackie trying to get help with her problem. Therapy for compulsive behavior wasn't customary, at least it was not made public. Years earlier the Kennedy family hushed up the facts about Jackie's electro-shock therapy to treat her dark depressions and wide mood swings. Old man Joe Kennedy, who had his own daughter lobotomized, felt that the best treatment for Jackie was to give her more money, buy her a house and let her start decorating. But after she decorated the White House, everything else must have been anti-climatic. Decorating Ari's homes was exciting at first, but that challenge quickly wore off. As for the yacht, it was Ari's special place and its decor reflected the man with his choice of whales scrotum skin covering the barstools. Not much challenge there for her, as the *Christina* was off limits to Jackie's trained eye.

Even if Jackie had been able to see that she had an enormous problem with compulsive behavior, she was too busy spending to even notice or think that she might be out of control. She had been successfully trained from childhood on how to ignore problems. Her entire life was a testament to her ability to put on a good show no matter what the reality was in her private life.

Jackie was a thoroughbred. Consequently she would not have normal compulsions like the rest of us. Chocolate would never be enough of an out of control experience for someone like Mrs. Onassis. Jackie had to cross the line in a much bigger way than most of us. Once she crossed the line, there would be no going back for Jackie.

Forget chocolate,

for Jackie spending was . . .

even better than sex!

EIGHTEEN

WHAT DESTROYED THE MARRIAGE?

THE CURSE ON PARADISE

*T*HERE WAS SO MUCH UNFINISHED KARMA
played out between Aristotle and Jacqueline that only the gods could attempt to understand or explain their relationship. They had so much and yet it all went wrong. The murder that brought them together would be their final undoing.

When Jackie sought refuge from the world's outrage on the private island of Skorpios, she could not know that her wedding night was the opening of a Greek tragedy that would play for the next seven years, a drama that was to plague her with a series of deaths and family scandals that would eventually rob her of the happiness she so desperately wanted.[1] The ancient Greeks were by nature a suspicious people and their fear of the gods instilled in them a strong belief in the supernatural. Today they are quick to speak of curses and evil within their midst. These are very real fears and are a part of their daily life.

This was apparent to Ari's friends, right from the beginning of his enchantment with Jackie. When Aristotle Onassis was in full cry after the widow of the martyred American president, perhaps it was inevitable mused his friend, Costa Gratos. "The Jackie affair was a classic case of the greatest social climber of all time meeting the greediest woman of all time." But

Ari didn't lack for warnings. Costa was Ari's best friend, a man who loved him. Onassis did not get angry with him when Costa told him, "You cannot do this with this woman." To his face Gratos described her with a phrase in Greek that is not polite, it is obscene, but which meant that she was poisonous. And he prophesied that she would bring him bad luck.[2]

To give him credit, Onassis seemed to recognize that his obsession with celebrities, very few of whom he actually liked, had become something in the nature of an addiction, not unlike a form of alcoholism. It was a compulsion followed by a hangover that arrived in the form of melancholy, accompanied by a resolve to go cold turkey and never touch the stuff again. His solution was typical of the man. His cure would be to take a cruise. He used to bring his yacht across the Atlantic alone for days with only his crew for company. At night in the grip of insomnia, he would prowl the deck for hours. It never worked, he always came back. And in the case of Jacqueline Kennedy, he came back not once, but many times.[3] She was his addiction. He was unhappy with her at times and then when they would be separated he would really be miserable. He was in the horrible position of not being happy with her or without her.

If his friends' reading of the situation was correct, Aristotle Onassis had gotten exactly what he had bargained for, and it was not what he had wanted at all.[4]

Ari was surrendering to the fact that his marriage to Jackie was on one level global property. He had some control over its disposal but not much. At the same time as the world's most famous displaced person, he was almost obsessively concerned with the world's evaluation of his activities, which was not always flattering. Although the attentions of the press and publishing houses greatly magnified the problems of the marriage, they were surmountable.

What could not be overcome was the weight of their respective pasts that drove them first gradually and later inexorably apart. As a former First Lady, Jackie was still greatly in demand for the various ceremonies which commemorate the late President's life and career. They were important to Jackie as a method of establishing an identity for her children. Such events put a severe strain on Onassis whose manhood was firmly based on the need to be a hero in his own legend. These events were a constant reminder of the fact that his wife's charisma had more to do with her dead husband than her living spouse.[5] Ari had disposed of the first husband but they could not escape him. The Camelot legend had taken on a life of its own that became bigger and more demanding than they could ever have anticipated. Basically they had created their own hell on earth and now they had to inhabit it.

Onassis didn't like the Kennedys, but he was a businessman. He got along with them fine. He would have gone to bed with the devil if it meant getting close to power.[6]

Yet despite their evident affection for each other, the marriage never seemed to develop that organic quality that characterizes the most happy unions. They satisfied important needs in each other but probably not the basic ones. It is difficult to see how they could, given the diversity of their backgrounds, concerns and endeavors. Jackie took her responsibilities as a mother very seriously and this dictated that she spend most of her time in New York. Onassis's most time-consuming business concerns were in Greece.

A series of minor disputes brought home to him the fact that his wife had a strong will often at odds with his own. Had it not been for the attentions of the press, such pinpricks might not have assumed such importance. One almost certainly unlooked-for consequence of their marriage was the shedding of the last vestiges of privacy. Not only were there more Jackie-watchers than ever before, they were more ruthless in their methods.[7]

The demands Onassis made upon his women were both complex and self-contradictory. They had to be satisfactory vehicles of self-promotion and, at the same time, adoring females. They had to accept his engulfing protectiveness and yet withstand his massive ego. Jackie was better equipped than most to deal with the man but hopelessly unequal to the problems presented by his family. It could be argued that Jackie fulfilled the contractual obligations implicit in their union. The trouble was that Onassis began to change the rules of the game.[8]

It came to pass, just as others had predicted, despite his bold announcements of husbandly indulgence, that Ari began to realize that Jackie was not the woman for him. "Within a year of the marriage," Gratos reported, "he would come into my office and say, 'My God, what a fool I have made of myself. This woman is a bore. Why didn't I see that before I married her?'" As is often the case when a man becomes disenchanted with a woman without quite knowing why, his bill of particulars was sparse and the items on it were not things that reasonable people would have found insoluble. It was just that everything was somehow wrong. He had publicly encouraged her to spend money to her heart's content and had likewise announced that she could do exactly as she pleased. Now, it seemed, she was to be blamed for doing precisely that.[9] It was almost as if they would have been far better off keeping their love a secret. Now that Ari could actually possess the woman of his dreams, the reality of living with her quickly destroyed the romance. Jackie had been his heart's desire until he had her. It is such a common ending, so disappointing.

Ari was worried about his children and, for the first time in his life, needed the support and strength of a real wife. Both Alexander and Christina perceived Jackie as an interloper who had deflected their father from the cherished possibility of a remarriage to their mother. Jackie was in no position to be supportive of Onassis. In fact, her very existence further complicated the already complex problems of communication between Onassis and his children.[10]

Alexander and Christina hated Jackie. Her arrival in their Father's life was an affront to their self-esteem. Jackie became the enemy. There was nothing she could do right. His children had felt the same way about Maria Callas. The only woman they would accept was their own mother, Tina. Christina referred to Jackie as, "My father's unhappy compulsion."[11] It made for an impossible situation.

"Jackie made the same mistake that Callas did," said Professor Georgakis, perhaps the one man in the Onassis entourage who was close to her. "She ignored the children. Unlike a Greek, she did not view the family as a horizontal entity but as a vertical one, as an American would view it. She didn't realize that in becoming part of the Onassis family, she was expected to develop deep and close relations with Alexander and Christina. She did not attempt to. That, and not the money she spent, was her greatest error. The children hadn't liked Callas and they didn't like Jackie. They saw the marriage as an extension of the same thing, Callas had been wrapped up in herself. In time, Onassis came to share this view."[12]

The children had amusing names for their father's women and toys. Callas was referred to as "the singer" and Jackie was "the geisha." The yacht was called "the tub" and the seaplane which Alexander disliked and mistrusted was "a heap of junk."[13]

About this time Jackie's popularity plummeted as the world appraised this unlikely marriage and critical books and articles were published. Before Jackie married Ari she had received nothing but praise from biographers, historians and memorists. After the marriage she began receiving the abuse. Her marriage put her in the annoying position of no longer being able to criticize people for exploiting the Kennedy tragedies. In marrying Onassis, Jackie had profited from them herself. It is safe to say that if she had not been the widow of the assassinated president, Onassis, the celebrity collector, would not have married her and shared his vast wealth with her.[14] Of course not, it was a package deal right from the get go. Her value lay in her widowhood and the only way to accomplish that and make her available would have been to eliminate Jack. It was such a simple solution but a difficult premise to accept, even now, for most people.

The marriage, according to Jacqueline's recounting to certain Bouvier relatives, worked until the death of Onassis's son, Alexander, in an air accident in January 1973. After that tragic event the marriage turned sour. A dispirited Onassis began regretting he had not married a younger woman who could have given him another son. He told Jackie that she was "bad luck." He could be a cruel and vulgar man.[15]

Alexander's death destroyed Onassis. It was a blow from which he would never recover, and Jackie would bear the brunt of the blame. Although Ari would never reveal his true feelings, his actions in the aftermath of his son's death tell us more than either Jackie or Ari would ever want the world to know. Possibly the guilt over what Ari had done to Joe Kennedy's son must have convinced Ari that he was being punished by the gods. For this he would blame Jackie and, in doing so, would reject her. His love changed to hate. He hated himself for being seduced by her and probably for ordering the murder of JFK. It was the worst time of their marriage. Jackie was evidently upset by the dark passion which stirred within the Onassis family, both because of its intensity and because it made her feel like the outsider. Her instinct was to bury pain and the Onassis instinct was to let it rip. This was hardly Jackie's fault, but it did not prevent Onassis from venting his feelings of frustration on his wife. His fury towards her was as vehement as his earlier generosity. "My God, what a fool I have made of myself," he told friends when asked about his wife. He felt he had been deluded and the realization was painful. He asserted that Jackie was "coldhearted and shallow." He felt cheated in his marriage and betrayed by his family. He seriously began to believe that his luck had deserted him.[16]

The loss of Alexander was the defining moment in Aristotle Onassis's life. On January 22, 1973, his beloved son who had exacted the pledge from his father not to nag him about his flying, was killed in an air crash shortly after he took off from Athens airport in a twin-engine amphibian Piaggio. Alexander was not flying the plane. Ari and Jackie who were in New York at the time rushed to the Athens hospital where they found that Alexander could survive only as a living vegetable. The next day, mercifully for him, Alexander died of a massive brain hemorrhage.

Onassis was devastated. The two patriarchs, Joe Kennedy and Aristotle Onassis, who had reveled in the making of money by crushing others, were crushed themselves by the deaths of their sons. Joe Kennedy could shut himself in his room at the big house on Cape Cod after his eldest son was killed in an air crash over the English Channel during World War II, listening for hours to symphonic music. Aristotle Onassis wept for days, cancelled all appointments and never again regained his zest for life, for love and for the acquisition of more wealth.[17] The only thing the two men had in common was their ability to blame others for their loss. Joe blamed FDR for getting us into a war that he opposed and Ari blamed Jackie. His obsession with her had caused him the loss of his son.

By 1973, the five year old marriage was unraveling at the seams. Ari complained about Jackie's indifference, her excessive spending and her hard outer crust. He even hired a private investigator to search for evidence of Jackie's infidelity. Said Stassinopoulos, Ari's friend, "His body had turned against itself and Onassis viciously turned against the woman whom he now irrationally considered the source of his accumulated woes."[18] What no one could know was that Ari was not being irrational. In his mind the crime they had committed together, which he could tell no one, was the reason his son had died. He was being punished and he deeply regretted the day he first laid eyes on Jacqueline Kennedy.

Onassis's grief was so extreme that at first he refused to bury Alexander. It was not altogether clear what he wanted instead. "In moments of tragedy," says Professor Georgakis, "a volatile character swings into unforeseen dimensions of illogic." His impression was that Onassis wanted the body "deep frozen," organically preserved against the day when brain surgery was sufficiently advanced to restore Alexander to life. In the end, Professor Georgakis, playing Antigone to Onassis' unwitting Creon, was impelled to write his friend an impassioned letter protesting that he had no right to dispose of the soul of his son in this way. Even in this, so ingrained was the habit and so instinctive the reaction, Onassis haggled. He would consent to the burial, but only if it were inside the chapel on Skorpios. The church would not allow it, since it was a privilege reserved for saints. A compromise was found. Alexander was buried beside the chapel, and an annex was later built to cover the grave.[19]

Now Ari entered into the most restless and unhappy time of his life. His son's death caused him to suffer a nervous breakdown. His grief was so overwhelming that it left him immobilized. Letitia Baldridge, Jackie's dear friend, recalls that Jackie and Ari had a falling out when Ari's personality changed after the death of Alexander. Greeks are very fate orientated and he felt that it was a curse upon himself when his only son perished. He unfairly and unconsciously blamed Jackie, and so it became inevitable for the marriage not to work.[20] It is a nice attempt by a close friend of Jackie's to explain away the reason Ari turned against her. No one would ever suspect the real reason.

Onassis was certain that the crash was no accident. The Athens rumor mill was busy and each rumor was more bizarre than the last. He was so convinced sabotage was the cause that he offered a million dollars to anyone who could prove it. It was murder, of course. The CIA had done it. The plane had been sabotaged in revenge for the death of his enemies, the Kouris brothers. Niarchos had done it for envy. Jackie had done it for reasons of her own. The theories were numerous.[21]

Onassis would give half a million to the informants and another half a million to the charity of their choice. Ari was trying to make a deal with the gods. He desperately felt that if someone had killed his son perhaps it would lessen his own guilt. He suspected others because it was the way he himself operated. Like JFK, Ari had many enemies and if someone could get to the President surely his son would be an easy target. If he could commit a perfect crime, others could do the same. As expected after a lengthy investigation, the report, that is still top secret, did little to clarify matters. The belief in sabotage and his blaming Jackie would be the only way Ari could carry on.

The most important human being in the world for Onassis was his only son, Alexander. For a Greek, any Greek, a son is a significant portion of himself. The fishing boat is built, the house is bought, the vines are sown, not just for the immediate needs of the family but for the future of the son. The son is a man's guarantee of immortality. For Onassis, with so much to bequeath and with an ego so overpowering, his son represented his own imperishable destiny.[22] That summer Onassis spent more time than usual on Skorpios. The trees, shrubs and flowers his ships had brought from all parts of the world were especially luxuriant. To his guests Onassis seemed almost his usual self, a considerate host and a skilled conversationalist. His relationship with Christina seemed much improved. His personal charm remained undiminished. For all his gregariousness, Onassis remained secretive about his emotions. He never spoke of his grief, though his suffering was plain enough. His insomnia became acute. Where in the past he had stayed up all night out of pleasure, he now would drink ouzo and sing the nostalgic Spanish and Greek songs that he loved. When there was no one around, he roamed the island alone, waiting for the dawn. He would spend much of the night outside the chapel sitting by the tomb of his son.

When he went to New York, he spent much of his time sitting in Gratos' office, talking about the past. "He really did not want to live," recalled Gratos. "He felt cheated and he blamed himself for having been cheated. He felt responsible for Alexander's death. But there was no self-pity. There was an extraordinary degree of stoicism in the way he took everything."[23] It was as if he knew why he was being punished and this sorrow visited upon him certainly fit the crime he and Jackie had committed together. He could have very easily felt a kinship to Adam in the Garden of Eden who had been tempted so similarly by Eve. As he was being banished from paradise, so too would he banish Jackie from his life.

Christina Onassis had her own demons to fight during this time. The loss of her brother devastated her and was soon followed by the tragic death of her mother, Tina. Tina's sudden demise was unexpected and rather mysterious. In his biography of Jackie Onassis, author Stephen Birmingham correctly gauges Christina's reaction. "Some superstitious strain out of her Smyrna peasant past suggested to Christina that some sinister force had to be connected with all these deaths in her family. It must be Jackie who was bringing all the bad luck to the family, undermining everything as her brother had predicted. To Christina it seemed as though Jackie killed every life she touched. She was the Angel of Death. This terrible conviction was all the more powerful because by then, Christina could see that her father was also dying."[24]

Her feelings would be validated by Ari who was now determined to push Jackie out of his life. Jackie was their curse and she was destroying their family just as she had destroyed the Kennedys. Although Ari could not share with Christina his own sordid involvement, he could understand his punishment because of his relationship with Jackie. She was the evil one and he was just another one of her victims. He had come under her spell and he cursed his family's fate at her hands.

"Christina was also highly distraught," confirmed Costa Gratos. "She felt Jackie was somehow to blame. Death was never very far from 'The Black Widow' as Christina now called her. Jackie was the world's most inveterate bystander to tragedy, just witness John and Robert Kennedy. Christina feared Jackie. She felt she had magical powers. Everyone around her had perished."[25]

Jackie's Greek in-laws did not want to have anything to do with her. Nor did they even want her around. She was banished from their life. Her hopes for a future with Ari in abundant wealth were lessening day by day. She knew he would never divorce her, but his disenchantment would play out in other ways. Jackie seemed more uncomfortable than ever on Skorpios. Guests sensed that she tried to be suitably hospitable, but her efforts showed and were not appreciated. She much preferred being alone. She would occasionally attempt to join in but she couldn't carry it off. The British diplomat, Sir John Russell, a Skorpios regular, thought the problem was social. "There was nobody there who had much in common with her, nobody she could be perfectly relaxed with."[26] Her season in the sun was coming to an end sooner than she ever expected. Jamie Auchincloss recalls, "I think everybody tried to make it work. It was just, so to speak, that there wasn't enough love to go around. It was a Greek tragedy."[27]

As the old Greeks might have said, it was a union ill begun, touched by the element of improbable and now sinister melodrama that Aristotle

Onassis seemed to carry with him wherever he went. The great house shadowed by a statesman's murder, the vulnerable heroine, the arrival of the interloper, and the inept young Cassandra who would not have been heeded even if she had been more skilled at her work of prophecy.[28]

In January 1974, they made their last trip together to Acapulco. It was not a happy expedition. Jackie had expressed a desire for a house in Acapulco. Ari did not want a house there and resented what he presumed to be Jackie's motives in asking for one. There were arguments on the ground and in the Lear jet on the way back to New York. He saw it as more of the same old thing, more needless extravagance, another attack on his wallet and he told her as much. As it happened, he was not the only one who had reached the end of a personal tether. Jackie screamed that she had given up her reputation to marry him, which was true. She had signed away her rights, which was also true. Furthermore she did not want any of his goddamn money which was, and would prove to be, debatable.[29]

It was in this acid mood that he wrote his last will on board the plane. Greek law is punctilious on the question of wills. They must be written out in the hand of the legator to avoid any suspicion of senility.[30]

Onassis was still scribbling when the plane landed in West Palm Beach for refueling. Jackie and Ari were seen in the airport coffee shop eating BLTs. Their sociable snack was a smoke screen for the benefit of the public. As soon as they returned to the plane, Onassis picked up where he had left off. "My yacht, the *Christina,* if my daughter and wife so wish, they can keep for their personal use." A separate clause made the same stipulation with regard to Skorpios. In both cases, the yacht as well as the island, he allotted Jackie one-quarter ownership rights, the remaining 75 percent to his daughter.[31] Ari's will adhered to the financial conditions set forth in Ari's prenuptial agreement with Jackie. It constituted the minimum he could possibly leave Jackie.[32]

In 1974, Ari was diagnosed as suffering from myasthenia gravis, a disease that causes abnormal fatigue. Often the most affected muscles involve the eyes. Onassis had to use tape on his eyelids to keep them from shutting. Although he wore dark glasses, the media soon discovered his illness. He was flown to Paris aboard a specially equipped Olympic Airways jet, and admitted to the American hospital on the outskirts of Paris. By this time the hostility between Jackie and Christina had escalated to the point where neither spoke to the other. Both would visit Ari at his hospital room and ignore each other. He would talk to his daughter in Greek and to Jackie in French. On March 10th, doctors told Jackie she could safely leave for the United States for a few days. She spoke to the hospital on March 14th and was told that Onassis was in stable condition. Later that night he went into a sharp decline and died the next morning. Three days later, Jackie buried her second husband on Skorpios next to his beloved son, Alexander.[33]

When she first heard the news of his death, Jackie made two phone calls. The first to Ted Kennedy who would be a sturdy ally in the inevitable battle over her share of Onassis' estate. True to form the second call she made was to the designer, Valentino. Jackie needed a new black dress to wear to the funeral.[34]

After the funeral Jacqueline issued a statement to the press that probably contained a morsel of truth. "Aristotle Onassis rescued me at a moment when my life was engulfed in shadows. He meant a lot to me. He brought me into a world where one could find both happiness and love. We lived through many beautiful experiences together which cannot be forgotten, and for which I will be eternally grateful."[35] What she could not say for public consumption but what she must have thought was thank God, I am free at last. Now there would be no other living soul who would know their secret. She was completely safe. She had known all along that Ari would never betray her since to do so would expose his own involvement. He would never do that intentionally. But it was worrisome, as he grew closer to his own death, that he might wish to purge himself and make a deathbed confession in hopes of saving his soul. The good news was that he didn't care to save his soul, only to escape this life, a life with unlimited potential filled with unlimited sorrow.

The death of Aristotle Onassis began an ugly series of lawsuits that eventually made Jackie a very wealthy woman. Surprising everyone, Ari left half his estate to the establishment of a charitable foundation in memory of Alexander Onassis. This was very likely due to Jackie's influence. Or it could have been done to make sure Jackie didn't get at it. His will written on the Lear jet returning to New York contained a stipulation that Jackie would lose her inheritance if she contested his will.[36]

Prior to his death, when the *New York Times* ran a story confirming Ari's intention to divorce his wife, Jackie became violently upset and called Chrisitna to deny the report, threatening to cause trouble if she didn't. Christina issued a statement which, while it proved totally false, mollified Jackie. "Miss Christina Onassis is very much distressed at the distorted stories and speculations that appeared in the international press about her father and Mrs. Jacqueline Onassis. These stories are totally untrue and she repudiates them. In fact, the marriage of the late Mr. Onassis and Mrs. Jacqueline Onassis was a happy marriage and all rumors of intended divorce are untrue. Her relationship with Mrs. Onassis was always and still is based on mutual friendship and respect. There are no financial or other disputes separating them."[37] This statement is such a fairy tale that it could be another version of Camelot. It was such a total crock that one can only wonder what Jackie must have threatened Christina with for her to agree to make this statement. Perhaps Christina did not relish the thought of a blood-bath lawsuit in the future. Or maybe Jackie even threatened to expose the darker side of Ari that no one knew about. At this point Jackie could say anything about her former husband and everyone would believe it. After his death, Ari could not defend himself and no one could that prove Jackie's accusations were all lies. Also Christina must have heard the truth about the Onassis marriage and fell into line for public consumption.

The harmony did not last long. Jackie and the stepdaughter she claimed to love jumped right into a bitter legal dispute. The gist of the battle centered around an interpretation of the will Ari had written in anger returning from Mexico. Jackie's attorney hoped to overthrow the document on the grounds that it was invalid. Greek law ordains that a last testament be composed in a single sitting in a single location. Onassis had interrupted the composition of the will to have lunch in the airport coffee shop and an airplane while airborne doesn't technically qualify as "a place." By invalidating the document according to Greek law Jackie would be entitled to 12.5 percent or $125 million of Ari's estimated billion-dollar estate.

Jackie appeared to hold all the cards due to this technicality in Greek law. Anticipating a protracted court fight and not wanting to further alienate Ted Kennedy since the Onassis empire still needed influential friends in Washington, Christina's advisors offered Jackie $20 million. With this offer, Jackie must relinquish all further claims on the estate including her one-quarter share in both Skorpios and the *Christina*. Taking into account the prenuptial payment, monthly allowance, jewelry and other gifts, clothes and travel that Jackie grossed for the period of her marriage, it came to more than $42 million. Jackie had earned nearly $7 million per year for each year they were married.[38] She had done quite well for herself. Both BlackJack and Janet could be very proud of their little girl.

Everyone was not happy for Jackie. Some were openly critical of this blatant attempt to collect more money than she had originally agreed upon when she married Ari. "Inexplicably, I feel sad...disillusioned if you will...about Jacqueline Kennedy," wrote Harriet Van Horn, the noted newspaper columnist. "With $26 million, Christina Onassis bought off her stepmother's threatened lawsuit, and Jackie bought herself another black eye in the public prints. It ought to disturb us that we suddenly see little green snakes of greed in Jackie's free-flowing hair. No doubt about it, we have idolized her overmuch. A betrayed wife and a gallant widow, she was transfigured in the light of President Kennedy's funeral tapers....I do not see virtue, or even sport, in wrestling $26 million from the corpse of the husband who was never the darling of your heart. Jackie will be grist for the mills of novelists and dramatists down through the ages."[39] The myth makes for great drama without anyone ever guessing what might be the real truth behind this facade of a sanitized life for public consumption.

The settlement afforded Jackie security and peace of mind. It gave Christina the assurance that she would never need to see her stepmother again. Their financial agreement stipulated that neither Jackie nor Christina could discuss the terms of the final settlement. Without mentioning the monetary aspect, Christina did talk about Jackie not long before the end of her life in 1988. "I don't like to talk about Jackie Kennedy," she said. "She is the most mercenary person I have ever met. She thinks, talks and dreams of nothing but money. What she doesn't realize is that I would have given her fifty times what I gave her for the pleasure of never having to see her again. I would have paid any price. What amazes me is that she survives while everybody around her drops dead. She's dangerous, she's deadly. She has decimated at least two families, the Kennedys and mine. If I never see her again as long as I live it will be too soon."[40]

This was quite an astounding comment for Christina to make publicly. One can see how Christina would feel that Jackie had destroyed the Onassis family, but the part where she slips in the destruction of the Kennedys leaves us to wonder what could she have been talking about. After all we know that the official Kennedy version makes Jackie out to be a survivor-saint. How could Jackie have hurt the Kennedys and how would Christina know this? Perhaps Jackie and Ari's secret had been revealed along the way but Christina would never reveal her father's involvement in anything so despicable as murder.

No one could ever argue with Christina's description of Jackie as the Angel of Death. The Onassis union was a marriage made in hell. The Black Widow had survived over the Scorpion but they had been worthy compatriots and then even worthier opponents. Their marriage dance was over. By his union with Jackie, Ari had received the same gift of immortality that had been given to Jack Kennedy. Only he would be forever known as Jackie's unsuitable second husband, an epitaph he would not have chosen for himself.

Perhaps Jackie will be kinder,
in her version of events to be released in 2044.

NINETEEN

*How did Jackie ensure
her place in history?*

THE CREATIVE HISTORY

*T*HERE WAS NOTHING NOW TO KEEP JACKIE IN Europe. Ari and Jackie had not lived happily ever after together. Their marriage ended horribly and the entire world knew it, but Jackie now had more money then she ever dreamed possible. It was all hers. She would never have to answer to any man again. Nor would she ever walk in any man's shadow again. She was truly a woman of independent means. This wealth was the answer to her quest for the meaning of life. She was finally safe and secure enough to find her own happiness and to become the person she always knew existed deep inside her. As for leaving Greece, she had no choice since in her final settlement with Christina, Jackie had signed off her 25% ownership of the island of Skorpios and the yacht, the *Christina.*

Jackie had truly grown to love Greece and she had cultivated an appreciation of all things Greek. It had started out as a way to please Onassis, but Jackie had became enchanted with the culture and history of Greece and the ambience on Skorpios. She would always treasure her fond memories, but there had been bad times too. She would leave it all behind knowing that her secret pact with Ari remained safely hidden from the entire world. Even at their worst, they had not betrayed each other. With

all his talk of divorcing Jackie, he never did it. He knew they would be
bound together for all time and eternity by their crime. It would bind them
in a way far stronger than marriage vows or promises. Neither one would
ever be rid of the other. They would take their secret with them to their
graves.

For Ari, it was all over. For Jackie, it was just beginning. She
would now return home. She had rushed into the waiting eager arms of
Aristotle Onassis who would save and protect her from the enemy . . .
America. It was time to make peace with the enemy. This would not be
easy for Jackie since the memory of her departure was still fresh in
everyone's minds. Caroline and John, Jr., had gone to school in the states
and it was their home. Jackie knew that for their sake she must put on a
good show. She would once again become the beloved, revered widow.

Going home would be a difficult journey for Jackie. Many Americans still felt the way Pete Hamill did about her when he wrote his column
for the *New York Post* when she married Onassis. "Many marriages are
put together the same way as the Jackie-Ari deal," he wrote. "Although
the brutally commercial nature of the contract is often disguised with romantic notions about love and time. Some women can be bought with a
guarantee of ham and eggs in the morning and a roof over their head,
others with a mink coat on the anniversary of the sealing of the contract...

"If it were possible to see the Aristotle Onassis -Jackie Kennedy
story as a novel, instead of a rather tedious serial, we could understand
Onassis' motives in light of what we know: a man in a long squalid feud
with his arch-rival, Stavos Niarchos, using his money and prestige to un-
dermine his business success, finally buying one of the few reigning international objects, the unapproachable widow of a slain prince, buying her
the way another might buy a Lear jet. But understanding Jackie Kennedy
is a more complicated matter. She spent part of her adult life hidden behind
the Kennedy publicity machine. She spent another crucial part, after the
murder of her husband, enshrined as some national object of veneration......

"She was not, of course, the victim of that veneration, she encouraged it, indulged it, created the desire for more knowledge by cultivating the image of aloofness. The price of an art object increases in direct ratio to its rarity.....

"Most American women understand that men often think of them only as objects. Some fight against the assumption, and carve out a position on the battlefield where a contest or a peace treaty is at least possible. Many others simply accept, some become glorified hostesses, laying the table for their men, others barter their sex and their presence for rewards. In a world in which men have most of the power and money, many women must use guile, intelligence or feigned submission to exist.....

"It is outrageous to think that someone will spend $120,000 a year on clothing in a world where so few people have no more than the clothes on their back. It is obscene that a woman would have more money in a month to use on applying paste to her face and spray to her hair than the average citizen of Latin America could earn in 100 years..."[1]

This column, written when Jackie originally left America to marry Ari, was not published until Jackie was back in the states a new widow and now dating Pete Hamill. Although it was meant to embarrass, it still accurately expressed what many Americans felt about Mrs. Onassis that "No courtesan....ever sold herself for more."[2]

It would be extremely difficult to resuscitate the love felt for her by many prior to her marriage. But she was determined to return to her role as an American icon. With her new wealth, Jackie believed she could do this. But this time it would all be on her terms. It was time for Jackie to write the final chapters of the Camelot history. Her image had been tarnished by her marriage to Onassis and the newly-acquired wealth was a bit much for the average American to comprehend. Jackie would have to quickly get rid of her cut-throat image and become what everyone remembered, still another role for Jackie, the consummate actress, to play. It would be an easy assignment since she had originated the role. This was a role of a lifetime and one that Jackie was born to play. Although she had been forced to marry well in order to survive, the truth was that she did not need to be married. She didn't like the restrictions it had imposed on her during both of her very short marriages. She would be much happier alone with just her money and her children to keep her company.

Jackie returned to America with a well thought out game plan. She would execute the Bouvier philosophy of not giving the public too much in order to keep them wanting more. It was the same basic strategy she had learned at her father's knee. After she had been named debutante-of-the-year , Jacqueline did not just play hard to get.....she was impossible to get. Her father had written her many times to remember that it was "fatal" to make herself seem "available". "Always keep them guessing," he would tell her.[3] Now Jackie would play hard to get with the entire country.

The commonly held belief is that Jacqueline Kennedy Onassis was a woman of unfathomable mystery. She herself fostered that opinion by cultivating a Mona Lisa image, never revealing what lay beneath her enigmatic smile. The events of her life have shown that she was not a complex puzzle at all.[4] In any given situation Jackie's behavior could be predicted if only one factor was considered. How did this event pertain to Jackie's financial situation? If it was a financially smart move, then Jackie would do it. This is obviously a trait that she has passed on to her magazine publishing son, John, Jr., when we witness his cover spoof of Drew Barrymore as Marilyn Monroe singing "Happy Birthday" to his father at Madison Square Garden in his magazine, *George,* or when he publicly criticizes his Kennedy cousins in order to sell more magazines.

Anything that would create more money in Jackie's life was appropriate. She taught John, Jr. well, as he was quoted, "I don't see what possible taste questions could be involved. If I don't find it tasteless, I don't know why anyone would. Just because people have clucked for decades, why does this make it strange that we would use that bit of iconography?"

If it was anything that would cost her money, Jackie was not interested. She had sacrificed too much of herself to just give away her hard earned money.

Jackie now had the luxury of being able to pick, choose and

control how she would market herself this time around. Although some segments of society weren't interested in Jackie's return, her American public was in general thrilled to have her back where she belonged. Not many had been excited about her relationship with Onassis. Everyone still wanted to remember their beautiful, beloved, weeping widow lady. She had done an incredible job of rewriting history with her Camelot fairytale. It would be easy for her to step back into her role and take her place once again on the American stage.

In order to downplay her incredible wealth, Jackie deliberately chose a very low key, understated lifestyle in New York City. She would become a New Yorker like no other New Yorker ever. She would make New York her passion. As Frank Sinatra serenades us in his famous lyrics, "If you can make it there, you can make it anywhere!"

Thus New York became her "kind of town" and she chose a high profile cause when she became the champion of architecture. "I am passionate about architecture," Jackie once said. "We are the only country in the world that trashes its old buildings. Too late we realize how very much we need them." As a trustee of the Municipal Art Society, Jackie became a full-fledged activist. When she learned of plans to erect two towers, one that was to be 925 feet high, at the southwest corner of Central Park, she became enraged at what she saw as the latest symptom of developer greed and excess. The traffic the structure would attract would clog the streets and dirty the air. She took on one of the largest development partnerships in the city and was so successful in applying legal and community pressure that the partners abandoned the project in 1993.

Although it was a designated landmark, the splendid Grand Central Terminal was threatened in 1968 by the owner of the Terminal and a developer, who wanted to acquire the air space above the Terminal for a fifty-three story office tower. Jackie became involved in 1977, taking her cause to the streets. She worked on the project full-time and in 1978 the Supreme Court of the United States ruled that the Terminal's air space must remain clear.

Two years later Jackie learned of a proposal to raze St. Bartholomew's Episcopalian Church on Lexington Avenue and Fiftieth Street to make way for a fifty-nine story office tower. Jackie quickly mobilized and formed the Committee To Save St. Bart's which she co-chaired with writer Brendan Gill. Jackie lobbied legislators and Governor Mario Cuomo to designate the church a landmark and spoke before a joint session of the New York Senate and Assembly. In 1991, the project was abandoned after the U.S. Supreme Court refused to hear the constitutional appeal for the developers.[5]

It is interesting to note that Jackie's three most important crusades in which she played a major role were about architecture. Her passion was about buildings not people. She cared more about terminals, churches and coliseum sites than the poor, needy or underprivileged. Jackie was very good at picking causes that would give her maximum exposure she could completely control with the minimum expense of her own personal finances. She was very good at getting other people to donate to her causes without having to do so herself. Her money was for keeping, not giving. She had worked and sacrificed far too much to get her own financial independence to just give it away. Jackie was very busy at all sorts of great causes just as long as it didn't cost her anything.

In order to fit in to the daily life of New York, Jackie decided to go back to work. It seems that she finally got tired of just shopping and wanted to do something that would give the appearance of productivity and creativity. A job would also give the impression that she was just a normal intelligent woman doing sensitive, meaningful work. For the sixteen years leading up to her death, Jackie worked for Doubleday Publishers, first as an associate editor and later as a senior editor. She edited an average of twelve books a year including many best sellers.

In 1975 she had begun her career at Viking. However she resigned two years later after Viking published a political thriller that contained an assassination attempt on Ted Kennedy. She also edited many celebrities' books. Jackie could recruit all sorts of writers who were thrilled to be working with her and using her name on their works as their editor. Of course, Jackie could never be just another editor. Her assistant at Viking claims that she habitually shredded her memos to keep them from falling into the hands of trivia seekers.[6]

Jackie's entrance into the work force was not without its problems. Her secretary at Viking despised her and felt demeaned having to take her personal messages and type her letters. Others were polite on the surface, but there was an unspoken feeling that Jackie was not to be taken seriously, that this job was merely a toy for her amusement. She was gently rebuffed in an editorial meeting when she suggested a coloring book based on architectural ruins.[7]

Jackie worked hard to achieve a delicate balance between power and celebrity. She knew full well that she had the former, which she believed, quite correctly, was essential to helping her achieve her goals. Her social life was not nearly as hectic as it was in the earlier years.[8] She deliberately cultivated a low profile. As she maintained discretion in all areas of her public life, it was crucial for Jackie to align herself back within the Kennedy fold. She supported Sargent Shriver's ill-fated run for the presidency in 1976 and even contributed $25,000 to his campaign. She supported a textile factory in Bedford-Stuyvesant area of Brooklyn because the project had meant so much to Robert Kennedy. She appeared at the ground-breaking of the John F. Kennedy Memorial Library in Massachusetts. She acted as an honorary chairman of a benefit at the Kennedy Center in Washington and surprised many by showing up. She changed her legal residence to Hyannis Port after Onassis' death.[9]

The JFK Memorial Library became a main focus of Jackie's interest, for this memorial would be the crowning achievement of her role in Camelot. She was active in every phase of the library's planning and execution. The library was her biggest priority and she gave it her *carte blanche* attention. This shrine to JFK would serve to enhance his memory and create a continuation of her rewriting of history. The Kennedy Library would give out the official Kennedy family version of all events, and Jackie would have complete control, exactly what she wanted.

Prior to the long-awaited dedication of the library, Jackie took time to have a little plastic surgery. She was fifty and even though she looked considerably younger, she felt it was time to have some work done on her eyes. The first public event she attended following her eye-lift was on October 20, 1979, for the dedication of the John F. Kennedy Presidential Library in Boston. [10] Needless to say, she looked fabulous.

When architect I.M. Pei's sweeping, heroic structure of concrete and glass was unveiled, it was truly Kennedyesque. Facing the ocean, like the homes Jack had loved, the building had something almost nautical about it, something yearning to be seaborne. After the assassination, Jackie decided that the Kennedy Library should be "more than just another Presidential Library." So it was built away from Cambridge on a spit of land at Columbia Point, more epic in scope. [11]

The hardest part of reentering the Kennedy circle again was the prospect of dealing with all the revelations about JFK's love life that were now surfacing everywhere. This was particularly painful because of her children. "The thing I care most about is the happiness of my children," she said. [12] Jackie made her children very aware of who they were. Both cherished their Kennedy name and the fact that they were the children of the late President . . . the heirs of Camelot. They had no material need that could not be satisfied. The trust funds established by Jack Kennedy and the Onassis settlement, made both Caroline and JFK, Jr., millionaires before they were 21 years old. [13] Due mainly to their mother's priorities, they were set for life. Jackie's main goal was to leave her children independently wealthy so they would never have to endure what she had gone through as a child and then as an adult. Just as she had been taught by her mother, so did she teach her children the value of money. It was her main mission in life to secure her fortune for her children. There would be no foundations or charitable works on the agenda for this branch of the Kennedy family.

As the wife of John F. Kennedy, Jackie became bitter and disillusioned but as the mother of his children she tried to consecrate his memory. She told close friends she would have paid any amount to suppress the revelations that came out in later years regarding the late President's private life. "They have been more painful to her as a mother than as a wife," said Jamie Auchincloss. "Each time a book or an article appears about one of Jack's mistresses, Jackie must tell Caroline and John that their father loved her and she loved him and they must love him too," he said. "It's excruciating for her, but she's powerless to do anything about it. Everyone in the family has had to deny the stories because Jackie does not want her children to remember that side of him. She says it has nothing to do with his role as their father. She has been successful in this deception because I don't think the children believe anything they have ever read about Kennedy's other women."

The late President's friends and former aides also conspired to protect his children from the assaults on his life. When Judith Campbell Exner was revealed in senate testimony to be one of the many women who knew Kennedy intimately in the White House, Kenny O'Donnell, Evelyn Lincoln and Dave Powers publicly denied any knowledge of her, although each had arranged her visits with the President. "The only Campbell I know is Campbell soup," said Dave Powers. Powers later privately admitted to Mrs. Exner's biographer that he did indeed know who she was, but he could never make such an admission publicly because he would lose his job as Director of the JFK Memorial Library.[14] The wrath of 'The Widow' was still feared by many JFK loyalists.

In order to occasionally escape New York, Jackie needed a place to enjoy some rest and relaxation. Jackie decided to build herself a 19-room cape cod-style mansion on 375 acres of oceanfront property on Martha's Vineyard. Jackie loved her new home that cost her approximately $3.5 million to build. It was good to see her spend her money for a change rather than hoard it as she was prone to do now that she was wealthy.

Among Jacqueline's first and most frequent visitors on Martha's Vineyard was Maurice Tempelsman. A somewhat elusive though politically powerful figure, Templesman had known Jackie for years . . . first as a friend, later as her financial advisor and now as her beau and companion. In Maurice, it seemed she had finally found the equilibrium and peace of mind she had so long sought and failed to find in either of her marriages.

At first glance, Tempelsman appeared to be an unlikely companion for Jackie. Born into an Orthodox Jewish family in Antwerp, Belgium, in 1929 (the same year as Jackie), his family fled Europe in 1940 to escape the Nazi onslaught. Maurice's current empire includes mining interests, diamond and mineral sales, the world's second largest petroleum corporation and a sprawling network of related concerns.[15]

Maurice's friendship with Jackie dated to the late 1950s during the Kennedy years. Maurice and his wife, Lily, were frequent guests at the White House. They had attended the gala dinner for the Pakistani President that the Kennedys gave at Mount Vernon.

For all his considerable accomplishments and wealth, Maurice Tempelsman struck many people as nothing more than a "poor man's Aristotle Onassis." Like Onassis, he was short, portly, older looking than his actual years. Both men smoked Dunhill cigars and collected rare art (such as Jacqueline Bouvier). Both men were financial wizards. Their other common denominator was a shared love of the sea.[16] It was clearly a replay of the Onassis relationship in that each had something the other wanted and could appreciate. Maurice admired Jackie and having her on his arm would give him an incredible sense of fulfillment. She was a jewel to admire, and he of all people knew the value of fine collectibles. As for Jackie, Maurice would fit perfectly her profile of an ideal man. First, he was incredibly wealthy. Secondly, he would be able to help her maintain and control her own wealth. His knowledge of money and investments would make him her dream man come true.

For Jackie her relationships were always based on some sort of money connection. "You can be sure Maurice Tempelsman gives Jackie lots of presents," said Truman Capote. "What's more, Jackie has made money on the basis of Tempelsman's advice on when to buy and sell in the volatile silver and gold markets. Girls like Jackie don't change."[17]

Of course not, Jackie would be able to use Maurice not only as her financial advisor, his most important function in her life, but also as her friend, confidante and lover. Jackie had no need ever again to have a husband. Now that she was independently wealthy, all she really needed was a man to advise her on how to preserve her wealth for her children. Maurice was also very good at staying in the background, necessary since his wife would not give him a divorce. They separated and remained on friendly terms but are still married, which was even better for Jackie since this would eliminate even a slim possibility of marriage. Jackie was growing to love her independence and her rich and famous lifestyle. She neither needed nor desired marriage in order to feel complete.

Maurice gave her complete peace of mind. Husbands did not always treat her the way she deserved. Maurice worshipped her but did not dominate her. They were equals.[18]

For Jackie everything was perfect. Caroline had married Edwin Schlossberg and soon made Jackie a grandmother which completely delighted her. She was sitting on top of the world. Her son, John, was incredibly handsome and so far not ready to marry. Perhaps he knew that finding someone who would please both Jackie and himself would be a rather difficult task.

If Jacqueline's days seemed more tranquil, if she managed to attain a self-confidence and softness she had previously lacked, she continued to deal harshly with anyone she felt had betrayed her. She never forgave her half-brother, Jamie Auchincloss, for having talked to Kitty Kelley when she wrote her version of Jackie's life. "It's impossible to be related to somebody as famous as Jacqueline Onassis," said Jamie in his own defense. "After talking to Kelley, they didn't talk very much anymore," relates Auchincloss. "I ended up writing her a letter of apology."[19] It didn't help mend their strained relationship. Jackie's cousin, John Davis, whose family portraits of the Bouviers and Kennedys annoyed Jackie immensely, received similar treatment. "That didn't bother me at all," said Davis. "What

did disturb me was that she also punished my mother."[20]   As for Gore
Vidal, her step-sibling, she stopped speaking to him. It was mutual with
them since neither would ever acknowledge the other anyway.

People wondered if Jackie had really changed or if they had simply
imagined a change. In 1986, she reduced her work load at Doubleday to
three half-days a week. She spent nearly as much time at the beauty parlor
on facials and comb-outs as she did at the office. She remained in psycho-
therapy once a week, having switched to a new $150 per session Park
Avenue practitioner.[21] Jackie particularly enjoyed her sessions talking to
professionals who were bound by the strict code of confidentiality.

As she was getting ready to grow older, Jackie was still determined
to protect her version of Camelot. She traveled to Cambridge, Massachusetts, for the dedication of a park to John F. Kennedy on what would have
been the late President's 70th birthday, but she refused to allow the JFK
Center for the performing arts in conjunction with ABC television to present
a filmed retrospective as a remembrance of the 25th year since the assassination. The Kennedy family was otherwise eager to participate, but Jackie's
voice carried more weight than theirs.[22]

This was not the time to let her guard down. There was already too
much about her life with Jack out there in the public domain floating
around waiting to embarrass her and possibly expose her. There were so
many lies, deceptions, cover-ups that she could not risk the possible exposure of her involvement lest it lead to other questions, questions she was not
prepared to answer or even listen to. The Kennedy official version of
events was all sugar coated lies. The marriage, the assassination, the Warren Commission, Camelot, the cover-ups . . . none of these events needed
any more scrutiny. So far the American public was quite accepting and
docile. We consumed only what Jackie was willing to serve up. She didn't
need any unnecessary or awkward questions at this stage of the game.

Jackie sealed her personal papers and her versions of events till the
year 2044. Now why would she do that? The only logical reason is to keep
something hidden from her children. There is something Jackie did not

want her children to know about. It certainly couldn't be that their Father was a womanizer since they can read and hear about their Dad's love life anytime they go past a newsstand, buy a copy of *George,* or turn on the television. In this era of total public scrutiny, Jackie's children already know more about their parents than anyone would want to know. It is doubtful in this day of total exposure that even they bought their mother's revisionist history.

It would make one wonder, what could be so secret,

that their mother must hide it from her own children?

TWENTY

How does a woman who had it all go quietly into the night?

THE LAST WORD

AS JACKIE APPROACHED THE FINAL YEARS OF her life, she ever so subtly distanced herself from the Kennedy clan. She never did like them or the life that they forced her to live. She married into the family to better her station in life. Both her marriages were stepping stones to acquiring her wealth. For Jackie it was always about money. Now that she had her own money there was no longer a need for her to be a Kennedy. She cared little about what any of them did or aimed to do in politics. She felt no obligation whatsoever to any of them.

Jackie always grimaced every time she had to go to the Cape or the Kennedy mansion in Palm Beach. There was always too much activity for her taste, too much emphasis on the physical and so little on the cultural. She never understood the Kennedy women who were not of her world of quiet sophistication and they, in turn, never accepted her. They were clam chowder, she was lobster bisque.

Among the Kennedy women, Ethel Kennedy was the ringleader of the anti-Jackie contingent. Jackie took an almost instant dislike to her, which deepened as the years passed, and Ethel had always despised Jackie. When Ethel heard that Jackie preferred to have her name pronounced "Jack-leen," Ethel said cuttingly, "like in queen?" Jackie grimaced at what she felt was a mishmash of decorating styles at Ethel's home. After watching Ethel and Eunice running and tumbling on the lawn during a touch football game, Jackie said contemptuously, "They're a bunch of gorillas falling all over one another."[1]

Jackie's dislike of Ethel intensified when Ethel led the Kennedy outcry against her marriage to Onassis. When Jackie returned to America several months after the wedding on Skorpios, she met Ethel for lunch. Diners at nearby tables heard Ethel ask scornfully, "Well, have you had enough of your Greek super tycoon?" Jackie was infuriated, "I won't sit here and listen to you talking about one of the sweetest men on earth!" Replied Ethel, "You've hurt the family, all this publicity about your obscene big spending . . . it's disgraceful."[2]

There was no love lost between Jackie and any of her in-laws. She never attended Thanksgiving and Christmas dinners, cherished family traditions at the compound. Caroline and John, Jr., are nearly always there. Dozens of Kennedys come from all over the country and Europe to be there. Family members used to comment on Jackie's absence at one time but no longer. Nobody expected her.[3]

Perhaps after all these years, Jackie no longer had to pretend to be something she never was. Maybe she felt awkward being with Jack's family after what she and Ari had done, especially since none of them ever suspected what had really happened. They didn't know who had destroyed their family. At least, Christina Onassis was smart enough to know who her enemy was and then proceed to quickly buy her off and get Jackie out of her life forever.

The only member of the Kennedy family that Jackie cared about or tried to stay close to was Joan Kennedy, Ted's wife. Both women shared a dislike of their roles in the Kennedy dynasty . . .the perpetual supporting cast. The husbands were the superstars and they were nothing. Jackie had once been close to Joan because she realized that she, too, was having trouble adjusting to her role as a political wife and fitting in with the Kennedys. They had many intimate conversations about the problems Joan had, but there was little Jackie could do when Joan began slipping into alcoholism. After Joan's divorce, Jackie called to offer support and advice but they soon drifted apart.[4] Jackie could have told Joan that being a Kennedy widow was a much easier than being a divorced wife.

Jackie and Maurice settled into their comfortable, supportive life in New York. They traveled together and presented themselves to the world as a devoted couple. Then in November 1993, Jackie noticed a swelling in her groin that responded to antibiotics. But while on vacation the following month in December, she reported flu-like symptoms to her doctor including swelling in her glands and abdominal pain. In January 1994, Jackie was diagnosed with non-Hodgkin's lymphoma. This type of cancer strikes about forty-five thousand Americans every year, however only about 10 percent of the cases involve cancer cells as aggressive as the ones found in Jackie. She publicly announced her diagnosis in February. Her lifelong friend, Nancy Tuckerman became her spokeswoman and claimed that Jackie was responding well to treatment.[5]

The cancer in her body had initially responded to chemotherapy but in March it was found in her brain and throughout her abdomen. In May, it was discovered in her liver and doctors told her there was nothing more they could do. Her spokeswoman, Nancy Tuckerman, made the statement, "The disease has progressed. She will not have any further treatment. There was nothing more to do for her."[6]

Jacqueline Bouvier Kennedy Onassis died at 10:15 p.m. on Thursday, May 19, 1994, "At home surrounded by her friends and family and her books, and the people and things she loved-in her own way, on her own terms," in the words of John F. Kennedy, Jr. He was at her beside along with Caroline and Maurice. She was sixty-four. The exact cause of death was not released.[7]

The afternoon before the funeral, there was a private wake at 1040 Fifth Avenue. Jackie's casket was closed beneath a colorful satin quilt from her bed. On a sunny Monday morning, her funeral was held at the same church where she had been baptized and confirmed, St. Ignatius Loyola. Her son, John, told the gathered friends, family and colleagues about the readings he and his sister had chosen. "Three things come to mind over and over again and ultimately dictated our selections. They were her love of words, the bonds of home and family and her spirit of adventure." After the readings, the cortege proceeded to Arlington National Cemetery to the spot where she had ignited the eternal flame for JFK's burial thirty-one years before.[8] It was fitting that she be buried alongside President Kennedy since it would be a beautiful ending to the Camelot legend. It would again touch the hearts of their adoring public just as it had so many years ago. The Navy Sea Chanters sang "Eternal Father" as they had thirty-one years before in honor of President Kennedy. John Kennedy, Jr., who had saluted at his Father's funeral in 1963, spontaneously leaned over to gently kiss the casket of his Mother. The service lasted only eleven minutes. No relatives of Aristotle Onassis were in attendance. Far from the cemetery, the "passing" bell at the gothic National Cathedral rang sixty-four times, once for each year of her life.[9]

And now as radio personality, Paul Harvey, would say, "Here's the rest of the story." Jackie made only two specific requests regarding her prized possessions. An ancient Hellenic marble head of a woman was to be given to Maurice Tempelsman and two Indian paintings to her friend, Bunny Mellon. She also willed a copy of JFK's Inaugural Address with an inscription by Robert Frost to her lawyer, Alexander Folger. Personal friends, maids, and the butler received cash gifts ranging from $25,000 to $250,000, with the instructions that her estate would pay the taxes on these gifts. To her children, Jackie left each $250,000 in cash, the Fifth Avenue apartment, the Martha's Vineyard home and the remainder of her belongings. The rest of her estate went to the C&J foundation. C&J stands for the names of her children, a charitable trust designed to last twenty-four years. Caroline, John, Maurice Tempelsman and Alexander Folger were named trustees. The foundation was directed to give annually eight percent of the value of the estate's assets to charities. After twenty-four years, the assets will pass on to her grandchildren. Her will also asked her children to keep her papers private.[10]

After reading her will from beginning to end, there is no doubt whatsoever that Jackie was an incredibly shrewd and wise woman when it came to her financial affairs. It is interesting to note that the foundation she created for her children will be their golden egg nest. The eight percent charitable gifts are merely token amounts that enable the foundation to reap tax write-offs. There was no desire on Jackie's part to donate any considerable amount to charities, just enough to make things look good, and laying the ground work to establish tax benefits for the foundation.

As to keeping her papers private, this would add the potential for enormous financial gains to the foundation, since no one else could use her papers or publish them to make money, only her children would have this option. In the future Caroline might write a biography of her Mother and, of course, John might serialize it in his magazine. It makes sense that Jackie would want only her children to have this opportunity since their slant would be the official line that has been fed to the public for years. By not writing her own memoirs, Jackie gave her children a nice rainy day fund if they ever were short of money in the future. Considering what she had left them, it would be a hard scenario to imagine, but Jackie vividly remembers her own father's fall from grace. Jackie could be counted on to plan well for any possible disaster in her children's future lives.

Would Jacqueline Onassis have someday written her memoirs? She made it clear that she would not. In 1967, she worked closely with writer, Molly Thayer, putting together an informal history of her years as First Lady. This was the only period of her life that Jackie felt qualified as public domain. Still in 1981, she expressed some ambivalence about not having written her memoirs. "It's really a shame that I sort of never wanted to. So many people, you know, hit the White House with their dictaphone running. I never even kept a journal. I thought, I want to live my life, not record it. And I'm still glad I did that. I think there's so many things that I've forgotten." At a later date, when Jackie was asked about her memoirs she was quoted as saying, "Maybe when I'm ninety. People change, the person she might have written about thirty-years ago is not the same person today. The imagination takes over. When Isak Dinesen wrote *Out of Africa*, she left out how badly her husband had treated her. She created a new past, in effect."[11]

This was Jackie's official reply. At other times when she was asked about writing her own biography, she would not reply or just ignore the question altogether. Do you really think that with her profound sense of history perhaps Jackie might have scribbled down a few thoughts and notes about her extraordinary life? Of course, she did. Especially after successfully creating Camelot and with her job experience as an editor, she would not be able to resist telling it all . . . her way. These papers are sealed until 2044 for a reason, to protect her children. The real story will be told by the person who lived it, most likely sometime in the next century.

The sad fact for current historians is that the John F. Kennedy Library's policy of keeping the most important resources closed to the public has hindered research. A veil of secrecy enshrouds the lives of several Kennedys and the Presidential Administration of John F. Kennedy. It was not until the Senate's Investigation of the Intelligence Agencies in 1975-1976 that some of the secrets of the Kennedy Administration, and the life of President Kennedy began coming to light. The researcher or writer bent on discovering new information about the Kennedy family or the JFK Administration will be amazed at how much information the library is still withholding from the public. In general, material closed to the public falls into three categories: papers classified for purposes of national security, papers relating to an individual's strictly personal affairs, and papers that "might be used in some way to harass any person."[12]

Further contributing to the atmosphere of secrecy is the welter of important material about the life and death of John F. Kennedy, and his administration from three major investigations that cannot be released to the public until the twenty-first century. These are composed of much of the Warren Commission testimony and exhibits, due to be released in 2014. The testimony by the Senate Select Committee of Governmental Operations with respect to intelligence activities to be released in 2025, and much of the testimony and evidence taken by the House Select Committee on Assassinations, to be released in 2029. Furthermore, some two hundred documents associated with the Warren Commission's inquiry were classified until 2039.[13] It would appear that there was quite a bit hidden from the American public. So far there has been no attempt to explain why. It does make one wonder.

As for keeping secrets, Jackie was very good at appearing to forgive. Her last will and testament would seem to prove that she did not forget when it came to her sister Lee's affair with Jack Kennedy. Lee's lack of standing at Jackie's funeral was the family's tacit acknowledgment of the frayed connection between the two women. During the brief burial ceremony at Arlington National

Cemetery, where Jackie was laid to rest next to JFK, Lee felt she was pushed into the background.

Her resentment that day was slight compared to the rage she felt the following week when Jackie's will was made public and Lee was cut out entirely. With not so much as a trinket left to her, at least as a gesture, Lee was deeply and publicly mortified. By the time she died, Jackie, through shrewd investments, had a lot of money to give away. Her will stated clearly that she was making no provision for Lee because she had already done so in her lifetime. So what if Jackie had helped her with money in the past, Lee fumed. What are families for anyway? Jackie should have left her something! After all, she left Lee's children, Anthony and Tina, the income from $500,000 trust funds that she had set up for each of them, and she helped them in the past, too. Those who were sympathetic to Lee thought that Jackie's decision was another indication of her mean streak. Those in Jackie's camp said that Lee was so chronically jealous and resentful of her sister that Jackie's decision was understandable. By her gesture, Jackie as expected, had the last word, once and for all.[14]

The more likely reason for Jackie leaving Lee out would have been her anger over Lee sleeping with Jack while Jackie was in the hospital giving birth to Caroline. She was never able to vent this anger since Jack's sexual escapades were all a part of the great Kennedy cover-up. So Jackie was never able to retaliate or take revenge against Lee until her own death. Obviously, she knew all about the affair from her step-sister, Nina Auchincloss, but for the sake of their mother and family harmony Jackie never mentioned it.

So obviously Lee would have been shocked by her omission from Jackie's will. As for leaving Lee's children set for life, Jackie felt no need to punish them, only their Mother. Jackie could well remember the stigma of being penniless while living within a wealthy family. She would not want any child to go through the humiliation she had suffered. She was fond of Lee's children and to her mind not to have money would be the worst thing that could happen to a child . . . or for that matter to an adult. It had happened to their grandfather, and Jackie would make sure that none of his grandchildren would ever experience this humiliation. Also by leaving Lee's children a generous inheritance, they wouldn't be sympathetic to any Jackie bashing by Lee in the future.

The amazing thing about Jackie was that she was so good at discretion. From not confronting her sister to keeping her secret with Ari, Jackie knew the importance of not drawing attention to herself. She had her pride and she would not subject it to public scrutiny . . . ever! Jackie's personal motto would become....never complain, and certainly never explain.

So what's it all about Jackie?

When all is said and done, the most important legacy Jackie left her children was her money and her things. Jackie had directed her children specifically to auction all of the things that they didn't want to keep for themselves. Thus America experienced the biggest garage sale to ever take place. It was also the biggest rip-off ever. From her grave Jackie must have been laughing at the spectacle of people paying incredible amounts of money for things just because they had been hers and Jacks. Many items were gifts they had received in the White House, put right into storage and never even used but sold for enormous amounts. It was an opportunistic event with Caroline and John laughing all the way to the bank.

A total of 5,914 of Jackie's personal items were sold in the public auction at Sotheby's in Manhattan from April 23 to 26, 1996. Sotheby's had estimated the total "fair market value," that is, the value the items would have had they not been owned by Jackie, at four million dollars. When the final gavel fell, the sale had earned her children $34.5 million. While several critics stepped forward to criticize the children who would benefit from the sale, others close to Jackie confirmed that it was her idea. "Jackie did mention in her will that her children should have an auction. She said that it would be the practical thing to do," said ever loyal Nancy Tuckerman, Jackie's White House Secretary and close friend.[15]

The catalog, which sold for $90 in hardcover and $55 in paperback, sold one hundred thousand copies before the auction. Proceeds from the catalog went to charities, including the John F. Kennedy Library Foundation, which received a total of one million dollars.[16] This seems like a small amount compared to what the children pocketed but remember they were only following their mother's wishes. Jackie had taught them well throughout her life and now her last lesson would be the most memorable.

MONEY MAKES YOUR LIFE MAGIC.

The top ten sellers in the auction were:
1. Jackie's engagement ring from Onassis . . . Value $500,000
   Sold for $2.5 million
2. Louis XVI desk which the nuclear test ban treaty was signed. $1,432,500. It was bought by an European foundation. The White House entered the bidding but lost out. Neither Jackie nor her children ever considered donating it to the White House as a part of American history.
3. JFK golf clubs sold for $772,500 to Arnold Schwarzenegger, husband of niece, Maria Shriver. Jackie interestingly enough was quoted by Steve Wasserman, a former executive editor of Doubleday, as saying about her nephew in-law, Arnold, whose movies she refused to see as saying, "I loathe everything he stands for."[17] His money was still acceptable no matter what kind of movies he has made.
4. JFK walnut cigar humidor given to the President by Milton Berle

sold for $574,500.

5. Oak rocking chair sold for $453,500.

6. Another oak rocking chair sold for $415,000.

7. Kunzite and diamond ring valued at $6,000 sold for $415,000.

8. Ben Hogan power thrust irons valued at $900 sold for much more.

9. Cabochon ruby and diamond ear clips sold for $360,000.

10. John Wooton painting sold for $343,500 valued at $25,000.[18]

The auction was Sotheby's seventh largest. Fifty-nine lots sold for more than one hundred times the high market value Sotheby's had estimated. It was one hell of a garage sale . . . the sale of the century.

This was the legacy Jackie left her children. The message comes through strong and clear . . . cherish your money, it is the most important thing in your life.

Jackie also left another message . . .one that her public must wait a long time to hear. It is one of the most valuable recordings in existence. Jackie's twelve-hour oral history, now hidden away in the archives of the John F. Kennedy Memorial Library. It will not be released until 2044, fifty years after her death and eighty-one years after her husband's murder.

TRIBUTES

She had considerable talent, considerable ambition and brains. You have to see her life as a significant and poignant mark in the evolution of women. She was the beautiful, sad heroine of our time . . . Betty Freiden [19]

She looked like a starlet who would never learn to act . . . Norman Mailer [20]

They were so wrong about Jackie. Of course she had talent, ambition and brains but she wasn't a sad heroine just a very good actress. She gave a performance of a lifetime her whole life long.

She was a success story. Remember, not many people can get away with murder. . .

plus get to keep all the money.

EPILOGUE

EPILOGUE

EPILOGUE

NOW THAT YOU HAVE READ AND CONSIDERED this theory, there are some facts that cannot be denied. Jackie and Ari both had as much motivation as any of the other possible assassins, and they had the means to order this murder. Their large egos would adore being able to commit not only the perfect crime but the crime of the century. They would be able to do this and walk away from it with no one ever to suspect or consider their involvement. However, this involvement did bind them together forever. Neither one could ever betray the other without betraying themselves. It truly was a union that would last throughout eternity. No matter what became of their own marriage, they would protect each other at all costs. Neither one would ever want to be connected with one of the most heinous crimes ever committed. This simply could never be revealed during their lifetimes.

It comes as no surprise that Jacqueline Kennedy would ensure that all her private papers and thoughts be sealed and kept private until the year 2044. This is 80 years after she recorded her thoughts. The papers are private and there is no public access to her personal life until it will be impossible to affect her children's lives.

Perhaps it is her opportunity to put her life in perspective for future

historians. Jackie will eventually show the world that she was not another
Rose Kennedy who stood helplessly by while her husband defiled their
marriage and her dignity. Jackie, with her sense of history, would not want
posterity to think of her as just another helpless wife who endured a marriage that made her the laughing stock of the entire world. She might very
well wish to add a postscript to the well-documented performance of JFK
and Marilyn Monroe at his birthday party at Madison Square Garden where
they vulgarly flaunted their love affair for everyone to see on national
television. Isn't there something said about.....Don't get mad, get even?

Jackie's story is not an unusual one, just as Evita tells us in the
musical....local girl makes good, marries famous man! Evita was considered a saint by many. However, there is no way to deny the fact that she
slept with men for money and that technically would make her a whore.
Jackie also slept with men to improve her station in life. When the union
between Jackie and the Onassis family was finally over, there is no doubt at
all that Jacqueline Bouvier Kennedy Onassis was one shrewd business woman.

This is truly a saga of epic proportions comparable to any fictional
Greek tragedy ever written. All of the characters in this story had more
fame and fortune then they could have ever wished for, yet there are no
happy endings. Oh yes, they had fame and fortune but it did not add to the
spiritual quality of their lives. For that matter their material lives did not
have particularly happy endings. It would appear that the money that Jackie
and Ari both felt was so necessary to their well-being did in fact carry a
curse with it. Both were consumed with greed and power. Yet they were
never able to put their wealth to any good use except for their outrageous
lifestyle that set them apart from the real world.

There were big lessons for both of them to learn. It would appear
that none of these lessons were learned at all. Their egos were much too
big to learn or even care about anything other than themselves. To all
appearances, they had it all yet they always wanted more.

In their case the saying, "What comes around goes around," came
true. Ari died a tragic death. He was separated from Jacqueline and still in

deep mourning for his beloved son, Alexander. All the money in the world couldn't give him happiness.

As for Jackie, true to form, she chose as her closest friend, Maurice Templesman, a man whose financial expertise would take her $25 million from the Onassis marriage to an estimated $150 million at her death. He would help to guide her amassed fortune from beyond the grave. Jackie's departure from this world was all about trust funds, auctions and their consequences, the things she really cared about in this lifetime. Isn't it also so appropriate that she would choose to lie beside JFK for her final resting place which is a nice touch for posterity and the legend?

Then there was the shopping thing. While writing this book, I would try to see her as the rest of the world views her. I tried to ennoble her life with thoughts of her style, class, and dignity. I never could get past the truth that Jackie was the original, authentic "Material Girl" of all time. Her shopping sprees and consumption excesses far exceeded the budgets of some small countries. It is hard to give or find value in a life that was mostly about amassing great amounts of money for herself and her children.

Speaking of children, it would appear that Jackie's legacy goes on not with great works of charity by her family, but with incredible money-making opportunities. For example, her auction generated an incredible amount of hard cold cash.

For those who are uncomfortable with the thought of Jackie and Aristotle Onassis having Jack whacked, please remember no one can prove who actually killed Kennedy, nor can anyone really disprove any theory that has been presented as an answer during the past thirty-five years. For the really sensitive souls out there, pretend this was just an outrageous work of fiction. Just pretend that the Kennedys are the fictional Cavanaughs and the President and his wife are Dan and Danielle. Her rescuer would be some Greek by the name of Nicos Stavos. Well, you get the idea. It would be just like the work of fiction that Ivana Trump wrote right after her divorce from "The Donald".

When I started out to write this, I decided to write it under a pseudonym. There is a perverse side of me that will enjoy the speculation about who would ever come up with such an off the wall theory. Is it someone close to Jackie or Ari? Is it an enemy from the past? Is it a political insider who wants to make a fast buck? Is it some rabid Kennedy hater? Is it another abused wife fulfilling her own desire to get even for Jackie? Is it some internet sick-o? Or is it just some ordinary person who happened to think one day....why not?

Remember as we know, real life can far exceed any fiction! Also what this country always needs is a new assassination theory, and here it is!

Ever since the assassination of John F. Kennedy, the American obsession has been .... Who killed Kennedy? Thirty-four years later, no one knows for sure.

America has been cynical since Kennedy was killed.
This cynicism has taken its toll.
Not knowing is worse than knowing the truth.

It is a cynicism that has crept into every aspect of American life. As a country we have not only lost our innocence, but we are still floundering in a sea of distrust and uncertainty. It is as if the entire country is paralyzed. America has lost its joy because there has never been an adequate explanation.

We have been treated like small children. We have not been told the truth for our own good. It has been decided for us what we can and cannot know. It is a demeaning way to treat a child, and to treat an entire country in this way is despicable. Yet, this is exactly what has been done to the American people since the assassination of Kennedy.

The very fabric of our lives was shredded to pieces leaving an entire country devastated by an event that we still do not understand. The people who killed Kennedy not only killed a man, they killed an entire country at the same time. Nothing will ever be the same again. Yet we all wait for things to go back to the way they were before Kennedy died. Those not yet born then still wonder and wish they could experience the Kennedy years.

It is as if an evil curse has been placed not only on one man and his family but this man's entire country. What happened to the Kennedys happened to all of us.

How could this happen to him? How could this happen to us? How could it happen to America?

Who did it? And why?

Who could have done this to us so effectively that we still do not know who our enemy was, or is?

There was a cover-up. Of that, we are certain. It began right from the very moment of the actual assassination. Nothing was right about the whole thing. To this day there are only theories. There are theories about everything from the plot, the gun shots, the grassy knoll, the motives, the assassin or assassins, to who did it and why.

Thirty-five years later the Warren Commission is a joke. When you read the original transcripts now and compare them with the testimony that was censored for our own protection, the truth is nowhere to be found. Who was protecting us from whom? And why? Why couldn't the American people be told the truth then? Why not now?

Americans, now, do not trust anyone. How can we when we have been lied to for over three generations? We have been demeaned by forces that have conspired to destroy our belief in everything we used to hold sacred. Who would do this to us?

This book has been written to help sort out the mess that we have found ourselves and our country in thirty-five years later.

Thirty-five years ago the Kennedy Presidency was very much like others that had preceded it. There were many things that were both good and bad about that administration. However, the Kennedys brought with them a past which was filled with bad karma.

Every president has enemies but for John Kennedy you practically had to take a number and get in line. He was not a nice person nor did he come from a nice family. This is a hard thing for us to accept. We all wanted so very much to not only like him but to love him. He was what we all wanted to be. He had it all- style, class, wealth- all the things that legends are made of. After his death, he became bigger than ever in our lives.

Who was it that got to him? Was it the Mafia? Why would they bother killing one Kennedy? What would that do since there were more at home. Was it the FBI? Why would J. Edgar Hoover need to kill Kennedy or any other president when he had so much dirt on them. He could tell them what to do. Was it labor? If they killed anyone, it would have been Bobby. Was it the CIA? Well, they were pissed off about getting hung out at the Bay of Pigs. But killing Kennedy would only bring out their assassination attempts on others such as Castro and Diem. Not a good idea! Could it have been the Communists? Oswald was a joke. Besides Kennedy was someone they could work with and he would be useful in the future. It could have been some lunatic. Some have taken credit for it, but not with any proof. Was it a government conspiracy that would include the military, etc, etc.? Why would they do it since they have always been able to do their own thing no matter who was president?

How about Lyndon Johnson? Well, he would have a great motive but he would be just a little too obvious.

How about the Warren Commission? Everyone still wonders about this investigation. It was a trip to never-neverland that was spoon fed to an American public. It was truly a great cover-up.

Kennedy's assassination was not by any means the first cover-up in the history of this country. This has been going on since the beginning of time. The interesting thing about the Warren Commission is that the cover-up really was that. No one, in government or the Kennedy family, wanted to find out who did kill Kennedy. It was easier on them not to know. This way if they, the government or the Kennedys, were responsible for JFK's death they would never have to take the blame. How convenient this approach was for the real killers.

As for the American people, they would believe what they were told! We did try. Oh, how we tried! But somehow it didn't work. Whether you do or do not believe in the forces of good and evil, read on and give some serious thought to what has actually happened since November 23, 1963.

Simply, a bad man was killed by two other bad people.

John Kennedy stood in the way of the happiness of Aristotle Onassis and Jacqueline Kennedy. They had the motivation, the money and the means to get rid of him. There were so many others who were suspects that they would never be considered themselves. Their alibis were airtight. Their contract killers were professionals. Thus no trail, no jail for anyone involved.

There now, the question is answered.
The unspeakable is spoken!
You finally know the answer.

There is nothing new under the stars. From the beginning of time, wives and lovers have killed husbands. Many have failed and gotten caught. Others have gotten away with it. More than you would think. It was just another crime like others before, no more, no less.

Although it may seem to have succeeded, on closer examination none of these people found happiness. Their lives only proved that what goes around comes around, over and over again.

There were big lessons to be learned here. Sadly, it does not appear that these lessons were learned.

What is the lesson here? What is the lesson for us, the American people?

It is hard to say because each country's and each person's lesson is within themselves. No one can answer that question for anyone else.

Hopefully, we can see that one man's death should not diminish us.

Perhaps we can finally put it behind us. It is time to rise above an unanswered question.

America needs to get well again.

Perhaps this theory will help some of us to move on.

Acknowledgments

Acknowledgments

ANY ONE WHO ATTEMPTS TO WRITE ABOUT THE Kennedys will come up against incredible but very subtle opposition. Perhaps a better description would be lack of cooperation or the unspoken fear of cooperating. The best example of this is the John F. Kennedy Presidential Library which is run with taxpayer's money from the National Archives Administration. This "public library" is not particularly helpful to even so called "friendly" journalists let alone anyone who might possibly be presenting a more controversial or unacceptable theory. Even though the three principals in this book are deceased, there still is an atmosphere of censoring and controlling any research which may prove to be contrary to the self-serving Kennedy version of the events that is their official history.

However there are people who, cloaked in anonymity, will express many and varied views which are surprising and in some cases shocking. It is impossible to thank all those who have spoken out with opinions that are contrary to the official Kennedy version. They know who they are and their revelations have contributed greatly to my research and my possible conclusions.

Since there was limited opportunity to meet with interviewers or to interview sources for this book, I gratefully wish to thank all the authors listed in the bibliography. They have fearlessly gone before me interviewing and documenting the entire history of the Kennedy family including all the triumphs and tragedies for posterity, making my research possible.

Then there are those whom I can't mention by name such as a favorite cousin's casual conversation which ignited the fuel to put pen to paper, and a dear friend's support, belief and advice which kept me on course whenever I was too discouraged to go on. A husband's love and his encouragement for an incredible concept and my children's constant belief in my ability and bravery to speak the unspeakable. I am most thankful for the opportunity to work side by side on this project with my daughter who became my sounding board, editing alter ego and computer consultant extraordinaire. My family was always there for me on the good days and even more so on the bad ones. Also I must thank those professionals who could not be a part of this project publicly but yet privately supported and encouraged all my efforts. It helped to know that they liked my way of telling a story and they believed in the plausibility of this theory. Lastly my heartfelt thanks to my friend whose patience and perseverance got this project on track and made it a reality.

In this book, I have implied that Jacqueline Bouvier Kennedy and Aristotle Onassis were capable of killing JFK. I know this will be very painful for their family members. How could it not be? Even though it is just another theory, it still is incredibly shocking and amazing.

I am amazed myself. The only thing I can tell you is that once it was out there it took on a life of its own. I have never written anything before in my life. When I would finally sit down to write late, late at night much of it was the closest thing to automatic writing that I can describe. I would just sit at my word processor and the words would start to appear. I would type long into the early hours of the morning and then fall into bed exhausted. I never would read anything until I awakened the next day. Then I would read it for the first time myself. It amazed me each day.

Why did I write it? I asked myself the same question many times and only found the answer after I finished the final draft. Like Jackie, my mother came from a divorced marriage with many of the same dysfunctional abuses that Jackie encountered. My mother also married a man just like her father and so the abuse continued. My Mom tried to leave my father several times but she could never do it. There was no one to help her escape. She was not financially independent and everyone was afraid of my father.

So she stayed with him for forty-six years. Two weeks before her death, she called me long distance in the middle of the day crying hysterically. She had watched the movie called "The Burning Bed" the night before. She told me that the movie was her life and she wished she had been able to kill my father just as Farrah Fawcett had killed her husband in the movie. I understood and felt her hopeless pain.

I asked her why she didn't do it? The answer was that she was afraid it would destroy her children's lives. She knew she couldn't get away with it and with a mother in prison, we would have no one. So she did nothing to save herself or us. I used to look at her with anger but when I looked at her in her coffin it was with so much relief that she had finally escaped from him. My mother couldn't pull off a murder so instead my father murdered her spirit in a slow, methodical, diabolical way yet all the while telling us how much he loved her.

If she had been able to do it or if someone had been able to help her, I would have understood. She was the victim. No one wants to think of their mother as a murderess but this is what happens sometimes. My mother was a great actress and put on an incredible front in order to avoid humiliation and salvage some dignity in her life. My father had other women. My mother died without telling me. She couldn't face more humiliation nor did she want to see the pity in my face. She could only take so much.

Did I want her to kill my father? Yes and No! Yes, he deserved it and you always want to see good triumph over evil. No, she couldn't have survived the notoriety and it would have diminished her virtue.

As I did my research, I was always looking for something that would let me believe that Onassis had forced Jackie to do this terrible deed. It would have been so much easier if he was just the bad guy.

After reading this some people will think of Jackie as the victim and others will think of her as the heroine. I think she was a strong woman who did what she had to do in order survive for herself and her children. I admire her.

This book was written because it makes more sense to me than anything else I have ever heard or read about JFK's death. In a long line of theories, it is not the first. . . .

and it surely will not be the last.

January Jones

BIBLIOGRAPHY

BIBLIOGRAPHY

ADAMS, CINDY AND CRIMP, SUSAN. *IRON ROSE:THE STORY OF ROSE FITZGERALD KENNEDY AND HER DYNASTY*. BEVERLY HILLS, CA:DOVE BOOKS, 1995

ADLER, BILL. *THE LAST WILL AND TESTAMENT OF JACQUELINE KENNEDY ONASSIS*. NEW YORK:CARROLL AND GRAF PUBLISHERS, 1997

ADLER, BILL. *THE UNCOMMON WISDOM OF JACQUELINE KENNEDY*. NEW YORK: A CITADEL PRESS BOOK PUBLISHED BY CAROL PUBLISHING CO.,1994

ANDERSEN, CHRISTOPHER, *JACKIE AFTER JACK*. NEW YORK: WILLIAM MOR-ROW AND COMPANY, INC., 1998

ANDERSEN, CHRISTOPHER. *JACK AND JACKIE:PORTRAIT OF AN AMERICAN MARRIAGE*. NEW YORK:WILLIAM MORROW AND COMPANY INC., 1996

ANTHONY, CARL SFERRAZZA. *AS WE REMEMBER HER*. NEW YORK: HARPERCOLLINS, 1997

BLY, NELLIE. *THE KENNEDY MEN: THREE GENERATIONS OF SEX, SCANDAL AND SECRETS*. NEW YORK:KENSINGTON PUBLISHING CORP.,1996

BRADLEE, BEN. *A GOOD LIFE*. NEW YORK:SIMON AND SCHUSTER, 1995

CAFARAKIS, CHRISTIAN. *THE FABULOUS ONASSIS:HIS LIFE AND LOVES.* NEW YORK:WILLIAM MORROW AND CO. INC., 1972

COLLIER, PETER AND HOROWITZ, DAVID. *THE KENNEDYS:AN AMERICAN DRAMA.* NEW YORK:WARNER BOOKS, 1984

CONDON, DIANNE RUSSELL. *JACKIE'S TREASURES.* NEW YORK:CLARKSON POTTER PUBLISHERS, 1996

DAVID, LESTER. *JACQUELINE KENNEDY ONASSIS.* NEW YORK:A BRICH LANE PRESS BOOK, 1994

DAVIS, JOHN H. *JACQUELINE BOUVIER: AN INTIMATE MEMOIR.* NEW YORK:JOHN WILEY AND SONS, INC., 1996

DAVIS, JOHN H. *THE KENNEDYS:DYNASTY AND DISASTER 1848-1983.* NEW YORK:MC GRAW-HILL BOOK CO., 1984

DAVIS, L.J. *ONASSIS:ARISTOTLE AND CHRISTINA.* NEW YORK:ST. MARTIN'S PRESS, 1986

DAVIS, LEE. *ASSASSINATION, TWENTY ASSASSINATIONS THAT CHANGED HISTORY.* NEW YORK:BDD SPECIAL EDITIONS, 1993

DU BOIS, DIANA. *IN HER SISTERS SHADOW.* BOSTON:LITTLE, BROWN AND CO., 1995

EVANS, PETER. *ARI:THE LIFE AND TIMES OF ARISTOTLE ONASSIS.* NEW YORK:SUMMIT BOOKS, 1986

FRASER, NICOLAS, JACOBSON, PHILIP, OTTAWAY MARK, CHESTER, LEWIS. *ARISTOTLE ONASSIS.* PHILADELPHIA AND NEW YORK:J. B. LIPPINCOTT CO, 1977

GENTRY, CURT. *J. EDGAR HOOVER:THE MAN AND THE SECRETS*. NEW YORK:W.W. NORTON AND CO., 1991

GOODWIN, DORIS KEARNS. *THE FITZGERALDS AND THE KENNEDYS AN AMERICAN SAGA*. NEW YORK: XT. MARTIN'S PRESS, 1987

HAMILTON, NIGEL. *JKF RECKLESS YOUTH*. NEW YORK:RANDOM HOUSE,1992

HERSH, SEYMOUR M.: *THE DARK SIDE OF CAMELOT*. BOSTON:LITTLE, BROWN AND COMPANY, 1997

HEYMANN, C. DAVID. *A WOMAN NAMED JACKIE*. NEW YORK:A LYLE STUART BOOK, 1989

HUBBELL, WEBB. *FRIENDS IN HIGH PLACES*. NEW YORK:WILLIAM MORROW AND COMPANY, 1997

HURT, HENRY. *REASONABLE DOUBT:AN INVESTIGATION INTO THE ASSASSINATION OF JOHN F. KENNEDY*. NEW YORK:HOLT, RINEHART AND WINSTON, 1985

KELLEY, KITTY. *JACKIE OH!*. NEW YORK:BALLANTINE BOOKS, 1979

KLEIN, EDWARD. *ALL TOO HUMAN:THE LOVE STORY OF JACK AND JACKIE KENNEDY*. NEW YORK:POCKET BOOKS, 1996

KOESTENBAUM, WAYNE. *JACKIE UNDER MY SKIN*. NEW YORK:A PLUME BOOK, 1996

LAWFORD, LADY MAY. *BITCH*. BROOKLINE VILLAGE, MA:BRANDEN PUBLISHING CO. INC.,1986

LEAMER, LAURENCE. *THE KENNEDY WOMEN*. NEW YORK:VILLARD BOOKS, 1994

MARTIN, RALPH G. *A HERO FOR OUR TIME:AN INTIMATE STORY OF THE KENNEDY YEARS*. NEW YORK:FAWCETT CREST, 1983

MARTIN, RALPH. *SEEDS OF DESTRUCTION*. NEW YORK:G. P. PUTNAM'S SONS,1995

OSBORNE, CLAIRE G. *JACKIE:A LEGEND DEFINED*. NEW YORK:AVON BOOKS, 1997

REEVES, RICHARD. *PRESIDENT KENNEDY:PROFILE OF POWER*. NEW YORK:SIMON AND SCHUSTER, 1993

REEVES, THOMAS C. *A QUESTION OF CHARACTER:A LIFE OF JOHN F. KENNEDY*. ROCKLIN, CA:PRIMA PUBLISHING, 1992

SCOTT, MICHAEL. *MARIA MENEGHINI CALLAS*. BOSTON:NORTHEASTERN UNIVERSITY PRESS, 1992

SLOAN, BILL. *JFK BREAKING THE SILENCE*. DALLAS, TEXAS:TAYLOR PUBLISHING CO., 1993

STROBER, DEBORAH H. AND GERALD S. *"LET US BEGIN ANEW":AN ORAL HISTORY OF THE KENNEDY PRESIDENCY*. NEW YORK:HARPER COLLINS, 1993

TROY, GIL. *AFFAIRS OF STATE*. NEW YORK:FREE PRESS, 1997

NOTES

NOTES

CHAPTER ONE

1   FRASER, NICOLAS, JACOBSON, PHILIP, OTTAWAY MARK,
     CHESTER, LEWIS. *ARISTOTLE ONASSIS*. PHILADELPHIA AND NEW
     YORK:J.B. LIPPINCOTT CO, 1977; "CHARLES DE GAULLE...", P.243

2   Ibid; "DE GAULLE HAD BEEN...", P.244

3   EVANS, PETER. *ARI:THE LIFE AND TIMES OF ARISTOTLE ONASSIS*.
     NEW YORK:SUMMIT BOOKS, 1986; "NO ONE WAS...", JACKET

4   FRASER, NICOLAS, JACOBSON, PHILIP, OTTAWAY MARK,
     CHESTER, LEWIS. *ARISTOTLE ONASSIS*. PHILADELPHIA AND NEW
     YORK:J. B. LIPPINCOTT CO, 1977; "THERE WAS ON...", P.168

5   EVANS, PETER. *ARI:THE LIFE AND TIMES OF ARISTOTLE ONASSIS*.
     NEW YORK:SUMMIT BOOKS, 1986; "HE LIKED THE...", P.164

6   HEYMANN, C. DAVID. *A WOMAN NAMED JACKIE*. NEW YORK:A
     LYLE STUART BOOK, 1989; "DOES THIS SORT...", P.392

CHAPTER TWO

1   DAVIS, JOHN H. *JACQUELINE BOUVIER: AN INTIMATE MEMOIR*.
     NEW YORK:JOHN WILEY AND SONS, INC., 1996; "JACQUELINE
     WAS THERE...", P.22

2   DAVIS, JOHN H. *JACQUELINE BOUVIER: AN INTIMATE MEMOIR*.
     NEW YORK:JOHN WILEY AND SONS, INC., 1996; "DURING THE
     FIRST...", P.39

3   LEAMER, LAURENCE. *THE KENNEDY WOMEN.* NEW YORK:
    VILLARD BOOKS,1994; "HER FATHER JACK...", P.428

4   DAVIS, JOHN H. *JACQUELINE BOUVIER: AN INTIMATE MEMOIR.*
    NEW YORK:JOHN WILEY AND SONS, INC., 1996; "JACK BOUVIER
    WAS...", P.24

5   HEYMANN, C. DAVID. *A WOMAN NAMED JACKIE.* NEW YORK:A
    LYLE STUART BOOK, 1989; "JACQUELINE WAS NEARLY...", P.63

6   ANDERSEN, CHRISTOPHER. *JACK AND JACKIE:PORTRAIT OF AN
    AMERICAN MARRIAGE.* NEW YORK:WILLIAM MORROW AND
    COMPANY INC., 1996; "AS THE MARRIAGE...", P.61

7   HEYMANN, C. DAVID. *A WOMAN NAMED JACKIE.* NEW YORK:A
    LYLE STUART BOOK, 1989; "AT AGE FIFTEEN...", P.63

8   ANDERSEN, CHRISTOPHER. *JACK AND JACKIE:PORTRAIT OF AN
    AMERICAN MARRIAGE.* NEW YORK:WILLIAM MORROW AND
    COMPANY INC., 1996; "JANET WAS THE...", P.57

9   DAVIS, JOHN H. *JACQUELINE BOUVIER: AN INTIMATE MEMOIR.*
    NEW YORK:JOHN WILEY AND SONS, INC., 1996; "THE LESSON
    WAS...", P.113

10 DAVIS, JOHN H. *JACQUELINE BOUVIER: AN INTIMATE MEMOIR.*
    NEW YORK:JOHN WILEY AND SONS, INC., 1996; "LIVING WITH
    THE...", P.112

11 ANDERSEN, CHRISTOPHER. *JACK AND JACKIE:PORTRAIT OF AN
    AMERICAN MARRIAGE.* NEW YORK:WILLIAM MORROW AND
    COMPANY INC., 1996; "YOU MUST REMEMBER...", P.69

12 KLEIN, EDWARD. *ALL TOO HUMAN:THE LOVE STORY OF JACK
    AND JACKIE KENNEDY.* NEW YORK:POCKET BOOKS, 1996;
    "JACKIE AND LEE...", P.28

13 KLEIN, EDWARD. *ALL TOO HUMAN:THE LOVE STORY OF JACK
    AND JACKIE KENNEDY.* NEW YORK:POCKET BOOKS, 1996;
    "BACK GROUND, WHERE SHE...", P.29

14 DAVIS, JOHN H. *JACQUELINE BOUVIER: AN INTIMATE MEMOIR.*
    NEW YORK:JOHN WILEY AND SONS, INC., 1996;"THE LESSON

WAS...", P.113

15 DAVIS, JOHN H. *JACQUELINE BOUVIER: AN INTIMATE MEMOIR.* NEW YORK:JOHN WILEY AND SONS, INC., 1996; "JACKIE'S RESPONSE...", P.114

16 DAVIS, JOHN H. *JACQUELINE BOUVIER: AN INTIMATE MEMOIR.* NEW YORK:JOHN WILEY AND SONS, INC., 1996; "EVEN HER BELOVED...", P.123

17 DAVIS, JOHN H. *JACQUELINE BOUVIER: AN INTIMATE MEMOIR.* NEW YORK:JOHN WILEY AND SONS, INC., 1996; "TELLING HER THAT...", P.124

18 HEYMANN, C. DAVID. *A WOMAN NAMED JACKIE.* NEW YORK: A LYLE STUART BOOK, 1989; "EILENE SLOCUM...", P.66

19 HEYMANN, C. DAVID. *A WOMAN NAMED JACKIE.* NEW YORK: A LYLE STUART BOOK, 1989; "ANOTHER ASPECT...", P.103

20 HEYMANN, C. DAVID. *A WOMAN NAMED JACKIE.* NEW YORK: A LYLE STUART BOOK, 1989; "SHE WAS A POOR...", P.95

21 KLEIN, EDWARD. *ALL TOO HUMAN:THE LOVE STORY OF JACK AND JACKIE KENNEDY.* NEW YORK:POCKET BOOKS, 1996; "WHAT NO ONE...", P.113

22 LEAMER, LAURENCE. *THE KENNEDY WOMEN.* NEW YORK: VILLARD BOOKS, 1994; "JANET, WAS A ...", P.428

23 DAVIS, JOHN H. *JACQUELINE BOUVIER: AN INTIMATE MEMOIR.* NEW YORK:JOHN WILEY AND SONS, INC., 1996; "THESE FIRST TWENTY...", P.XII

24 KELLEY, KITTY. *JACKIE OH!.* NEW YORK:BALLANTINE BOOKS, 1979; "BEING THE PRODUCT...", P.23

25 DAVIS, JOHN H. *JACQUELINE BOUVIER: AN INTIMATE MEMOIR.* NEW YORK:JOHN WILEY AND SONS, INC., 1996; "JACQUELINE WOULD ALWAYS...", P.39

CHAPTER THREE

1   BLY, NELLIE. *THE KENNEDY MEN: THREE GENERATIONS OF
        SEX, SCANDAL AND SECRETS.* NEW YORK:KENSINGTON
        PUBLISHING CORP.,1996; "WHERE ELSE…", P.8

2   BLY, NELLIE. *THE KENNEDY MEN: THREE GENERATIONS OF
        SEX, SCANDAL AND SECRETS.* NEW YORK:KENSINGTON
        PUBLISHING CORP.,1996; "THE BOYS ALSO…", P.2

3   BLY, NELLIE. *THE KENNEDY MEN: THREE GENERATIONS OF
        SEX, SCANDAL AND SECRETS.* NEW YORK:KENSINGTON
        PUBLISHING CORP.,1996; "IT CAME ASHORE…", P.16

4   BRADLEE, BEN. *A GOOD LIFE.* NEW YORK:SIMON AND
        SCHUSTER, 1995; "JUST BEFORE HIS…", P.38

5   MARTIN, RALPH G. *SEEDS OF DESTRUCTION.* NEW YORK:
        G.P.PUTNAM'S SONS, 1995; "A UNITED STATE…", P.XX

6   BLY, NELLIE. *THE KENNEDY MEN: THREE GENERATIONS OF
        SEX, SCANDAL AND SECRETS.* NEW YORK:KENSINGTON
        PUBLISHING CORP.,1996; "WHEN IT WAS TIME…", P.10

7   BLY, NELLIE. *THE KENNEDY MEN: THREE GENERATIONS OF
        SEX, SCANDAL AND SECRETS.* NEW YORK:KENSINGTON PUB-
        LISHING CORP.,1996; "THE GREAT DISAPPOINTMENT…", P.11

8   REEVES, THOMAS C. *A QUESTION OF CHARACTER:A LIFE OF
        JOHN F. KENNEDY.* ROCKLIN, CA:PRIMA PUBLISHING, 1992;
        "IN THIRTY-TWO MONTHS…", P.289

9   REEVES, THOMAS C. *A QUESTION OF CHARACTER:A LIFE OF
        JOHN F. KENNEDY.* ROCKLIN, CA:PRIMA PUBLISHING, 1992;
        "THE VITAL FORCE…", P.33

10   MARTIN, RALPH G. *SEEDS OF DESTRUCTION.* NEW YORK:
        G.P.PUTNAM'S SONS, 1995; "IN THESE EARLY…", P.XVIII

11   MARTIN, RALPH G. *SEEDS OF DESTRUCTION.* NEW YORK:
        G.P.PUTNAM'S SONS, 1995; "THEN SELECTED THE…", P.XIX

12   MARTIN, RALPH G. *SEEDS OF DESTRUCTION.* NEW

YORK:G.P.PUTNAM'S SONS, 1995; "I'D JUST COME...", P.XVII

13   BLY, NELLIE. *THE KENNEDY MEN: THREE GENERATIONS OF SEX, SCANDAL AND SECRETS.* NEW YORK:KENSINGTON PUBLISHING CORP.,1996; "YEARS AGO, WE...", P.14

14   MARTIN, RALPH G. *SEEDS OF DESTRUCTION.* NEW YORK: G.P.PUTNAM'S SONS, 1995; "IT WAS ALWAYS...", P.13

15   MARTIN, RALPH G. *SEEDS OF DESTRUCTION.* NEW YORK:G.P.PUTNAM'S SONS, 1995; "NO MATTER WHAT...", P.XXI

16   REEVES, THOMAS C. *A QUESTION OF CHARACTER:A LIFE OF JOHN F. KENNEDY.* ROCKLIN, CA:PRIMA PUBLISHING, 1992; "ATTENDING WEEKLY MASS...", P.31

17   REEVES, THOMAS C. *A QUESTION OF CHARACTER:A LIFE OF JOHN F. KENNEDY.* ROCKLIN, CA:PRIMA PUBLISHING, 1992; "JACK WAS NEVER...", P.33

18   MARTIN, RALPH G. *SEEDS OF DESTRUCTION.* NEW YORK: G.P.PUTNAM'S SONS, 1995; "FROM THEIR FATHER...", P.XVIII

19   REEVES, THOMAS C. *A QUESTION OF CHARACTER:A LIFE OF JOHN F. KENNEDY.* ROCKLIN, CA:PRIMA PUBLISHING, 1992; "JACK GREW UP...", P.41

20   REEVES, THOMAS C. *A QUESTION OF CHARACTER:A LIFE OF JOHN F. KENNEDY.* ROCKLIN, CA:PRIMA PUBLISHING, 1992; "AS JOE BECAME...", P.31

21   MARTIN, RALPH G. *SEEDS OF DESTRUCTION.* NEW YORK: G.P.PUTNAM'S SONS, 1995; "MOTHER WAS NOT...", P.11

22   REEVES, THOMAS C. *A QUESTION OF CHARACTER:A LIFE OF JOHN F.KENNEDY.* ROCKLIN, CA:PRIMA PUBLISHING, 1992; "HE WAS NOT...", P.40

23   BLY, NELLIE. *THE KENNEDY MEN: THREE GENERATIONS OF SEX, SCANDEL AND SECRETS.* NEW YORK:KENSINGTON PUBLISHING CORP.,1996; "THE KENNEDY FAMILY MYTH...", P.9

CHAPTER FOUR

1　HEYMANN, C. DAVID. *A WOMAN NAMED JACKIE*. NEW YORK:A LYLE STUART BOOK, 1989; "HOW DID IT ALL...", P.106

2　ANDERSEN, CHRISTOPHER. *JACK AND JACKIE:PORTRAIT OF AN AMERICAN MARRIAGE*. NEW YORK:WILLIAM MORROW AND COMPANY INC., 1996; "JACK, THIRTY-FOUR AT THE...", P.87

3　HEYMANN, C. DAVID. *A WOMAN NAMED JACKIE*. NEW YORK:A LYLE STUART BOOK, 1989; "JACK SEEMED DULY...", P.107

4　KELLEY, KITTY. *JACKIE OH!*. NEW YORK:BALLANTINE BOOKS, 1979; "AT THAT TIME...", P.18

5　HEYMANN, C. DAVID. *A WOMAN NAMED JACKIE*. NEW YORK:A LYLE STUART BOOK, 1989; "JACKIE FELT...", P.112

6　HEYMANN, C. DAVID. *A WOMAN NAMED JACKIE*. NEW YORK:A LYLE STUART BOOK, 1989; "FOR THE PRESENT THOUGH...", P.112

7　KELLEY, KITTY. *JACKIE OH!*. NEW YORK:BALLANTINE BOOKS, 1979; "WHAT I WON'T...", P.7

8　REEVES, THOMAS C. *A QUESTION OF CHARACTER:A LIFE OF JOHN F. KENNEDY*. ROCKLIN, CA:PRIMA PUBLISHING, 1992; "JACKIE HAD ALMOST...", P.111

9　KELLEY, KITTY. *JACKIE OH!*. NEW YORK:BALLANTINE BOOKS, 1979; "IN ORDER TO SURVIVE...", P.24

10　REEVES, THOMAS C. *A QUESTION OF CHARACTER:A LIFE OF JOHN F. KENNEDY*. ROCKLIN, CA:PRIMA PUBLISHING, 1992; "AS FOR JACK...", P.111

11　KLEIN, EDWARD. *ALL TOO HUMAN:THE LOVE STORY OF JACK AND JACKIE KENNEDY*. NEW YORK:POCKET BOOKS, 1996; "EVEN JACK'S TRUSTED...", P.96

12　KLEIN, EDWARD. *ALL TOO HUMAN:THE LOVE STORY OF JACK AND JACKIE KENNEDY*. NEW YORK:POCKET BOOKS, 1996; "THE WOMEN CHASED HIM...", P.135

13　KLEIN, EDWARD. *ALL TOO HUMAN:THE LOVE STORY OF JACK AND*

JACKIE KENNEDY. NEW YORK:POCKET BOOKS, 1996; "HE COULD NOT...", P.135

14   KLEIN, EDWARD. *ALL TOO HUMAN:THE LOVE STORY OF JACK AND JACKIE KENNEDY*. NEW YORK:POCKET BOOKS, 1996; "THERE WAS ALSO...", P.93

15   KELLEY, KITTY. *JACKIE OH!*. NEW YORK:BALLANTINE BOOKS, 1979; "TO JACK'S WAY...", P.23

16   ANDERSEN, CHRISTOPHER. *JACK AND JACKIE:PORTRAIT OF AN AMERICAN MARRIAGE*. NEW YORK:WILLIAM MORROW AND COMPANY INC., 1996; "THEY HAD BOTH...", P.108

17   KELLEY, KITTY. *JACKIE OH!*. NEW YORK:BALLANTINE BOOKS, 1979; "SHE WAS SO...", P.20

18   HEYMANN, C. DAVID. *A WOMAN NAMED JACKIE*. NEW YORK:A LYLE STUART BOOK, 1989; "RUN IN PLACE...", P.116

19   KLEIN, EDWARD. *ALL TOO HUMAN:THE LOVE STORY OF JACK AND JACKIE KENNEDY*. NEW YORK:POCKET BOOKS, 1996; "JACKIE WAS NO...", P.122

20   HEYMANN, C. DAVID. *A WOMAN NAMED JACKIE*. NEW YORK:A LYLE STUART BOOK, 1989; "JOE KENNEDY NOT...", P.117

21   KLEIN, EDWARD. *ALL TOO HUMAN:THE LOVE STORY OF JACK AND JACKIE KENNEDY*. NEW YORK:POCKET BOOKS, 1996; "A GIRL DOESN'T...", P.138

22   KLEIN, EDWARD. *ALL TOO HUMAN:THE LOVE STORY OF JACK AND JACKIE KENNEDY*. NEW YORK:POCKET BOOKS, 1996; "JACKIE WAS GRIPPED...", P.144

23   KLEIN, EDWARD. *ALL TOO HUMAN:THE LOVE STORY OF JACK AND JACKIE KENNEDY*. NEW YORK:POCKET BOOKS, 1996; "SHE RESUMED HER...", P.148

24   ANDERSEN, CHRISTOPHER. *JACK AND JACKIE:PORTRAIT OF AN AMERICAN MARRIAGE*. NEW YORK:WILLIAM MORROW AND COMPANY INC., 1996; "YOU CAN'T MARRY...", P.117

25   KELLEY, KITTY. *JACKIE OH!*. NEW YORK:BALLANTINE BOOKS,

1979; "HE WENT OUT…", P.21

26   KLEIN, EDWARD. *ALL TOO HUMAN:THE LOVE STORY OF JACK AND JACKIE KENNEDY*. NEW YORK:POCKET BOOKS, 1996; "SEND THEM TO…", P.155

27   KELLEY, KITTY. *JACKIE OH!*. NEW YORK:BALLANTINE BOOKS, 1979;"IN JACKIE, JOE…", P.36

28   KELLEY, KITTY. *JACKIE OH!*. NEW YORK:BALLANTINE BOOKS, 1979; "JOE PAVED THE…", P.32

29   ANDERSEN, CHRISTOPHER. *JACK AND JACKIE:PORTRAIT OF AN AMERICAN MARRIAGE*. NEW YORK:WILLIAM MORROW AND COMPANY INC., 1996; "JOE DID NOT…", P.116

30   KLEIN, EDWARD. *ALL TOO HUMAN:THE LOVE STORY OF JACK AND JACKIE KENNEDY*. NEW YORK:POCKET BOOKS, 1996; "DURING THIS PERIOD…", P.127

31   KLEIN, EDWARD. *ALL TOO HUMAN:THE LOVE STORY OF JACK AND JACKIE KENNEDY*. NEW YORK:POCKET BOOKS, 1996; "JOE HAD …", P.133

32   ANDERSEN, CHRISTOPHER. *JACK AND JACKIE:PORTRAIT OF AN AMERICAN MARRIAGE*. NEW YORK:WILLIAM MORROW AND COMPANY INC., 1996; "SHE OUT JACKIED…", P.103

33   KLEIN, EDWARD. *ALL TOO HUMAN:THE LOVE STORY OF JACK AND JACKIE KENNEDY*. NEW YORK:POCKET BOOKS, 1996; "IT WAS ONE…", P.165

34   ANDERSEN, CHRISTOPHER. *JACK AND JACKIE:PORTRAIT OF AN AMERICAN MARRIAGE*. NEW YORK:WILLIAM MORROW AND COMPANY INC., 1996; "HE WAS HALFWAY…", P.123

35   KLEIN, EDWARD. *ALL TOO HUMAN:THE LOVE STORY OF JACK AND JACKIE KENNEDY*. NEW YORK:POCKET BOOKS, 1996; "NOBODY WAS FOOLED…", P.162

36   DAVIS, JOHN H. *JACQUELINE BOUVIER: AN INTIMATE MEMOIR*. NEW YORK:JOHN WILEY AND SONS, INC., 1996; "PICKING UP WOMEN…", P.182

37   ANDERSEN, CHRISTOPHER. *JACK AND JACKIE:PORTRAIT OF AN AMERICAN MARRIAGE*. NEW YORK:WILLIAM MORROW AND   COM PANY INC., 1996; "JACKIE MARRIED JACK...", P.106

38   ANDERSEN, CHRISTOPHER. *JACK AND JACKIE:PORTRAIT OF AN AMERICAN MARRIAGE*. NEW YORK:WILLIAM MORROW AND COMPANY INC., 1996; "I USED TO SAY...", P.106

39   KLEIN, EDWARD. *ALL TOO HUMAN:THE LOVE STORY OF JACK AND JACKIE KENNEDY*. NEW YORK:POCKET BOOKS, 1996; "JOE KENNEDY WOULD...", P.160

40   DAVIS, JOHN H. *JACQUELINE BOUVIER: AN INTIMATE MEMOIR*. NEW YORK:JOHN WILEY AND SONS, INC., 1996; "THE REASON WAS...", P.186

41   KELLEY, KITTY. *JACKIE OH!*. NEW YORK:BALLANTINE BOOKS, 1979; "WE ALL KNEW...", P.14

42   DAVIS, JOHN H. *JACQUELINE BOUVIER: AN INTIMATE MEMOIR*. NEW YORK:JOHN WILEY AND SONS, INC., 1996; "THE RADIANCE...", P.195

43   LEAMER, LAURENCE. *THE KENNEDY WOMEN*. NEW YORK:VILLARD BOOKS, 1994; "I WARNED THEM...", P.433

44   ANDERSEN, CHRISTOPHER. *JACK AND JACKIE:PORTRAIT OF AN AMERICAN MARRIAGE*. NEW YORK:WILLIAM MORROW AND COMPANY INC., 1996; "SOME OF THOSE...", P.118

45   ANDERSEN, CHRISTOPHER. *JACK AND JACKIE:PORTRAIT OF AN AMERICAN MARRIAGE*. NEW YORK:WILLIAM MORROW AND COMPANY INC., 1996; "THEY WERE NOT...", P.105

46   ANDERSEN, CHRISTOPHER. *JACK AND JACKIE:PORTRAIT OF AN AMERICAN MARRIAGE*. NEW YORK:WILLIAM MORROW AND COMPANY INC., 1996; "THERE WERE NO...", P.100

CHAPTER FIVE

1   ANDERSEN, CHRISTOPHER. *JACK AND JACKIE:PORTRAIT OF AN*

AMERICAN MARRIAGE. NEW YORK:WILLIAM MORROW AND COMPANY INC., 1996; "BEFORE HE LEFT...", P.128

2   KELLEY, KITTY. *JACKIE OH!.* NEW YORK:BALLANTINE BOOKS, 1979; "JACKIE DIDN'T HAVE...", P.37

3   MARTIN, RALPH G. *A HERO FOR OUR TIME:AN INTIMATE STORY OF THE KENNEDY YEARS.* NEW YORK:FAWCETT CREST, 1983; "HE WOULD FIND...", P.83

4   ANDERSEN, CHRISTOPHER. *JACK AND JACKIE:PORTRAIT OF AN AMERICAN MARRIAGE.* NEW YORK:WILLIAM MORROW AND COMPANY INC., 1996; "I'M SURE THIS...", P.128

5   DAVIS, JOHN H. *JACQUELINE BOUVIER: AN INTIMATE MEMOIR.* NEW YORK:JOHN WILEY AND SONS, INC., 1996; "KENNEDY MEN ARE...", P.183

6   MARTIN, RALPH G. *SEEDS OF DESTRUCTION.* NEW YORK: G.P.PUTNAM'S SONS, 1995; "I ONLY GOT...", P.192

7   KELLEY, KITTY. *JACKIE OH!.* NEW YORK:BALLANTINE BOOKS, 1979; "IT WAS MOST...", P.48

8   DAVIS, JOHN H. *JACQUELINE BOUVIER: AN INTIMATE MEMOIR.* NEW YORK:JOHN WILEY AND SONS, INC., 1996; "FINALLY, HER MONEY...", P.177

9   KLEIN, EDWARD. *ALL TOO HUMAN:THE LOVE STORY OF JACK AND JACKIE KENNEDY.* NEW YORK:POCKET BOOKS, 1996; "IN FACT, JACK...", P.181

10   KLEIN, EDWARD. *ALL TOO HUMAN:THE LOVE STORY OF JACK AND JACKIE KENNEDY.* NEW YORK:POCKET BOOKS, 1996; "IN LATE MAY...", P.197

11   BLY, NELLIE. *THE KENNEDY MEN: THREE GENERATIONS OF SEX, SCANDAL AND SECRETS.* NEW YORK:KENSINGTON PUBLISHING CORP.,1996; "JACKIE LEFT JACK...", P.79

12   DU BOIS, DIANA. *IN HER SISTERS SHADOW.* BOSTON:LITTLE, BROWN AND CO., 1995; "THEIR LIVES WERE...", P.81

13   KLEIN, EDWARD. *ALL TOO HUMAN:THE LOVE STORY OF JACK AND*

JACKIE KENNEDY. NEW YORK:POCKET BOOKS, 1996; "JACK AND JACKIE WENT...", P.199

14   BLY, NELLIE. *THE KENNEDY MEN: THREE GENERATIONS OF SEX, SCANDAL AND SECRETS.* NEW YORK:KENSINGTON PUBLISHING CORP.,1996; "ACCORDING TO A FRIEND...", P.80

15   KELLEY, KITTY. *JACKIE OH!.* NEW YORK:BALLANTINE BOOKS, 1979; "JACKIE WOULD TRY...", P.57

16   ANDERSEN, CHRISTOPHER. *JACK AND JACKIE:PORTRAIT OF AN AMERICAN MARRIAGE.* NEW YORK:WILLIAM MORROW AND COMPANY INC., 1996; "WHAT MADE THE...", P.172

17   HEYMANN, C. DAVID. *A WOMAN NAMED JACKIE.* NEW YORK:A LYLE STUART BOOK, 1989; "SOME OF THE CONCESSIONS...", P.194

18   ANDERSEN, CHRISTOPHER. *JACK AND JACKIE:PORTRAIT OF AN AMERICAN MARRIAGE.* NEW YORK:WILLIAM MORROW AND COMPANY INC., 1996; "AS PART OF THE...", P.171

19   KLEIN, EDWARD. *ALL TOO HUMAN:THE LOVE STORY OF JACK AND JACKIE KENNEDY.* NEW YORK:POCKET BOOKS, 1996; "IT'S UP TO THE...", P.221

20   MARTIN, RALPH G. *A HERO FOR OUR TIME:AN INTIMATE STORY OF THE KENNEDY YEARS.* NEW YORK:FAWCETT CREST, 1983; "IT'S NOT THE RIGHT...", P.86

21   BLY, NELLIE. *THE KENNEDY MEN: THREE GENERATIONS OF SEX, SCANDAL AND SECRETS.* NEW YORK:KENSINGTON PUBLISHING CORP.,1996; "CAROLINE BOUVIER KENNEDY...", P.81

22   HEYMANN, C. DAVID. *A WOMAN NAMED JACKIE.* NEW YORK:A LYLE STUART BOOK, 1989; "JACKIE ONCE DESCRIBED...", P.146

23   KELLEY, KITTY. *JACKIE OH!.* NEW YORK:BALLANTINE BOOKS, 1979; "JACKIE WAS SO BITTER...", P.53

24   HEYMANN, C. DAVID. *A WOMAN NAMED JACKIE.* NEW YORK:A LYLE STUART BOOK, 1989; "THE DAY AFTER...", P.191

25   HEYMANN, C. DAVID. *A WOMAN NAMED JACKIE.* NEW YORK:A LYLE STUART BOOK, 1989; "AS OFTEN HAPPENS...", P.192

26 BLY, NELLIE. *THE KENNEDY MEN: THREE GENERATIONS OF SEX, SCANDAL AND SECRETS.* NEW YORK:KENSINGTON PUBLISHING CORP.,1996; "ON THE EVE...", P.86

27 LEAMER, LAURENCE. *THE KENNEDY WOMEN.* NEW YORK:VILLARD BOOKS, 1994; "FOR JACK'S VISITS...", P.535

28 BLY, NELLIE. *THE KENNEDY MEN: THREE GENERATIONS OF SEX, SCANDAL AND SECRETS.* NEW YORK:KENSINGTON PUBLISHING CORP.,1996: "*GRADUALLY DR. FEELGOOD...*", *P.105*

29 MARTIN, RALPH G. *SEEDS OF DESTRUCTION.* NEW YORK: G.P.PUTNAM'S SONS, 1995; "NO PRESIDENT...", P.350

30 BLY, NELLIE. *THE KENNEDY MEN: THREE GENERATIONS OF SEX, SCANDAL AND SECRETS.* NEW YORK:KENSINGTON PUBLISHING CORP.,1996; "THE GOVERNMENT ...", P.105

CHAPTER SIX

1 KELLEY, KITTY. *JACKIE OH!.* NEW YORK:BALLANTINE BOOKS, 1979; "KENNEDY MEN HAD...", P.59

2 KELLEY, KITTY. *JACKIE OH!.* NEW YORK:BALLANTINE BOOKS, 1979; "THE OTHER WOMEN...", P.59

3 HEYMANN, C. DAVID. *A WOMAN NAMED JACKIE.* NEW YORK:A LYLE STUART BOOK, 1989; "WE WERE UP...", P.61

4 HEYMANN, C. DAVID. *A WOMAN NAMED JACKIE.* NEW YORK:A LYLE STUART BOOK, 1989; "FBI FILES...", P.180

5 ANDERSEN, CHRISTOPHER. *JACK AND JACKIE:PORTRAIT OF AN AMERICAN MARRIAGE.* NEW YORK:WILLIAM MORROW AND   COMPANY INC., 1996; "AUDREY HEPBURN...", P.156

6 ANDERSEN, CHRISTOPHER. *JACK AND JACKIE:PORTRAIT OF AN AMERICAN MARRIAGE.* NEW YORK:WILLIAM MORROW AND   COMPANY INC., 1996; "J. EDGAR HOOVER...", P.192

7 HEYMANN, C. DAVID. *A WOMAN NAMED JACKIE.* NEW YORK:A

LYLE STUART BOOK, 1989; "SECRET SERVICE AGENT...", P.279

8   ANDERSEN, CHRISTOPHER. *JACK AND JACKIE:PORTRAIT OF AN AMERICAN MARRIAGE*. NEW YORK:WILLIAM MORROW AND COMPANY INC., 1996; "JACK WAS ASSURING...", P.209

9   HEYMANN, C. DAVID. *A WOMAN NAMED JACKIE*. NEW YORK:A LYLE STUART BOOK, 1989; "IN HER BOOK...", P.235

10   KELLEY, KITTY. *JACKIE OH!*. NEW YORK:BALLANTINE BOOKS, 1979; "HOOVER DID NOT...", P.126

11   HEYMANN, C. DAVID. *A WOMAN NAMED JACKIE*. NEW YORK:A LYLE STUART BOOK, 1989; "OF ALL HIS OTHER...", P.236

12   HEYMANN, C. DAVID. *A WOMAN NAMED JACKIE*. NEW YORK:A LYLE STUART BOOK, 1989; "NEWS OF JACK...", P.238

13   HEYMANN, C. DAVID. *A WOMAN NAMED JACKIE*. NEW YORK:A LYLE STUART BOOK, 1989; "THEN ON ANOTHER...", P.287

14   HEYMANN, C. DAVID. *A WOMAN NAMED JACKIE*. NEW YORK:A LYLE STUART BOOK, 1989; "PETER LAWFORD...", P.181

15   HEYMANN, C. DAVID. *A WOMAN NAMED JACKIE*. NEW YORK:A LYLE STUART BOOK, 1989; "ANOTHER LAWFORD ...", P.285

16   HEYMANN, C. DAVID. *A WOMAN NAMED JACKIE*. NEW YORK:A LYLE STUART BOOK, 1989; "ONE OF JFK'S...", P.181

17   HEYMANN, C. DAVID. *A WOMAN NAMED JACKIE*. NEW YORK:A LYLE STUART BOOK, 1989; "THERE MAY NOT HAVE...", P.182

18   HEYMANN, C. DAVID. *A WOMAN NAMED JACKIE*. NEW YORK:A LYLE STUART BOOK, 1989; "I CAN VOUCH...", P.182

19   HEYMANN, C. DAVID. *A WOMAN NAMED JACKIE*. NEW YORK:A LYLE STUART BOOK, 1989; "ALTHOUGH ANGIE HAS...", P.246

21   HEYMANN, C. DAVID. *A WOMAN NAMED JACKIE*. NEW YORK:A LYLE STUART BOOK, 1989; "THE CLOSER JOHN KENNEDY...", P.225

22   HEYMANN, C. DAVID. *A WOMAN NAMED JACKIE*. NEW YORK:A LYLE STUART BOOK, 1989; "DURING THE PRESIDENTIAL...", P.229

23   KELLEY, KITTY. *JACKIE OH!*. NEW YORK:BALLANTINE BOOKS, 1979; "THIS PICTURE NEVER...", P.129

24   KELLEY,KITTY. *JACKIE OH!*. NEW YORK:BALLANTINE BOOKS,
     1979;"WHENEVER THE FIRST...", P.122

25   BLY, NELLIE. *THE KENNEDY MEN: THREE GENERATIONS OF SEX,
     SCANDAL AND SECRETS.* NEW YORK:KENSINGTON PUBLISHING
     CORP.,1996; "AREN'T YOU AFRAID...", P.103

26   KELLEY, KITTY. *JACKIE OH!*. NEW YORK:BALLANTINE BOOKS,
     1979; "BEING MARRIED...", P.130

27   HEYMANN, C. DAVID. *A WOMAN NAMED JACKIE.* NEW YORK:A
     LYLE STUART BOOK, 1989; "THE OTHER WOMAN...", P.292

28   MARTIN, RALPH G. *A HERO FOR OUR TIME:AN INTIMATE STORY OF
     THE KENNEDY YEARS.* NEW YORK:FAWCETT CREST, 1983; "THE
     SECRET SERVICE...", P.445

29   BLY, NELLIE. *THE KENNEDY MEN: THREE GENERATIONS OF SEX,
     SCANDAL AND SECRETS.* NEW YORK:KENSINGTON PUBLISHING
     CORP.,1996; "JACKIE KNEW WHAT...", P.103

30   BLY, NELLIE. *THE KENNEDY MEN: THREE GENERATIONS OF SEX,
     SCANDAL AND SECRETS.* NEW YORK:KENSINGTON PUBLISHING
     CORP.,1996; "IT'S SAID THAT...", P.109

31   BLY, NELLIE. *THE KENNEDY MEN: THREE GENERATIONS OF SEX,
     SCANDAL AND SECRETS.* NEW YORK:KENSINGTON PUBLISHING
     CORP.,1996; "AS THE AFFAIR...", P.119

32   KELLEY, KITTY. *JACKIE OH!*. NEW YORK:BALLANTINE BOOKS,
     1979; "THIS WAS DELIBERATELY...", P.131

33   KELLEY, KITTY. *JACKIE OH!*. NEW YORK:BALLANTINE BOOKS,
     1979; "WHEN MARILYN...", P.131

34   KELLEY, KITTY. *JACKIE OH!*. NEW YORK:BALLANTINE BOOKS,
     1979; "JACKIE ASKED ME...", P.60

35   KELLEY, KITTY. *JACKIE OH!*. NEW YORK:BALLANTINE BOOKS,
     1979; "THEN THERE WAS...", P.124

36   KELLEY, KITTY. *JACKIE OH!*. NEW YORK:BALLANTINE BOOKS,
     1979; "MARY CONFIDED...", P.124

37   KELLEY, KITTY. *JACKIE OH!*. NEW YORK:BALLANTINE BOOKS,

1979; "THE FACT WAS...", P.77

38   KELLEY, KITTY. *JACKIE OH!*. NEW YORK:BALLANTINE BOOKS,
     1979; "SHE IS NOT...", P.75

39   KLEIN, EDWARD. *ALL TOO HUMAN:THE LOVE STORY OF JACK AND
     JACKIE KENNEDY.* NEW YORK:POCKET BOOKS, 1996; "LEE TOLD
     ME...", P.236

40   REEVES, THOMAS C. *A QUESTION OF CHARACTER:A LIFE OF JOHN
     F. KENNEDY.* ROCKLIN, CA:PRIMA PUBLISHING, 1992; "FROM THE
     FIRST...", P.116

CHAPTER SEVEN

1   TROY, GIL. *AFFAIRS OF STATE.* NEW YORK:FREE PRESS, 1997; "THE
     PUBLIC LIFE...", P.99

2   HEYMANN, C. DAVID. *A WOMAN NAMED JACKIE.* NEW YORK:A
     LYLE STUART BOOK, 1989; "AS OFTEN HAPPENS...", P.192

3   KELLEY, KITTY. *JACKIE OH!*. NEW YORK:BALLANTINE BOOKS,
     1979; "OTHER AREAS...", P.48

4   HEYMANN, C. DAVID. *A WOMAN NAMED JACKIE.* NEW YORK:A
     LYLE STUART BOOK, 1989; "THERE WAS CERTAINLY...", P.192

5   KLEIN, EDWARD. *ALL TOO HUMAN:THE LOVE STORY OF JACK AND
     JACKIE KENNEDY.* NEW YORK:POCKET BOOKS, 1996; "THE FIRST
     JOURNALIST...", P.219

6   LEAMER, LAURENCE. *THE KENNEDY WOMEN.* NEW YORK:
     VILLARD BOOKS, 1994; "HE'S GONE...", P.514

7   HEYMANN, C. DAVID. *A WOMAN NAMED JACKIE.* NEW YORK:A
     LYLE STUART BOOK, 1989; "IT'S POSSIBLE...", P.193

8   KLEIN, EDWARD. *ALL TOO HUMAN:THE LOVE STORY OF JACK AND
     JACKIE KENNEDY.* NEW YORK:POCKET BOOKS, 1996; "YOU'RE TOO
     OLD...", P.218

9   LAWFORD, LADY MAY. *BITCH.* BROOKLINE VILLAGE, MA:
     BRANDEN PUBLISHING CO. INC.,1986; "OLD JOE ...",   P.77

10   LAWFORD, LADY MAY. *BITCH*. BROOKLINE VILLAGE, MA: BRANDEN PUBLISHING CO. INC.,1986; "I WON'T STAY…" P.78

11   KLEIN, EDWARD. *ALL TOO HUMAN:THE LOVE STORY OF JACK AND JACKIE KENNEDY*. NEW YORK:POCKET BOOKS, 1996; "IF I DON'T…", P.247

12   MARTIN, RALPH G. *A HERO FOR OUR TIME:AN INTIMATE STORY OF THE KENNEDY YEARS*. NEW YORK:FAWCETT CREST, 1983; "SHE WAS GETTING…", P.446

13   TROY, GIL. *AFFAIRS OF STATE*. NEW YORK:FREE PRESS, 1997; "THE PRESIDENT…", P.122

14   TROY, GIL. *AFFAIRS OF STATE*. NEW YORK:FREE PRESS, 1997; "THE PRESIDENT AND FIRST…", P.124

15   HEYMANN, C. DAVID. *A WOMAN NAMED JACKIE*. NEW YORK:A LYLE STUART BOOK, 1989; "HARD, TOUGH…", P.268

16   KELLEY, KITTY. *JACKIE OH!*. NEW YORK:BALLANTINE BOOKS, 1979; "PEOPLE WERE…", P.115

17   TROY, GIL. *AFFAIRS OF STATE*. NEW YORK:FREE PRESS, 1997; "THE KENNEDY'S DID …", P.106

18   HEYMANN, C. DAVID. *A WOMAN NAMED JACKIE*. NEW YORK:A LYLE STUART BOOK, 1989; "COME ON NOW…", P.293

19   ANDERSEN, CHRISTOPHER. *JACK AND JACKIE:PORTRAIT OF AN AMERICAN MARRIAGE*. NEW YORK:WILLIAM MORROW AND COMPANY INC., 1996; "AT ONE OF THEIR…", P.350

20   KLEIN, EDWARD. *ALL TOO HUMAN:THE LOVE STORY OF JACK AND JACKIE KENNEDY*. NEW YORK:POCKET BOOKS, 1996; "LATER ON, JACKIE…", P.316

21   KLEIN, EDWARD. *ALL TOO HUMAN:THE LOVE STORY OF JACK AND JACKIE KENNEDY*. NEW YORK:POCKET BOOKS, 1996; "IF YOU LEAVE…", P.220

CHAPTER EIGHT

1 ANTHONY, CARL SFERRAZZA. *AS WE REMEMBER HER.* NEW YORK: HARPERCOLLINS, 1997; "MR. KENNEDY SAID...", P.80

2 KELLEY, KITTY. *JACKIE OH!.* NEW YORK:BALLANTINE BOOKS, 1979; "JACKIE LIVED BY...", P.83

3 KELLEY, KITTY. *JACKIE OH!.* NEW YORK:BALLANTINE BOOKS, 1979; "I WAS ALONE...", P.47

4 REEVES, THOMAS C. *A QUESTION OF CHARACTER:A LIFE OF JOHN F. KENNEDY.* ROCKLIN, CA:PRIMA PUBLISHING, 1992; "ASKING JACKIE...", P.115

5 HEYMANN, C. DAVID. *A WOMAN NAMED JACKIE.* NEW YORK:A LYLE STUART BOOK, 1989; "POLITICS IS IN...", P.208

6 HEYMANN, C. DAVID. *A WOMAN NAMED JACKIE.* NEW YORK:A LYLE STUART BOOK, 1989; "ONE DAY A REPORTER...", P.208

7 HEYMANN, C. DAVID. *A WOMAN NAMED JACKIE.* NEW YORK:A LYLE STUART BOOK, 1989; "NOTHING DISTURBS...", P.208

8 HEYMANN, C. DAVID. *A WOMAN NAMED JACKIE.* NEW YORK:A LYLE STUART BOOK, 1989; "JACKIE LOOKED DOWN...", P.209

9 HEYMANN, C. DAVID. *A WOMAN NAMED JACKIE.* NEW YORK:A LYLE STUART BOOK, 1989; "JACKIE WAS A...", P.209

10 HEYMANN, C. DAVID. *A WOMAN NAMED JACKIE.* NEW YORK:A LYLE STUART BOOK, 1989; "EARLY IN THEIR...", P.177

11 HEYMANN, C. DAVID. *A WOMAN NAMED JACKIE.* NEW YORK:A LYLE STUART BOOK, 1989; "JANET DES ROSIERS...", P.229

12 ANDERSEN, CHRISTOPHER. *JACK AND JACKIE:PORTRAIT OF AN AMERICAN MARRIAGE.* NEW YORK:WILLIAM MORROW AND COMPANY INC., 1996; "SHE HATED...", P.132

13 HEYMANN, C. DAVID. *A WOMAN NAMED JACKIE.* NEW YORK:A LYLE STUART BOOK, 1989; "SHE WAS A DIFFICULT...", P.222

14 HEYMANN, C. DAVID. *A WOMAN NAMED JACKIE.* NEW YORK:A LYLE STUART BOOK, 1989; "WHATEVER ELSE...", P.221

15 HEYMANN, C. DAVID. *A WOMAN NAMED JACKIE*. NEW YORK:A
    LYLE STUART BOOK, 1989; "I FELT JACKIE...",P.220

16 HEYMANN, C. DAVID. *A WOMAN NAMED JACKIE*. NEW YORK:A
    LYLE STUART BOOK, 1989; "JACKIE'S MALAISE...", P.221

17 "HE WAS UTTERLY...":JEFFERY POTTER,*MEN, MONEY, AND
    MAGIC*:P.261

18 REEVES, RICHARD. *PRESIDENT KENNEDY:PROFILE OF POWER*. NEW
    YORK:SIMON AND SCHUSTER, 1993; "EARLY IN
    ADMINISTRATION...", P.154

19 COLLIER, PETER AND HOROWITZ, DAVID. *THE KENNEDYS:AN
    AMERICAN DRAMA*. NEW YORK:WARNER BOOKS, 1984;
    "JACQUELINE KENNEDY HAD...", P.353

20 HEYMANN, C. DAVID. *A WOMAN NAMED JACKIE*. NEW YORK:A
    LYLE STUART BOOK, 1989; "AFTER JACKIE MOVED...", P.266

21 HEYMANN, C. DAVID. *A WOMAN NAMED JACKIE*. NEW YORK:A
    LYLE STUART BOOK, 1989; "ACUTELY AWARE...", P.266

22 HEYMANN, C. DAVID. *A WOMAN NAMED JACKIE*. NEW YORK:A
    LYLE STUART BOOK, 1989; "JACKIE'S SHYNESS...", P.272

23 HEYMANN, C. DAVID. *A WOMAN NAMED JACKIE*. NEW YORK:A
    LYLE STUART BOOK, 1989; "I FEEL STRONGLY...", P.267

24 HEYMANN, C. DAVID. *A WOMAN NAMED JACKIE*. NEW YORK:A
    LYLE STUART BOOK, 1989; "JACKIE WAS DOING...", P.275

25 ANDERSEN, CHRISTOPHER. *JACK AND JACKIE:PORTRAIT OF AN
    AMERICAN MARRIAGE*. NEW YORK:WILLIAM MORROW AND
    COMPANY INC., 1996; "I SYMPATHIZE..." P.283

26 HEYMANN, C. DAVID. *A WOMAN NAMED JACKIE*. NEW YORK:A
    LYLE STUART BOOK, 1989; "JACKIE'S OTHER PROBLEM...", P.278

27 ANDERSEN, CHRISTOPHER. *JACK AND JACKIE:PORTRAIT OF AN
    AMERICAN MARRIAGE*. NEW YORK:WILLIAM MORROW AND
    COMPANY INC., 1996; "IF MRS. KENNEDY...", P.275

28 ANDERSEN, CHRISTOPHER. *JACK AND JACKIE:PORTRAIT OF AN
    AMERICAN MARRIAGE*. NEW YORK:WILLIAM MORROW AND

COMPANY INC., 1996; "NOT EVEN THE PRESIDENT...", P.278

29   ANDERSEN, CHRISTOPHER. *JACK AND JACKIE:PORTRAIT OF AN AMERICAN MARRIAGE.* NEW YORK:WILLIAM MORROW AND COMPANY INC., 1996; "JACKIE DIDN'T WANT...", P.277

30. HEYMANN, C. DAVID. *A WOMAN NAMED JACKIE.* NEW YORK:A LYLE STUART BOOK, 1989, "OFF THE RECORD...", P.266

31. BLY, NELLIE. *THE KENNEDY MEN: THREE GENERATIONS OF SEX, SCANDAL AND SECRETS.* NEW YORK:KENSINGTON PUBLISHING CORP.,1996; "THE FIRST CALLER..." P. 121

CHAPTER NINE

1   HEYMANN, C. DAVID. *A WOMAN NAMED JACKIE.* NEW YORK:A LYLE STUART BOOK, 1989; "JACK GAVE JACKIE...", P.387

2   CAFARAKIS, CHRISTIAN. *THE FABULOUS ONASSIS:HIS LIFE AND LOVES.* NEW YORK:WILLIAM MORROW AND CO. INC., 1972; "BUT OF COURSE...", P.99

3   CAFARAKIS, CHRISTIAN. *THE FABULOUS ONASSIS:HIS LIFE AND LOVES.* NEW YORK:WILLIAM MORROW AND CO. INC., 1972; "WHY NOT ASK...", P.100

4   EVANS, PETER. *ARI:THE LIFE AND TIMES OF ARISTOTLE ONASSIS.* NEW YORK:SUMMIT BOOKS, 1986; "NO ONE WAS RICHER...", JACKET

5   HEYMANN, C. DAVID. *A WOMAN NAMED JACKIE.* NEW YORK:A LYLE STUART BOOK, 1989; "LAID DOWN THE LAW...", P.389

6   HEYMANN, C. DAVID. *A WOMAN NAMED JACKIE.* NEW YORK:A LYLE STUART BOOK, 1989; "THE GOLDEN GREEK'S", P.388

7   HEYMANN, C. DAVID. *A WOMAN NAMED JACKIE.* NEW YORK:A LYLE STUART BOOK, 1989; "I CAN'T POSSIBLY...", P.388

8   CAFARAKIS, CHRISTIAN. *THE FABULOUS ONASSIS:HIS LIFE AND LOVES.* NEW YORK:WILLIAM MORROW AND CO. INC., 1972; "I PERSONALLY THINK...", P.99

9	KLEIN, EDWARD. *ALL TOO HUMAN:THE LOVE STORY OF JACK AND JACKIE KENNEDY*. NEW YORK:POCKET BOOKS, 1996; "HIS DECISION TO...", P.214

10	KELLEY, KITTY. *JACKIE OH!*. NEW YORK:BALLANTINE BOOKS, 1979; "THE STRAINS IMPOSED...", P.75

11	LEAMER, LAURENCE. *THE KENNEDY WOMEN*. NEW YORK:VILLARD BOOKS, 1994; "JACKIE'S ATTITUDE...", P.586

12	DAVIS, L.J. *ONASSIS:ARISTOTLE AND CHRISTINA*. NEW YORK:ST. MARTIN'S PRESS, 1986; "THE PRESIDENT'S RELATIONS...", P.125

13	FRASER, NICOLAS, JACOBSON, PHILIP, OTTAWAY MARK, CHESTER, LEWIS. *ARISTOTLE ONASSIS*. PHILADELPHIA AND NEW YORK:J. B. LIPPINCOTT CO, 1977; "THE CRUISE WAS...", P.247

14	ANDERSEN, CHRISTOPHER. *JACK AND JACKIE:PORTRAIT OF AN AMERICAN MARRIAGE*. NEW YORK:WILLIAM MORROW AND COMPANY INC., 1996; "ONASSIS FELL...", P.356

15	HEYMANN, C. DAVID. *A WOMAN NAMED JACKIE*. NEW YORK:A LYLE STUART BOOK, 1989; "ARI ENTERTAINED...", P.393

16	KLEIN, EDWARD. *ALL TOO HUMAN:THE LOVE STORY OF JACK AND JACKIE KENNEDY*. NEW YORK:POCKET BOOKS, 1996; "JACKIE WAS EXCITED...", P.336

17	LEAMER, LAURENCE. *THE KENNEDY WOMEN*. NEW YORK: VILLARD BOOKS, 1994; "THE FAVORITE GAMES..."6, P.587

18	DAVIS, L.J. *ONASSIS:ARISTOTLE AND CHRISTINA*. NEW YORK:ST. MARTIN'S PRESS, 1986; "HE HAD LEARNED...", P.125

19	KLEIN, EDWARD. *ALL TOO HUMAN:THE LOVE STORY OF JACK AND JACKIE KENNEDY*. NEW YORK:POCKET BOOKS, 1996; "AS THE CHRISTINA...", P.336

20	KLEIN, EDWARD. *ALL TOO HUMAN:THE LOVE STORY OF JACK AND JACKIE KENNEDY*. NEW YORK:POCKET BOOKS, 1996; "THE ONLY WAY...", P.336

21	HEYMANN, C. DAVID. *A WOMAN NAMED JACKIE*. NEW YORK:A LYLE STUART BOOK, 1989; "ON BOARD ARI AND JACKIE...", P.393

22   HEYMANN, C. DAVID. *A WOMAN NAMED JACKIE*. NEW YORK:A
      LYLE STUART BOOK, 1989; "WALKING TOGETHER...", P.391

23   KELLEY, KITTY. *JACKIE OH!*. NEW YORK:BALLANTINE BOOKS,
      1979; "IN ISTANBUL...", P.216

24   KLEIN, EDWARD. *ALL TOO HUMAN:THE LOVE STORY OF JACK AND
      JACKIE KENNEDY*. NEW YORK:POCKET BOOKS, 1996; "WHILE
      JACKIE WAS...", P.339

25   KELLEY, KITTY. *JACKIE OH!*. NEW YORK:BALLANTINE BOOKS,
      1979; "WHEN JACKIE LEFT..." P.210

26   CAFARAKIS, CHRISTIAN. *THE FABULOUS ONASSIS:HIS LIFE AND
      LOVES*. NEW YORK:WILLIAM MORROW AND CO. INC., 1972;
      "WHEN JACKIE RETURNED...", P.101

27   KELLEY, KITTY. *JACKIE OH!*. NEW YORK:BALLANTINE BOOKS,
      1979; "SHE WAS IMMENSELY...", P.217

28   KELLEY, KITTY. *JACKIE OH!*. NEW YORK:BALLANTINE BOOKS.
      1979; "SHE HAD MADE...", P.219

CHAPTER TEN

1   HUBBELL, WEBB. *FRIENDS IN HIGH PLACES*. NEW YORK:WILLIAM
      MORROW AND CO., 1997 "WEBB,IF I...", P.282

2   HEYMANN, C. DAVID. *A WOMAN NAMED JACKIE*. NEW YORK:A
      LYLE STUART BOOK, 1989; "ALL OF A SUDDEN...", P.395

3   HEYMANN, C. DAVID. *A WOMAN NAMED JACKIE*. NEW YORK:A
      LYLE STUART BOOK, 1989; "WHAT I IMAGINED...", P.395

4   MARTIN, RALPH G. *A HERO FOR OUR TIME:AN INTIMATE STORY OF
      THE KENNEDY YEARS*. NEW YORK:FAWCETT CREST, 1983;
      "RECONSTRUCTING THE SCENE...", P.511

5   HEYMANN, C. DAVID. *A WOMAN NAMED JACKIE*. NEW YORK:A
      LYLE STUART BOOK, 1989; "I DON'T KNOW...", P.396

6   MARTIN, RALPH G. *SEEDS OF DESTRUCTION*. NEW YORK:G.P.

PUTNAM'S SONS, 1995; "THE PRESIDENT'S SECRETARY...", P.452

7   MARTIN, RALPH G. *A HERO FOR OUR TIME:AN INTIMATE STORY OF THE KENNEDY YEARS.* NEW YORK:FAWCETT CREST, 1983; "NO, I DON'T THINK...", P.511

8   HEYMANN, C. DAVID. *A WOMAN NAMED JACKIE.* NEW YORK:A LYLE STUART BOOK, 1989; "A SPLIT IN...", P.396

9   HEYMANN, C. DAVID. *A WOMAN NAMED JACKIE.* NEW YORK:A LYLE STUART BOOK, 1989; "JACKIE SUNBATHING...", P.392

10   KLEIN, EDWARD. *ALL TOO HUMAN:THE LOVE STORY OF JACK AND JACKIE KENNEDY.* NEW YORK:POCKET BOOKS, 1996; "INSTEAD, HE SEIZED...", P.341

11   COLLIER, PETER AND HOROWITZ, DAVID. *THE KENNEDYS:AN AMERICAN DRAMA.* NEW YORK:WARNER BOOKS, 1984; "SENATOR FULLBRIGHT...", P.256

12   HEYMANN, C. DAVID. *A WOMAN NAMED JACKIE.* NEW YORK:A LYLE STUART BOOK, 1989; "GOD, I HATE TO...", P.397

13   BLY, NELLIE. *THE KENNEDY MEN: THREE GENERATIONS OF SEX, SCANDAL AND SECRETS.* NEW YORK:KENSINGTON PUBLISHING CORP.,1996; "AS SHOCKING AS THE...", P.143

14   MARTIN, RALPH G. *SEEDS OF DESTRUCTION.* NEW YORK: G.P.PUTNAM'S SONS, 1995; "DID YOU EVER...", P.446

15   MARTIN, RALPH G. *A HERO FOR OUR TIME:AN INTIMATE STORY OF THE KENNEDY YEARS.* NEW YORK:FAWCETT CREST, 1983; "KENNEDY TALKED ABOUT...", P.500

16   BLY, NELLIE. *THE KENNEDY MEN: THREE GENERATIONS OF SEX, SCANDAL AND SECRETS.* NEW YORK:KENSINGTON PUBLISHING CORP.,1996; "IT WAS NOV. 22,...", P.138

17   KLEIN, EDWARD. *ALL TOO HUMAN:THE LOVE STORY OF JACK AND JACKIE KENNEDY.* NEW YORK:POCKET BOOKS, 1996; "LAST NIGHT WOULD...", P.343

18   ANDERSEN, CHRISTOPHER. *JACK AND JACKIE:PORTRAIT OF AN AMERICAN MARRIAGE.* NEW YORK:WILLIAM MORROW AND

COMPANY INC., 1996; "WE'RE GOING IN...", P.363

19 KELLEY, KITTY. *JACKIE OH!*. NEW YORK:BALLANTINE BOOKS, 1979; "THERE WAS A LARGE...", P.399

20 MARTIN, RALPH G. *SEEDS OF DESTRUCTION*. NEW YORK: G.P. PUTNAM'S SONS, 1995; "'WELL',SAID MRS. CONNALLY...", P.453

21 HEYMANN, C. DAVID. *A WOMAN NAMED JACKIE*. NEW YORK:A LYLE STUART BOOK, 1989; "IN HER MOMENT...", P.400

22 ANDERSEN, CHRISTOPHER. *JACK AND JACKIE:PORTRAIT OF AN AMERICAN MARRIAGE*. NEW YORK:WILLIAM MORROW AND COMPANY INC., 1996; "FINALLY, AT ONE...", P.366

23 KELLEY, KITTY. *JACKIE OH!*. NEW YORK:BALLANTINE BOOKS, 1979; "AS THE FUNERAL...", P.232

CHAPTER ELEVEN

1 EVANS, PETER. *ARI:THE LIFE AND TIMES OF ARISTOTLE ONASSIS*. NEW YORK:SUMMIT BOOKS, 1986; "ON NOVEMBER 22,...", P.197

2 ANDERSEN, CHRISTOPHER.*JACKIE AFTER JACK*. WILLIAM MORROW AND COMPANY,INC.,1998,"JACKIE DREW ONASSIS..."P.47

3 HEYMANN, C. DAVID. *A WOMAN NAMED JACKIE*. NEW YORK:A LYLE STUART BOOK, 1989; "JACKIE'S TWIN...", P.413

4 HEYMANN, C. DAVID. *A WOMAN NAMED JACKIE*. NEW YORK:A LYLE STUART BOOK, 1989; "MAX JACOBSON WHO...", P.412

5 KELLEY, KITTY. *JACKIE OH!*. NEW YORK:BALLANTINE BOOKS, 1979; "IT'S JUST LIKE...", P.238

6 KELLEY, KITTY. *JACKIE OH!*. NEW YORK:BALLANTINE BOOKS, 1979; "UPSTAIRS IN THE ...", P.240

7 HEYMANN, C. DAVID. *A WOMAN NAMED JACKIE*. NEW YORK:A LYLE STUART BOOK, 1989; "RISING ABOVE HER...", P.414

8 KELLEY, KITTY. *JACKIE OH!*. NEW YORK:BALLANTINE BOOKS, 1979; "WHEN JACKIE LEARNED...", P.239

9 MARTIN, RALPH G. *SEEDS OF DESTRUCTION*. NEW YORK: G.P.PUTNAM'S SONS, 1995; "CARDINAL CUSHING...", P.462

10   ANDERSEN, CHRISTOPHER. *JACK AND JACKIE:PORTRAIT OF AN*
        AMERICAN MARRIAGE. NEW YORK:WILLIAM MORROW AND
        COMSPANY INC., 1996; "THE IMAGES GENERATED...", P.367

11   KLEIN, EDWARD. *ALL TOO HUMAN:THE LOVE STORY OF JACK AND*
        JACKIE KENNEDY. NEW YORK:POCKET BOOKS, 1996; "FIRST TO
        LAST...", P.347

12   KLEIN, EDWARD. *ALL TOO HUMAN:THE LOVE STORY OF JACK AND*
        JACKIE KENNEDY. NEW YORK:POCKET BOOKS, 1996; "THE CAM
        ERAS WERE...", P.352

13   MARTIN, RALPH G. *SEEDS OF DESTRUCTION.* NEW YORK:
        G.P.PUTNAM'S SONS, 1995; "BOBBY'S PAIN WAS...", P.463

14   MARTIN, RALPH G. *SEEDS OF DESTRUCTION.* NEW YORK:
        G.P.PUTNAM'S SONS, 1995; "IT WAS A MASS...", P.465

15   HEYMANN, C. DAVID. *A WOMAN NAMED JACKIE.* NEW YORK:A
        LYLE STUART BOOK, 1989; "JOHN DAVIS, HAVING...", P.416

16   TROY, GIL. *AFFAIRS OF STATE.* NEW YORK:FREE PRESS, 1997;
        "MRS. KENNEDY ACHIEVED...", P.129

17   TROY, GIL. *AFFAIRS OF STATE.* NEW YORK:FREE PRESS, 1997;
        "THE KENNEDYS...", P.132

18   TROY, GIL. *AFFAIRS OF STATE.* NEW YORK:FREE PRESS, 1997;
        "SUCH REVELATIONS...", P.92

19   KELLEY, KITTY. *JACKIE OH!.* NEW YORK:BALLANTINE BOOKS,
        1979; "NO LESS ASTONISHING...", P.239

20   DAVIS, L.J. *ONASSIS:ARISTOTLE AND CHRISTINA.* NEW YORK:ST.
        MARTIN'S PRESS, 1986; "AFTER DINNER...", P.126

21   FRASER, NICOLAS, JACOBSON, PHILIP, OTTAWAY MARK,
        CHESTER, LEWIS. *ARISTOTLE ONASSIS.* PHILADELPHIA AND NEW
        YORK:J. B. LIPPINCOTT CO, 1977; "ONASSIS' IMPOSED ..."P.248

CHAPTER TWELVE

1   ANDERSEN, CHRISTOPHER. *JACK AND JACKIE:PORTRAIT OF AN*

AMERICAN MARRIAGE. NEW YORK:WILLIAM MORROW AND COMPANY INC., 1996; "IN CHILDHOOD GAMES...", P.59

2   DAVIS, JOHN H. *JACQUELINE BOUVIER: AN INTIMATE MEMOIR.* NEW YORK:JOHN WILEY AND SONS, INC., 1996; "JACKIE WAS AN ARTISTE...", P.27

3   DAVIS, JOHN H. *JACQUELINE BOUVIER: AN INTIMATE MEMOIR.* NEW YORK:JOHN WILEY AND SONS, INC., 1996; "HER GRAND-FATHER...", P.35

4   DAVIS, JOHN H. *JACQUELINE BOUVIER: AN INTIMATE MEMOIR.* NEW YORK:JOHN WILEY AND SONS, INC., 1996; "SHE PREFERRED MYTH...", PXII

5   HEYMANN, C. DAVID. *A WOMAN NAMED JACKIE.* NEW YORK:A LYLE STUART BOOK, 1989; "A WEEK AFTER THE...", P.418

6   HEYMANN, C. DAVID. *A WOMAN NAMED JACKIE.* NEW YORK:A LYLE STUART BOOK, 1989; "JACKIE REGURGITATED...", P.418

7   DAVID, LESTER. *JACQUELINE KENNEDY ONASSIS.* NEW YORK:A BRICH LANE PRESS BOOK, 1994; "BIG BUSINESS...", P.86

8   HEYMANN, C. DAVID. *A WOMAN NAMED JACKIE.* NEW YORK:A LYLE STUART BOOK, 1989; "JACKIE PROCEEDED TO...", P.417

9   OSBORNE, CLAIRE G. *JACKIE:A LEGEND DEFINED.* NEW YORK: AVON BOOKS, 1997; "THE MAGIC OF CAMELOT...", P.465

10   OSBORNE, CLAIRE G. *JACKIE:A LEGEND DEFINED.* NEW YORK: AVON BOOKS, 1997; "ANOTHER, SUCH AS ARTHUR...", P.468

11   MARTIN, RALPH G. *SEEDS OF DESTRUCTION.* NEW YORK: G.P.PUTNAM'S SONS, 1995; "THAT STORY OF HERS...", P.470

12   OSBORNE, CLAIRE G. *JACKIE:A LEGEND DEFINED.* NEW YORK: AVON BOOKS, 1997; "CAMELOT WAS AN...", P.465

13   OSBORNE, CLAIRE G. *JACKIE:A LEGEND DEFINED.* NEW YORK: AVON BOOKS, 1997; "DEAN RUSK...", P.465

14   OSBORNE, CLAIRE G. *JACKIE:A LEGEND DEFINED.* NEW YORK: AVON BOOKS, 1997; "ADAM YARMOLINSKY ASKS...", P.465

15   OSBORNE, CLAIRE G. *JACKIE:A LEGEND DEFINED.* NEW YORK:

AVON BOOKS, 1997; "WILLIAM SLAONE COFFIN...", P.469

16   OSBORNE, CLAIRE G. *JACKIE:A LEGEND DEFINED*. NEW YORK:
        AVON BOOKS, 1997; "AS WILLIAM SMITH...", P.468

17   OSBORNE, CLAIRE G. *JACKIE:A LEGEND DEFINED*. NEW YORK:
        AVON BOOKS, 1997; "CAMELOT IS RIDICULOUS...", P.470

18   OSBORNE, CLAIRE G. *JACKIE:A LEGEND DEFINED*. NEW YORK:
        AVON BOOKS, 1997; "LLOYD CUTTER SAYS...", P.471

19   BLY, NELLIE. *THE KENNEDY MEN: THREE GENERATIONS OF SEX,
        SCANDAL AND SECRETS*. NEW YORK:KENSINGTON PUBLISHING
        CORP.,1996; "DURING THE AFTERMATH...", P.144

20   DAVIS, JOHN H. *THE KENNEDYS:DYNASTY AND DISASTER 1848-1983*.
        NEW YORK:MC GRAW-HILL BOOK CO., 1984; "THE PERSONALITY
        OF JFK...", P.505

21   DAVIS, JOHN H. *THE KENNEDYS:DYNASTY AND DISASTER 1848-1983*.
        NEW YORK:MC GRAW-HILL BOOK CO., 1984; "ALONG WITH THE
        GLORIFICATION...", P.505

22   DAVIS, JOHN H. *THE KENNEDYS:DYNASTY AND DISASTER 1848-1983*.
        NEW YORK:MC GRAW-HILL BOOK CO., 1984; "UNFORTUNATELY
        WHAT PROCEEDED...", P.505

CHAPTER THIRTEEN

1   HERSH, SEYMOUR. *THE DARK SIDE OF CAMELOT*. BOSTON:LITTLE,
        BROWN AND COMPANY, 1997, "THE PRESIDENT'S FILES...",P.32
        HEYMANN, C. DAVID. *A WOMAN NAMED JACKIE*. NEW YORK:A
        LYLE STUART BOOK, 1989; "JACKIE'S COUSIN...", P.415

3   DAVIS, LEE. *ASSASSINATION, TWENTY ASSASSINATIONS THAT
        CHANGED HISTORY*. NEW YORK:BDD SPECIAL EDITIONS, 1993;
        "THE WARREN COMMISSION...", P.90

4   HURT, HENRY. *REASONABLE DOUBT:AN INVESTIGATION INTO THE
        ASSASSINATION OF JOHN F. KENNEDY*. NEW YORK:HOLT,
        RINEHART AND WINSTON, 1985; "INITIALLY, THE DISAGREE-

MENT...", P.16

5   STROBER, DEBORAH H. AND GERALD S. *"LET US BEGIN ANEW":AN ORAL HISTORY OF THE KENNEDY PRESIDENCY.* NEW YORK:HARPER COLLINS, 1993; "I DO HAVE ONE...", P.464

6   STROBER, DEBORAH H. AND GERALD S. *"LET US BEGIN ANEW":AN ORAL HISTORY OF THE KENNEDY PRESIDENCY.* NEW YORK:HARPER COLLINS, 1993; "I KNEW THE PEOPLE...", P.462

7   DAVIS, JOHN H. *THE KENNEDYS:DYNASTY AND DISASTER 1848-1983.* NEW YORK:MC GRAW-HILL BOOK CO., 1984; "WHAT A CONTRAST..", P.506

8   DAVIS, JOHN H. *THE KENNEDYS:DYNASTY AND DISASTER 1848-1983.* NEW YORK:MC GRAW-HILL BOOK CO., 1984; "JOHNSON ASKED THE CIA...", P.478

9   GENTRY, CURT. *J. EDGAR HOOVER:THE MAN AND THE SECRETS.* NEW YORK:W.W. NORTON AND CO., 1991; "IN WHAT MUST...",P.557

10   MARTIN, RALPH G. *SEEDS OF ESTRUCTION.* NEWYORK:G.P.PUTNAM'S SONS, 1995; "ARTHUR SCHLESINGER RECORDED..", P.485

11   MARTIN, RALPH G. *SEEDS OF DESTRUCTION.* NEW YORK: G.P.PUTNAM'S SONS, 1995; "HE HAD SEEN NO...", P.486

12   OSBORNE, CLAIRE G. *JACKIE:A LEGEND DEFINED.* NEW YORK: AVON BOOKS, 1997; "THE OLIVER STONE...", P.463

13   SLOAN, BILL. *JFK BREAKING THE SILENCE.* DALLAS, TEXAS: TAYLOR PUBLISHING CO., 1993; "IN 1992 A BOOK...", P.247

14   HURT, HENRY. *REASONABLE DOUBT:AN INVESTIGATION INTO THE ASSASSINATION OF JOHN F. KENNEDY.* NEW YORK:HOLT, RINEHART AND WINSTON, 1985; "IN EARLY 1977...", P.414

15   HURT, HENRY. *REASONABLE DOUBT:AN INVESTIGATION INTO THE ASSASSINATION OF JOHN F. KENNEDY.* NEW YORK:HOLT, RINEHART AND WINSTON, 1985; "EVEN MORE STARTLING...", P.419

16   HURT, HENRY. *REASONABLE DOUBT:AN INVESTIGATION INTO THE ASSASSINATION OF JOHN F. KENNEDY.* NEW YORK:HOLT, RINEHART AND WINSTON, 1985; "THREE FRENCHMEN...", P.419

17   HURT, HENRY. *REASONABLE DOUBT:AN INVESTIGATION INTO THE ASSASSINATION OF JOHN F. KENNEDY.* NEW YORK:HOLT, RT AND WINSTON, 1985; "A BREIF FILED...", P.417

18   HURT, HENRY. *REASONABLE DOUBT:AN INVESTIGATION INTO THE ASSASSINATION OF JOHN F. KENNEDY.* NEW YORK:HOLT, RINEHART AND WINSTON, 1985; "THE POINT IS THAT...", P.417

19.   DAVIS, JOHN. *THE KENNEDY:DYNASTY AND DISASTER 1848-1983.* NEW YORK:MC GRAW-HILL BOOK CO., 1984, "JOHNSON KNEW..."P.526

CHAPTER FOURTEEN

1   TROY, GIL. *AFFAIRS OF STATE.* NEW YORK:FREE PRESS, 1997; "ON JANUARY 14, ...", P.130

2   TROY, GIL. *AFFAIRS OF STATE.* NEW YORK:FREE PRESS, 1997; "NOW NO ONE...", P.130

3   HEYMANN, C. DAVID. *A WOMAN NAMED JACKIE.* NEW YORK:A LYLE STUART BOOK, 1989; "IN THIS ROOM...", P.422

4   ANTHONY, CARL SFERRAZZA. *AS WE REMEMBER HER.* NEW YORK: HARPERCOLLINS, 1997; "IN HER CLOSING DAYS...", P.204

5   ANTHONY, CARL SFERRAZZA. *AS WE REMEMBER HER.* NEW YORK: HARPERCOLLINS, 1997; "THROUGHOUT THE SPRING...", P.213

6   HEYMANN, C. DAVID. *A WOMAN NAMED JACKIE.* NEW YORK:A LYLE STUART BOOK, 1989; "PRESIDENT JOHNSON...", P.423

7   KELLEY, KITTY. *JACKIE OH!.* NEW YORK:BALLANTINE BOOKS, 1979; "ON THE FINANCIAL...", P.253

8   KELLEY, KITTY. *JACKIE OH!.* NEW YORK:BALLANTINE BOOKS, 1979; "JACKIE FELT THESE...", P.270

9   KELLEY, KITTY. *JACKIE OH!.* NEW YORK:BALLANTINE BOOKS, 1979; "SHE DEMANDED THAT...", P.272

10   KELLEY, KITTY. *JACKIE OH!.* NEW YORK:BALLANTINE BOOKS, 1979; "THEY HAD NO IDEA...", P.272

11   KELLEY, KITTY. *JACKIE OH!*. NEW YORK:BALLANTINE BOOKS,
      1979; "PAUL FAY'S BOOK...", P.271

12   HEYMANN, C. DAVID. *A WOMAN NAMED JACKIE*. NEW YORK:A
      LYLE STUART BOOK, 1989; "HOW CAN I REFUSE...", P.458

13   HEYMANN, C. DAVID. *A WOMAN NAMED JACKIE*. NEW YORK:A
      LYLE STUART BOOK, 1989; "JACKIE'S RATIONALE...", P.458

14   HEYMANN, C. DAVID: *A WOAMN NAMED JACKIE*. NEW YORK:A
      LYLE STUART BOOK, 1989; "MRS. KENNEDY BECAME...", P.461

15   KELLEY, KITTY. *JACKIE OH!*. NEW YORK:BALLANTINE BOOKS,
      1979; "ANYBODY WHO IS...", P.274

16   HEYMANN, C. DAVID. *A WOMAN NAMED JACKIE*. NEW YORK:A
      LYLE STUART BOOK, 1989; "WHY SHE CO-OPERATED...", P.462

17   HEYMANN, C. DAVID. *A WOMAN NAMED JACKIE*. NEW YORK:A
      LYLE STUART BOOK, 1989; "JACKIE KENNEDY WAS THE...", P.472

18   HEYMANN, C. DAVID. *A WOMAN NAMED JACKIE*. NEW YORK:A
      LYLE STUART BOOK, 1989; "JACKIE'S NATURAL...", P.479

19   KELLEY, KITTY. *JACKIE OH!*. NEW YORK:BALLANTINE BOOKS,
      1979; "HOWEVER, THERE WAS...", P.266

20   KELLEY, KITTY. *JACKIE OH!*. NEW YORK:BALLANTINE BOOKS,
      1979; "RUMORS CONTINUED...", P.285

21   ANDERSEN, CHRISTOPHER. *JACKIE AFTER JACK*.NEWYORK:WILLIAM
      MORROW AND COMPANY INC., 1998,"THE TRIP WAS...",P.163

CHAPTER FIFTEEN

1   CAFARAKIS, CHRISTIAN. *THE FABULOUS ONASSIS:HIS LIFE AND
      LOVES*. NEW YORK:WILLIAM MORROW AND CO. INC., 1972;
      "EVEN IF JOHN KENNEDY...", P.101

2   CAFARAKIS, CHRISTIAN. *THE FABULOUS ONASSIS:HIS LIFE AND
      LOVES*. NEW YORK:WILLIAM MORROW AND CO. INC., 1972; "IN
      A LETTER...", P.100

3   CAFARAKIS, CHRISTIAN. *THE FABULOUS ONASSIS:HIS LIFE AND

LOVES. NEW YORK:WILLIAM MORROW AND CO. INC., 1972; "WHEN JACKIE RETURNED…", P.101

4   CAFARAKIS, CHRISTIAN. *THE FABULOUS ONASSIS:HIS LIFE AND LOVES*. NEW YORK:WILLIAM MORROW AND CO. INC., 1972; "INHERITANCE I WASN'T…", P.105

5   CAFARAKIS, CHRISTIAN. *THE FABULOUS ONASSIS:HIS LIFE AND LOVES*. NEW YORK:WILLIAM MORROW AND CO. INC., 1972; "HE THEN RELATES THAT ONASSIS…", P.106

6   CAFARAKIS, CHRISTIAN. *THE FABULOUS ONASSIS:HIS LIFE AND LOVES*. NEW YORK:WILLIAM MORROW AND CO. INC., 1972; "COUNTING HER TRIPS…", P.109

7   FRASER, NICOLAS, JACOBSON, PHILIP, OTTAWAY MARK, CHESTER, LEWIS. *ARISTOTLE ONASSIS*. PHILADELPHIA AND NEW YORK:J. B. LIPPINCOTT CO, 1977; "I ONLY WISH…", P.187

8   CAFARAKIS, CHRISTIAN. *THE FABULOUS ONASSIS:HIS LIFE AND LOVES*. NEW YORK:WILLIAM MORROW AND CO. INC., 1972; "AFTER MARIA WAS GONE…", P.102

9   CAFARAKIS, CHRISTIAN. *THE FABULOUS ONASSIS:HIS LIFE AND LOVES*. NEW YORK:WILLIAM MORROW AND CO. INC., 1972; "ARI SPENT TWO…", P.102

10   CAFARAKIS, CHRISTIAN. *THE FABULOUS ONASSIS:HIS LIFE AND LOVES*. NEW YORK:WILLIAM MORROW AND CO. INC., 1972; "JUST AS IT WAS…", P.103

11   CAFARAKIS, CHRISTIAN. *THE FABULOUS ONASSIS:HIS LIFE AND LOVES*. NEW YORK:WILLIAM MORROW AND CO. INC., 1972; "ARI LEFT QUICKLY…", P.104

12   DAVIS, L.J. *ONASSIS:ARISTOTLE AND CHRISTINA*. NEW YORK:ST. MARTIN'S PRESS, 1986; "THE PRESS WAS NOT…", P.122

13   ANTHONY, CARL SFERRAZZA. *AS WE REMEMBER HER*. NEW YORK: HARPERCOLLINS, 1997; "THE FIRST TIME…", P.240

14   HEYMANN, C. DAVID. *A WOMAN NAMED JACKIE*. NEW YORK:A LYLE STUART BOOK, 1989; "SHE IS TOTALLY…", P.482

15   HEYMANN, C. DAVID. *A WOMAN NAMED JACKIE.* NEW YORK:A
      LYLE STUART BOOK, 1989; "THIS CANNOT GO ON...", P.486

16   HEYMANN, C. DAVID. *A WOMAN NAMED JACKIE.* NEW YORK:A
      LYLE STUART BOOK, 1989; "BOTH WOMEN PLAYED...", P.482

17   HEYMANN, C. DAVID. *A WOMAN NAMED JACKIE.* NEW YORK:A
      LYLE STUART BOOK, 1989; "JACKIE SPENT THE SUMMER...", P.486

18   EVANS, PETER. *ARI:THE LIFE AND TIMES OF ARISTOTLE ONASSIS.*
      NEW YORK:SUMMIT BOOKS, 1986; "ALL THAT SUMMER...", P.218

19   EVANS, PETER. *ARI:THE LIFE AND TIMES OF ARISTOTLE ONASSIS.*
      NEW YORK:SUMMIT BOOKS, 1986; "I GUESS THE KID...", P.217

20   ANDERSEN, CHRISTOPHER.*JACKIE AFTER JACK.* WILLIAM MORROW
      AND COMPANY,INC.,1998,"ALTHOUGH J.EDGAR HOOVER..."P.180

21   EVANS, PETER. *ARI:THE LIFE AND TIMES OF ARISTOTLE ONASSIS.*
      NEW YORK:SUMMIT BOOKS, 1986; "HOWEVER IT WAS A...", P.218

22   HEYMANN, C. DAVID. *A WOMAN NAMED JACKIE.* NEW YORK:A
      LYLE STUART BOOK, 1989; "I HATE THIS COUNTRY...", P.486

23   HEYMANN, C. DAVID. *A WOMAN NAMED JACKIE.* NEW YORK:A
      LYLE STUART BOOK, 1989; "ONASSIS, HAVING ...", P.489

24   KELLEY, KITTY. *JACKIE OH!.* NEW YORK:BALLANTINE BOOKS,
      1979; "MUMMY WAS HYSTERICAL...", P.305

25   KELLEY, KITTY. *JACKIE OH!.* NEW YORK:BALLANTINE BOOKS,
      1979; "TWO HOURS LATER...", P.307

26   HEYMANN, C. DAVID. *A WOMAN NAMED JACKIE.* NEW YORK:A
      LYLE STUART BOOK, 1989; "IT WAS THE MOST...", P.496

CHAPTER SIXTEEN

1   DAVIS, JOHN H. *THE KENNEDYS:DYNASTY AND DISASTER 1848-1983.*
      NEW YORK:MC GRAW-HILL BOOK CO., 1984; "ON OCTOBER
      18TH...", P.569

2   DAVIS, JOHN H. *THE KENNEDYS:DYNASTY AND DISASTER 1848-1983.*

     NEW YORK:MC GRAW-HILL BOOK CO., 1984; "BUT NOT
     EVERYBODY...", P.569

3   DAVIS, JOHN H. *THE KENNEDYS:DYNASTY AND DISASTER 1848-1983.*
     NEW YORK:MC GRAW-HILL BOOK CO., 1984; "FINALLY JACKIE
     COULD...", P.570

4   KELLEY, KITTY. *JACKIE OH!.* NEW YORK:BALLANTINE BOOKS,
     1979; "WELL, WE ASSUME...", P.310

5   DAVIS, JOHN H. *THE KENNEDYS:DYNASTY AND DISASTER 1848-1983.*
     NEW YORK:MC GRAW-HILL BOOK CO., 1984; "STILL HER
     REPUTATION...", P.248

6   ANTHONY, CARL SFERRAZZA. *AS WE REMEMBER HER.* NEW YORK:
     HARPERCOLLINS, 1997; "THE FRANKEST PUBLIC...", P.248

7   FRASER, NICOLAS, JACOBSON, PHILIP, OTTAWAY MARK,
     CHESTER, LEWIS. *ARISTOTLE ONASSIS.* PHILADELPHIA AND NEW
     YORK: J. B. LIPPINCOTT CO, 1977; "THE DISPARITY IN...", P.258

8   FRASER, NICOLAS, JACOBSON, PHILIP, OTTAWAY MARK,
     CHESTER, LEWIS. *ARISTOTLE ONASSIS.* PHILADELPHIA AND NEW
     YORK:J. B.LIPPINCOTT CO, 1977; "THEIR IDEAS WERE...", P.258

9   EVANS, PETER. *ARI:THE LIFE AND TIMES OF ARISTOTLE ONASSIS.*
     NEW YORK:SUMMIT BOOKS, 1986; "WHEN THE CHIPS...", P.215

10   OSBORNE, CLAIRE G. *JACKIE:A LEGEND DEFINED.* NEW YORK:
     AVON BOOKS, 1997, "YOU DON'T KNOW...", P.102

11   KELLEY, KITTY. *JACKIE OH!.* NEW YORK:BALLANTINE BOOKS,
     1979; "MEANWHILE, SOME 250...", P.312

12   FRASER, NICOLAS, JACOBSON, PHILIP, OTTAWAY MARK,
     CHESTER, LEWIS. *ARISTOTLE ONASSIS.* PHILADELPHIA AND NEW
     YORK:J. B. LIPPINCOTT CO, 1977; "AN AGREEMENT WAS...", P.306

13   KELLEY, KITTY. *JACKIE OH!.* NEW YORK:BALLANTINE BOOKS,
     1979; "THE GUESTS RETIRED...", P.318

14   EVANS, PETER. *ARI:THE LIFE AND TIMES OF ARISTOTLE ONASSIS.*
     NEW YORK:SUMMIT BOOKS, 1986; "ARI GAVE HIM...", P.229

15   FRASER, NICOLAS, JACOBSON, PHILIP, OTTAWAY MARK,

CHESTER, LEWIS. *ARISTOTLE ONASSIS*. PHILADELPHIA AND NEW
YORK:J. B. LIPPINCOTT CO, 1977; "AS FOR ARI,...", P.306

16   DAVID, LESTER. *JACQUELINE KENNEDY ONASSIS*. NEW YORK:A
BRICH LANE PRESS BOOK, 1994; "HE LOVED BEAUTY...", P.122

17   DAVID, LESTER. *JACQUELINE KENNEDY ONASSIS*. NEW YORK:A
BRICH LANE PRESS BOOK, 1994; "HE PAYS ABSOLUTELY...", P.122

18   ANTHONY, CARL SFERRAZZA. *AS WE REMEMBER HER*. NEW YORK:
HARPERCOLLINS, 1997; "ARI WAS A ...", P.257

19   FRASER, NICOLAS, JACOBSON, PHILIP, OTTAWAY MARK,
CHESTER, LEWIS. *ARISTOTLE ONASSIS*. PHILADELPHIA AND NEW
YORK:J. B. LIPPINCOTT CO, 1977; "ONASSIS IS DYNAMIC...", P.308

20   ANTHONY, CARL SFERRAZZA. *AS WE REMEMBER HER*. NEW YORK:
HARPERCOLLINS, 1997; "HER MARRIAGE TO JACK...", P.246

21   HEYMANN, C. DAVID. *A WOMAN NAMED JACKIE*. NEW YORK:A
LYLE STUART BOOK, 1989; "ONASSIS AMUSED HIMSELF...", P.501

22   DAVID, LESTER. *JACQUELINE KENNEDY ONASSIS*. NEW YORK:A
BRICH LANE PRESS BOOK, 1994; "ONCE, WHILE BOTH...", P.124

23   DAVID, LESTER. *JACQUELINE KENNEDY ONASSIS*. NEW YORK:A
BRICH LANE PRESS BOOK, 1994; "THEY SAT CLOSE...", P.125

24   ANTHONY, CARL SFERRAZZA. *AS WE REMEMBER HER*. NEW YORK:
HARPERCOLLINS, 1997; "ALL THE HAPPINESS...", P.247

25   ANTHONY, CARL SFERRAZZA. *AS WE REMEMBER HER*. NEW YORK:
HARPER COLLINS, 1997; "I REMEMBER GOING...", P.249

26   ANTHONY, CARL SFERRAZZA. *AS WE REMEMBER HER*. NEW YORK:
HARPER COLLINS, 1997; "IT WAS AN ABSOLUTELY...", P.252

27   ANTHONY, CARL SFERRAZZA. *AS WE REMEMBER HER*. NEW YORK:
HARPERCOLLINS, 1997; "JACKIE LOVES TRAVELING...", P.252

28   HEYMANN, C. DAVID. *A WOMAN NAMED JACKIE*. NEW YORK:A
LYLE STUART BOOK, 1989; "AFTER ARI MARRIED...", P.507

CHAPTER SEVENTEEN

1   DAVIS, L.J. *ONASSIS:ARISTOTLE AND CHRISTINA*. NEW YORK:ST. MARTIN'S PRESS, 1986; "THAT JACKIE,...", P.140

2   FRASER, NICOLAS, JACOBSON, PHILIP, OTTAWAY MARK, CHESTER, LEWIS. *ARISTOTLE ONASSIS*. PHILADELPHIA AND NEW YORK:J. B. LIPPINCOTT CO, 1977; "ACCORDING TO BEN...", P.244

3   HEYMANN, C. DAVID. *A WOMAN NAMED JACKIE*. NEW YORK:A LYLE STUART BOOK, 1989; "BRUCE GOULD, THEN...", P.202

4   HEYMANN, C. DAVID. *A WOMAN NAMED JACKIE*. NEW YORK:A LYLE STUART BOOK, 1989; "I COULDN'T SPEND...", P.223

5   HEYMANN, C. DAVID. *A WOMAN NAMED JACKIE*. NEW YORK:A LYLE STUART BOOK, 1989; "JACKIE'S GREATEST ASSETS...", P.358

6   DAVIS, L.J. *ONASSIS:ARISTOTLE AND CHRISTINA*. NEW YORK:ST. MARTIN'S PRESS, 1986; "THE RETAILER'S BEST...", P.140

7   KELLEY, KITTY. *JACKIE OH!*. NEW YORK:BALLANTINE BOOKS,

9   HEYMANN, C. DAVID. *A WOMAN NAMED JACKIE*. NEW YORK:A LYLE STUART BOOK, 1989; "SHE WAS A SPEED...", P.513

10 FRASER, NICOLAS, JACOBSON, PHILIP, OTTAWAY MARK, CHESTER, LEWIS. *ARISTOTLE ONASSIS*. PHILADELPHIA AND NEW YORK:J. B. LIPPINCOTT CO, 1977; "SHE IS LIKE A...", P.307

11 FRASER, NICOLAS, JACOBSON, PHILIP, OTTAWAY MARK, CHESTER, LEWIS. *ARISTOTLE ONASSIS*. PHILADELPHIA AND NEW YORK:J. B. LIPPINCOTT CO, 1977; "YET, THERE CAN...", P.307

12 HEYMANN, C. DAVID. *A WOMAN NAMED JACKIE*. NEW YORK:A LYLE STUART BOOK, 1989; "IT WAS THE LAST...", P.513

13 CAFARAKIS, CHRISTIAN. *THE FABULOUS ONASSIS:HIS LIFE AND LOVES*. NEW YORK:WILLIAM MORROW AND CO. INC., 1972; "JACKIE RECEIVES...", P.112

14 HEYMANN, C. DAVID. *A WOMAN NAMED JACKIE*. NEW YORK:A LYLE STUART BOOK, 1989; "IN ADDITION TO...", P.562

15 DAVIS, L.J. *ONASSIS:ARISTOTLE AND CHRISTINA*. NEW YORK:ST. MARTIN'S PRESS, 1986; "ARI WAS OUT...", P.148

16 DAVIS, L.J. *ONASSIS:ARISTOTLE AND CHRISTINA*. NEW YORK:ST.

MARTIN'S PRESS, 1986; "EXPENDITURES UNDER A...", P.198

17 DAVIS, L.J. *ONASSIS:ARISTOTLE AND CHRISTINA.* NEW YORK:ST.
MARTIN'S PRESS, 1986; "DURING THE FIRST...", P.148

18 HEYMANN, C. DAVID. *A WOMAN NAMED JACKIE.* NEW YORK:A
LYLE STUART BOOK, 1989; "ARI MAINTAINED...", P.560

19 DAVIS, L.J. *ONASSIS:ARISTOTLE AND CHRISTINA.* NEW YORK:ST.
MARTIN'S PRESS, 1986; "THERE WAS A ...", P.197

20 KELLEY, KITTY. *JACKIE OH!.* NEW YORK:BALLANTINE BOOKS,
1979; "IN HER MORE...", P.323

CHAPTER EIGHTEEN

1 KELLEY, KITTY. *JACKIE OH!.* NEW YORK:BALLANTINE BOOKS,
1979; "WHEN JACKIE SOUGHT...", P.322

2 DAVIS, L.J. *ONASSIS:ARISTOTLE AND CHRISTINA.* NEW YORK:ST.
MARTIN'S PRESS, 1986; "THE JACKIE AFFAIR...", P.122

3 DAVIS, L.J. *ONASSIS:ARISTOTLE AND CHRISTINA.* NEW YORK:ST.
MARTIN'S PRESS, 1986; "TO GIVE HIM...", P.122

4 DAVIS, L.J. *ONASSIS:ARISTOTLE AND CHRISTINA.* NEW YORK:ST.
MARTIN'S PRESS, 1986; "IF HIS FRIENDS...", P.139

5 FRASER, NICOLAS, JACOBSON, PHILIP, OTTAWAY MARK,
CHESTER, LEWIS. *ARISTOTLE ONASSIS.* PHILADELPHIA AND NEW
YORK:J. B. LIPPINCOTT CO, 1977; "ALTHOUGH THE ATTENTIONS...",
P.314

6 DAVIS, L.J. *ONASSIS:ARISTOTLE AND CHRISTINA.* NEW YORK:ST.
MARTIN'S PRESS, 1986; "ONASSIS DIDN'T LIKE...", P.120

7 FRASER, NICOLAS, JACOBSON, PHILIP, OTTAWAY MARK,
CHESTER, LEWIS. *ARISTOTLE ONASSIS.* PHILADELPHIA AND NEW
YORK:J. B. LIPPINCOTT CO, 1977; "NOT ONLY WERE...", P.309

8 FRASER, NICOLAS, JACOBSON, PHILIP, OTTAWAY MARK,
CHESTER, LEWIS. *ARISTOTLE ONASSIS.* PHILADELPHIA AND NEW
YORK:J. B. LIPPINCOTT CO, 1977; "THE DEMANDS...", P.315

9   DAVIS, L.J. *ONASSIS:ARISTOTLE AND CHRISTINA*. NEW YORK:ST.
     MARTIN'S PRESS, 1986; "IT HAD COME...", P.147

10   FRASER, NICOLAS, JACOBSON, PHILIP, OTTAWAY MARK,
     CHESTER, LEWIS. *ARISTOTLE ONASSIS*. PHILADELPHIA AND NEW
     YORK:J. B. LIPPINCOTT CO, 1977; "HER VERY EXISTENCE...", P.315

11   DAVIS, L.J. *ONASSIS:ARISTOTLE AND CHRISTINA*. NEW YORK:ST.
     MARTIN'S PRESS, 1986; "MY FATHER'S ...", P.127

12   DAVIS, L.J. *ONASSIS:ARISTOTLE AND CHRISTINA*. NEW YORK:ST.
     MARTIN'S PRESS, 1986; "JACKIE MADE...", P.143

13   DAVIS, L.J. *ONASSIS:ARISTOTLE AND CHRISTINA*. NEW YORK:ST.
     MARTIN'S PRESS, 1986; "THE CHILDREN HAD...", P.143

14   DAVIS, JOHN H. *THE KENNEDYS:DYNASTY AND DISASTER 1848-1983*.
     NEW YORK:MC GRAW-HILL BOOK CO., 1984; "UNFLATTERING
     BOOKS BECAME...", P.572

15   DAVIS, JOHN H. *THE KENNEDYS:DYNASTY AND DISASTER 1848-1983*.
     NEW YORK:MC GRAW-HILL BOOK CO., 1984; "THE MARRIAGE
     ACCORDING...", P.572

16   FRASER, NICOLAS, JACOBSON, PHILIP, OTTAWAY MARK,
     CHESTER, LEWIS. *ARISTOTLE ONASSIS*. PHILADELPHIA AND NEW
     YORK:J. B. LIPPINCOTT CO, 1977; "JACKIE WAS EVIDENTLY...",
     P.319

17   DAVID, LESTER. *JACQUELINE KENNEDY ONASSIS*. NEW YORK:A
     BRICH LANE PRESS BOOK, 1994; "ON JANUARY 22,...", P.126

18   DAVID, LESTER. *JACQUELINE KENNEDY ONASSIS*. NEW YORK:A
     BRICH LANE PRESS BOOK, 1994; "HIS BODY HAD...", P.127

19   FRASER, NICOLAS, JACOBSON, PHILIP, OTTAWAY MARK,
     CHESTER, LEWIS. *ARISTOTLE ONASSIS*. PHILADELPHIA AND NEW
     YORK:J. B. LIPPINCOTT CO, 1977; "ONASSIS' GREIF WAS...", P.330

20   ANTHONY, CARL SFERRAZZA. *AS WE REMEMBER HER*. NEW YORK:
     HARPERCOLLINS, 1997; "JACKIE AND ARI HAD...", P.259

21   DAVIS, L.J. *ONASSIS:ARISTOTLE AND CHRISTINA*. NEW YORK:ST.
     MARTIN'S PRESS, 1986; "THE CIA HAD...", P.185

22   FRASER, NICOLAS, JACOBSON, PHILIP, OTTAWAY MARK,
CHESTER, LEWIS. *ARISTOTLE ONASSIS.* PHILADELPHIA AND NEW
YORK:J. B. LIPPINCOTT CO, 1977; "THE MOST IMPORTANT...",P.320

23   FRASER, NICOLAS, JACOBSON, PHILIP, OTTAWAY MARK,
CHESTER, LEWIS. *ARISTOTLE ONASSIS.* PHILADELPHIA AND NEW
YORK:J. B. LIPPINCOTT CO, 1977; "WHEN HE WENT...", P.338

24   HEYMANN, C. DAVID. *A WOMAN NAMED JACKIE.* NEW YORK:A
LYLE STUART BOOK, 1989; "SOME SUPERSTITIONS...", P.558

25   HEYMANN, C. DAVID. *A WOMAN NAMED JACKIE.* NEW YORK:A
LYLE STUART BOOK, 1989; "CHRISTINA WAS HIGHLY...", P.558

26   FRASER, NICOLAS, JACOBSON, PHILIP, OTTAWAY MARK,
CHESTER, LEWIS. *ARISTOTLE ONASSIS.* PHILADELPHIA AND NEW
YORK:J. B. LIPPINCOTT CO, 1977; "JACKIE SEEMED...", p.347

27   DAVIS, L.J. *ONASSIS:ARISTOTLE AND CHRISTINA.* NEW YORK:ST.
MARTIN'S PRESS, 1986; "I THINK EVERYBODY...", P.129

28   DAVIS, L.J. *ONASSIS:ARISTOTLE AND CHRISTINA.* NEW YORK:ST.
MARTIN'S PRESS, 1986; "AS THE OLD...", P. 129

29   DAVIS, L.J. *ONASSIS:ARISTOTLE AND CHRISTINA.* NEW YORK:ST.
MARTIN'S PRESS, 1986; "IT WAS NOT A HAPPY...", P.200

30   FRASER, NICOLAS, JACOBSON, PHILIP, OTTAWAY MARK,
CHESTER, LEWIS. *ARISTOTLE ONASSIS.* PHILADELPHIA AND NEW
YORK:J. B. LIPPINCOTT CO, 1977; "IT WAS IN THIS MOOD...", P.347

31   HEYMANN, C. DAVID. *A WOMAN NAMED JACKIE.* NEW YORK:A
LYLE STUART BOOK, 1989; "MY YACHT...", P.556

32   HEYMANN, C. DAVID. *A WOMAN NAMED JACKIE.* NEW YORK.A
LYLE STUART BOOK, 1989; "ARI'S WILL...", P.555

33   DAVID, LESTER. *JACQUELINE KENNEDY ONASSIS.* NEW YORK:A
BRICH LANE PRESS BOOK, 1994; "BY THIS TIME...", P.129

34   ANDERSEN, CHRISTOPHER.*JACKIE AFTER JACK.* WILLIAM MORROW
AND COMPANY,INC.,1998,"WHEN SHE FIRST..."P.291

35   OSBORNE, CLAIRE G. *JACKIE:A LEGEND DEFINED.* NEW
YORK:AVON BOOKS, 1997; "THE DEATH OF ARISTOTLE...", P.105

36 HEYMANN, C. DAVID. *A WOMAN NAMED JACKIE*. NEW YORK:A
LYLE STUART BOOK, 1989; "MISS CHRISTINA...", P.566

37 HEYMANN, C. DAVID. *A WOMAN NAMED JACKIE*. NEW YORK:A
LYLE STUART BOOK, 1989; "JACKIE APPEARED...", P.567

38 DAVIS, L.J. *ONASSIS:ARISTOTLE AND CHRISTINA*. NEW YORK:ST.
MARTIN'S PRESS, 1986; "INEXPLICABLY, I FEEL...", P.242

39 HEYMANN, C. DAVID. *A WOMAN NAMED JACKIE*. NEW YORK:A
LYLE STUART BOOK, 1989; "I DON'T LIKE TO...", P.569

CHAPTER NINETEEN

1 KELLEY, KITTY. *JACKIE OH!*. NEW YORK:BALLANTINE BOOKS,
1979; "MANY MARRIAGES...", P.369

2 KELLEY, KITTY. *JACKIE OH!*. NEW YORK:BALLANTINE BOOKS,
1979; "NO COURTESIAN...", P.369

3 DAVIS, JOHN H. *JACQUELINE BOUVIER: AN INTIMATE MEMOIR*.
NEW YORK:JOHN WILEY AND SONS, INC., 1996; "HER FATHER
HAD...", P.108

4 DAVID, LESTER. *JACQUELINE KENNEDY ONASSIS*. NEW YORK:A
BRICH LANE PRESS BOOK, 1994; "THE COMMONLY HELD...", P.248

5 OSBORNE, CLAIRE G. *JACKIE:A LEGEND DEFINED*. NEW YORK:
AVON BOOKS, 1997; "TWO YEARS LATER...", P.107

6 OSBORNE, CLAIRE G. *JACKIE:A LEGEND DEFINED*. NEW YORK:
AVON BOOKS, 1997; "OF COURSE...", P.109

7 KELLEY, KITTY. *JACKIE OH!*. NEW YORK:BALLANTINE BOOKS,
1979; "HER SECRETARY...", P.366

8 DAVID, LESTER. *JACQUELINE KENNEDY ONASSIS*. NEW YORK:A
BRICH LANE PRESS BOOK, 1994; "JACKIE WORKED...", P.249

9 KELLEY, KITTY. *JACKIE OH!*. NEW YORK:BALLANTINE BOOKS,
1979; "SHE SUPPORTED SARGENT...", P.368

10 HEYMANN, C. DAVID. *A WOMAN NAMED JACKIE*. NEW YORK:A
LYLE STUART BOOK, 1989; "THE FIRST PUBLIC...", P.598

11 COLLIER, PETER AND HOROWITZ, DAVID. *THE KENNEDYS:AN AMERICAN DRAMA*. NEW YORK:WARNER BOOKS, 1984; "WHEN ARCHITECT...", P.544

12 KELLEY, KITTY. *JACKIE OH!*. NEW YORK:BALLANTINE BOOKS, 1979; "THE THING I CARE...", P.372

13 KELLEY, KITTY. *JACKIE OH!*. NEW YORK:BALLANTINE BOOKS, 1979; "JACKIE MADE HER...", P.373

14 KELLEY, KITTY. *JACKIE OH!*. NEW YORK:BALLANTINE BOOKS, 1979; "THEY HAVE BEEN...", P.373

15 HEYMANN, C. DAVID. *A WOMAN NAMED JACKIE*. NEW YORK:A LYLE STUART BOOK, 1989; "AT FIRST GLANCE...", P.602

16 HEYMANN, C. DAVID. *A WOMAN NAMED JACKIE*. NEW YORK:A LYLE STUART BOOK, 1989; "MAURICE'S FRIENDSHIP...", P.603

17 HEYMANN, C. DAVID. *A WOMAN NAMED JACKIE*. NEW YORK:A LYLE STUART BOOK, 1989; "YOU CAN BE SURE...", P.604

18 ANTHONY, CARL SFERRAZZA. *AS WE REMEMBER HER*. NEW YORK: HARPERCOLLINS, 1997; "MAURICE GAVE HER...", P.304

19 HEYMANN, C. DAVID. *A WOMAN NAMED JACKIE*. NEW YORK:A LYLE STUART BOOK, 1989; "IF JACKIE'S DAYS...", P.624

20 HEYMANN, C. DAVID. *A WOMAN NAMED JACKIE*. NEW YORK:A LYLE STUART BOOK, 1989; "THAT DIDN'T BOTHER...", P.625

21 HEYMANN, C. DAVID. *A WOMAN NAMED JACKIE*. NEW YORK:A LYLE STUART BOOK, 1989; "PEOPLE WONDERED IF...", P.626

22 HEYMANN, C. DAVID. *A WOMAN NAMED JACKIE*. NEW YORK:A LYLE STUART BOOK, 1989; "SHE TRAVELED TO ...", P.626

CHAPTER TWENTY

1 DAVID, LESTER. *JACQUELINE KENNEDY ONASSIS*. NEW YORK:A BRICH LANE PRESS BOOK, 1994; "ETHEL KENNEDY WAS...", P.211

2 DAVID, LESTER. *JACQUELINE KENNEDY ONASSIS*. NEW YORK:A BRICH LANE PRESS BOOK, 1994; "JACKIE'S DISLIKE...", P.211

3   DAVID, LESTER. *JACQUELINE KENNEDY ONASSIS.* NEW YORK:A
     BRICH LANE PRESS BOOK, 1994; "SHE NEVER ATTENDED..", P.206

4   DAVID, LESTER. *JACQUELINE KENNEDY ONASSIS.* NEW YORK:A
     BRICH LANE PRESS BOOK, 1994; "JACKIE HAD ONCE...", P.212

5   OSBORNE, CLAIRE G. *JACKIE:A LEGEND DEFINED.* NEW YORK:
     AVON BOOKS, 1997; "JACKIE NOTICED...", P.137

6   OSBORNE, CLAIRE G. *JACKIE:A LEGEND DEFINED.* NEW YORK:
     AVON BOOKS, 1997; "HER SPOKESPERSON...", P.139

7   OSBORNE, CLAIRE G. *JACKIE:A LEGEND DEFINED.* NEW YORK:
     AVON BOOKS, 1997; "JACQUELINE KENNEDY ONASSIS...", P.141

8   "THE AFTERNOON BEFORE...", P.354

9   OSBORNE, CLAIRE G. *JACKIE:A LEGEND DEFINED.* NEW YORK:
     AVON BOOKS, 1997; "THE NAVY SEA...", P.145

10   OSBORNE, CLAIRE G. *JACKIE:A LEGEND DEFINED.* NEW YORK:
     AVON BOOKS, 1997; "JACKIE MADE ONLY...", P.147

11   FRASER, NICOLAS, JACOBSON, PHILIP, OTTAWAY MARK,
     CHESTER, LEWIS. *ARISTOTLE ONASSIS.* PHILADELPHIA AND NEW
     YORK:J. B. LIPPINCOTT CO, 1977; "WOULD JACQUELINE
     ONASSIS...", P.337

12   DAVIS, JOHN H. *THE KENNEDYS:DYNASTY AND DISASTER 1848-1983.*
     NEW YORK:MC GRAW-HILL BOOK CO., 1984; "THE JFK LIBRARY...",
     P.649

13   DAVIS, JOHN H. *THE KENNEDYS:DYNASTY AND DISASTER 1848-1983.*
     NEW YORK:MC GRAW-HILL BOOK CO., 1984; "FURTHER
     CONTRIBUTING...", P.649

14   DU BOIS, DIANA. *IN HER SISTERS SHADOW.* BOSTON:LITTLE,
     BROWN AND CO., 1995; "HER RESENTMENT...", P.380

15   OSBORNE, CLAIRE G. *JACKIE:A LEGEND DEFINED.* NEW YORK:
     AVON BOOKS, 1997; "A TOTAL OF 5914...", P.147

16   OSBORNE, CLAIRE G. *JACKIE:A LEGEND DEFINED.* NEW YORK:
     AVON BOOKS, 1997; "THE CATALOG...", P.148

17   FRASER, NICOLAS, JACOBSON, PHILIP, OTTAWAY MARK,

CHESTER, LEWIS. *ARISTOTLE ONASSIS.* PHILADELPHIA AND NEW
YORK:J. B. LIPPINCOTT CO, 1977; "I LOATHE THIS...", P.335

18 OSBORNE, CLAIRE G. *JACKIE:A LEGEND DEFINED.* NEW YORK:
AVON BOOKS, 1997; "THE TOP TEN...", P.148

19 OSBORNE, CLAIRE G. *JACKIE:A LEGEND DEFINED.* NEW YORK:
AVON BOOKS, 1997; "SHE HAD CONSIDERATE...", P.168

20 OSBORNE, CLAIRE G. *JACKIE:A LEGEND DEFINED.* NEW YORK:
AVON BOOKS, 1997; "SHE LOOKED...", P.171

INDEX